Community Action Against Poverty

COMMUNITY ACTION AGAINST POVERTY

POVERTY

Readings from the Mobilization Experience

Edited by

George A. Brager and Francis P. Purcell

COLLEGE & UNIVERSITY PRESS · *Publishers*

NEW HAVEN, CONN.

MANUFACTURED IN THE UNITED STATES OF AMERICA
UNITED PRINTING SERVICES, INC.
NEW HAVEN, CONN.

This book is dedicated to those who staffed Mobilization for Youth during the agency's early years and who devoted their knowledge, imagination, and crusading zeal to creative innovation in social service.

Foreword

The community demonstration projects developed under the sponsorship of the President's Committee on Juvenile Delinquency and Youth Crime were each required to include in their operations a plan for evaluating the impact of the action programs on juvenile delinquency and youth crime, as well as on other related community conditions. These evaluations were to be of the effects of specific activities as well as of the over-all programs. Although it was recognized that this extremely difficult requirement would probably not be met with any considerable degree of precision, it was nevertheless anticipated that even approximate results would be of substantial value for future planning and design.

In addition to the formal requirements of evaluation, a strong hope was expressed (but never given specific implementation) that each project would arrange for a skillful and mature project historian who would have intimate access to all participants and records and who would faithfully record and preserve this unique experience in planned social change and mobilization of community resources to cope with the problems of youth. Only a few of the demonstration projects undertook to capture this kind of material, Mobilization for Youth being one, but how adequate these efforts have been is not yet manifest.

At any rate, all of this is to underscore the point that the present volume, valuable in its own right, is doubly valuable because it at least partially fills the unfortunate gap noted above. What we have here are reports of observations and experiences maturely reflected upon by persons who occupied key staff positions in Mobilization for Youth during the most dynamic and problematic period of its history, when the boldest and most exciting innovations were being planned and mounted and the greatest resistances and threats were being confronted.

Further enhancing the special value of this collection is the fact that Mobilization for Youth is the "granddaddy" of the community demonstration programs. Its conception and the initiation of its research and planning stages with a substantial grant from the National Institute of Mental Health antedate the passage of Public Law 87-274 and establishment of the President's Committee on Juvenile Delinquency and Youth Crime by two years. In consequence, Mobilization was able to mount its action programs under the sponsorship of the President's Committee well in advance of the other demonstration communities, at a time when there were few, if any, precedents or guidelines. Pioneering and trail blazing, terms frequently misapplied, are apt and precisely descriptive in this instance. And the rewards of zestful adventure and creative innovation were balanced by the costs of errors, false starts, massive resistance and outright assaults by interests that saw themselves threatened. This latter included a full-scale McCarthyite attack based on false charges that the agency was dominated by communists. It is testimony to the tough vitality of the program that it survived this assault; but the victory was costly in demoralization, loss of momentum, and almost complete erosion of key staff.

Notwithstanding the hazards and penalties of innovation, Mobilization for Youth has been enormously influential, not only in setting new patterns of thought and action which have been heavily used in other communities, but in its impact on the conceptions emerging in later Federal welfare programs. As already indicated, the conceptualizations and experience growing out of Mobilization for Youth had a large role in the crystallization of the basic conceptions and rationale of the President's Committee itself. And it is no secret that the community action section of the Economic Opportunities Act was drawn largely from the experience and working documents of the President's Committee.

Perhaps in the long run the most significant contribution of Mobilization for Youth will be its impact on the social work profession itself. For in striving to enhance the competence of a community to deal effectively with the conditions affecting its youth, Mobilization for Youth brought into clear, concrete and dramatic focus the inadequacies of the profession for grappling with the problems it is now called upon to deal with. This challenge, of course, did not originate with Mobilization for Youth, but it is doubtful if the case was ever before put so concretely and convincingly and on such a scale.

It is certainly no strain on the facts to credit Mobilization for Youth and subsequent projects following its lead with being a powerful stimulus impelling the social work profession to reappraise its position and responsibilities. Consideration of the needs and demands of the community as it seeks to increase its capacity to cope and the question of the appropriate roles of the social worker vis-à-vis the various components of the community inevitably focuses attention on what has hitherto been a rather anemic curriculum in what has been called community organization. Indeed, the profession is now engaged in a broad study of this whole problem. Confrontation with social processes and problems not amenable to theories and practices of individual therapy has accelerated the demand for a more adequate command of social science knowledge by the professional practitioner. The traditional centrality of casework as the chief orientation and instrumentality of the profession and as the dominant component of training has now been so thoroughly challenged that profound changes in the schools of social work are inevitable. This is not to say that work with individual cases will be regarded as unimportant. Indeed, casework strengthened by a broader social contextual and interactional perspective and sophistication will again become a powerful component of professional theory and practice.

But it is not enough to demonstrate the inadequacy of traditional methods and approaches. The new knowledge and skills required to upgrade the capabilities of the profession must be identified, and experience put into form that can be communicated and thus utilized in more adequate programs of training. This is a major objective of the authors and editors of this volume. And it is urgently hoped that staffs of other similar projects will follow their example.

Mobilization for Youth has led us a long way on the steep and sometimes perilous trail to a new and more comprehensive view of the task of raising the level of competence of American communities to define goals and implement them through effective joint action. But the authors of this book will be the first to assert that there is still quite a way to go before we see the full implications of the direction their programs have taken. Given its mission and the situation confronting it, Mobilization for Youth could not avoid giving top priority to actions designed to render the institutional resources of the community more accessible, flexible, and adapted to the needs of the most deprived segments —"the lowest 20 per cent"—and to focus attention on ways and means of enhancing the capabilities of this segment for participating effectively in shaping its world. But a community as such does not necessarily become more competent by making its voiceless elements more articulate and its weak components more vigorous and effective in action, as necessary and important a step as this is. The better off and more articulate segments are themselves not necessarily equipped with the qualities and capabilities that are requisite for participation in collaborative effort to identify needs, set goals and implement them. A community falls short of its competence to act as such to the extent that any of its significant component parts are unable to interact effectively with the others. And the new community practitioner can no more afford to concentrate on one part of the community system than can his casework counterpart fail to view the personality as a total dynamic system.

If the assumption that effective interaction among the components of a community is a major criterion of its competence is accepted, then it follows that economic plenty is no guarantee of competence. And, indeed, to judge from the witless fumbling and futile whining that goes on when they are confronted by rebellious waywardness among their pampered youth of our chrome-plated ex-urbian paradises, they are no more competent than the inner city slum communities to function as such. This condition expands considerably, of course, the arena for the exercise of the skills and talents of the new community specialist. It also places a heavy demand on social scientists to get out of the rut of correlating all their findings with the magic variable, socioeconomic class, and to develop some new hypotheses about conditions that enhance the quality and human development potentialities of group living.

LEONARD S. COTTRELL, JR.

Russell Sage Foundation
November 24, 1965

Acknowledgments

To acknowledge individual contributions to a group enterprise is to risk unjust omissions, but this is a risk that we must take. Without James E. McCarthy and Richard A. Cloward, who, with George A. Brager, were co-directors of Mobilization during its first turbulent program years and its earlier planning phase, there would have been no Mobilization for Youth. Inestimable as well were the contributions of the following executives, who are no longer with the project: Charles F. Grosser, who was Assistant Executive Director; Melvin Herman, Chief of Work Programs; Edward Sparer, Chief of the Legal Services Unit; Harry Specht, Assistant Chief of Community Development; and Abraham Tannenbaum, Education Chief. Together with such current staff as Marilyn Bibb, Chief of Community Development, and Margaret Shea and Sherman Barr, Chief and Assistant Chief of Services to Individuals and Families, they were responsible for much of Mobilization's impact upon the welfare scene.

* * * * *

Just as Mobilization owes its existence to the persons listed above, this volume is, in large measure, the consequence of the editorial assistance provided by Gladys Topkis. The editors wish to acknowledge their debt and their gratitude.

GEORGE A. BRAGER
FRANCIS P. PURCELL

October 1966

Contents

Contributors

SHERMAN BARR — Assistant Chief of Services to Individuals and Families, Mobilization for Youth

GEORGE A. BRAGER — Formerly co-Director of Mobilization for Youth and Consultant to the Manpower Administration, U. S. Department of Labor; Associate Professor of Social Work, Columbia University

RICHARD A. CLOWARD — Director of Research, Mobilization for Youth; Professor of Social Work, Columbia University

RICHARD ELMAN — Research Associate, Columbia University

IRWIN EPSTEIN — Research Assistant, Columbia University

CHARLES F. GROSSER — Formerly Assistant Executive Director of Mobilization for Youth; Associate Professor, Graduate School of Social Work, New York University

MARVIN E. FRANKEL — Federal Judge, U. S. District Court, Southern District of N. Y.; formerly member of the Board of Directors, Mobilization for Youth

GERTRUDE GOLDBERG — Formerly co-Supervisor of Visiting Homemaker Program, Mobilization for Youth; Research Associate, School of Education, Yeshiva University

MELVIN HERMAN — Formerly Chief of Work Programs, Mobilization for Youth; Professor, Graduate School of Social Work, New York University; Co-Director, Center for Study of Unemployed Youth

MARVIN E. LARSON — Director, State Department of Social Welfare, Kansas; President, American Public Welfare Association

OSCAR A. ORNATI — Professor of Economics, New York University

FRANCES PIVEN — Formerly Program Consultant, Mobilization for Youth; Assistant Professor, Columbia University School of Social Work

FRANCIS P. PURCELL — Formerly Chief of Training, Mobilization for Youth; Professor Social Work, Rutgers University

FRANK REISSMAN — Formerly Social Science Specialist, Mobilization for Youth; Professor of Education, New York University

BERNARD ROSENBERG — Consultant to Work Programs, Mobilization for Youth; Associate Professor of Sociology and Anthropology, City College of the City University of New York

EDWARD V. SPARER — Formerly Chief of Legal Services Unit, Mobilization for Youth; Legal Director, Center on Social Welfare Policy and Law, Columbia University School of Social Work

HARRY SPECHT — Formerly Assistant Chief of Community-Development Program, Mobilization for Youth; Associate Professor of Social Work, Graduate School of Social Work, San Francisco State College

Introduction

It is no exaggeration to suggest that the Economic Opportunities Act of 1964 and many of the programs that have sprung up to implement it stem in large measure from the experience of Mobilization for Youth. The impact of Mobilization's first years upon social work, education, and, even more significantly, upon government, law, and the moral climate of the nation, has been remarkable. For this reason, we have here collected a number of papers prepared by Mobilization for Youth personnel or for MFY institutes. The problems dealt with in this collection, the experiences reported, and the reflections the papers give rise to, all have urgent implications for attempts to reduce poverty.

Mobilization for Youth was the first comprehensive attempt to combat delinquency through intervention involving an entire community (a sizable portion of New York's Lower East Side). The basic assumption underlying the program is that deviant behavior is but one aspect of a larger social problem. Patterns of conduct are therefore explained, not only or mainly as the result of internal and psychological processes or of past social experiences, but also—and primarily—as a response to present social conditions. In this view, an adolescent's lack of motivation to seek employment, for example, is not necessarily due to intrapsychic factors (e.g., poor identification with the father figure). Nor can it be accounted for purely in socio-psychological or cultural terms (e.g., as the product of cultural strain resulting from poverty or particular group patterns). Rather, it reflects a current social fact—the New York City Department of Welfare policy to reduce the income of families on welfare when youngsters in these families are working.[1] Thus Mobilization has placed major emphasis on efforts to bring about change in social institutions both structurally, through its mandate as a demonstration project (see Frances Piven, "The Demonstration Project: A Federal Strategy for Local Change"), and programatically, through its community-development and legal-services programs. Its over-

---

[1] The New York City Department of Welfare has revised this policy as a consequence of Mobilization's intercession.

all goal is "to demonstrate ways of helping residents of the inner-city slum to deal with problems caused by living under conditions of poverty, deprivation, and discrimination."[2]

Mobilization's program is based on the theory set forth in the proposal that

> . . . much delinquent behavior is engendered because opportunities for conformity are limited. Delinquency therefore represents not a lack of motivation to conform but quite the opposite: the desire to meet social expectations itself becomes the source of delinquent behavior if the possibility of doing so is limited or nonexistent.[3]

To reduce delinquency, then, it is necessary to expand the objective opportunities available to impoverished youth; thus youth-employment and educational efforts became major components of the MFY program. It is also necessary, in this schema, to attack the factors which prevent youth from taking advantage of whatever opportunities do exist; a network of specialized services to individuals, group members, and their families was therefore developed as well.

But Mobilization's mandate was the development of programs which represented innovation in content, method, structure, or auspices. It does not require theoretical sophistication to hold that slum youngsters need jobs, that their education should be better, or that individuals in trouble require help in order to maximize their life chances. Nor does espousal of these notions guarantee programmatic innovation. Perhaps the major contribution of the Mobilization program, and its primary source of innovation, stems from the rather simple idea that if services are to be organized meaningfully, social-class variables must be systematically taken into account in program planning. An understanding, in class terms, of the reciprocal relationship between "defects" of the clients and those of the institutions with which they deal suggests specific targets for efforts to bring about institutional change.

[2] *Action on the Lower East Side* (New York: Mobilization for Youth, 1964), p. 1.

[3] *A Proposal for the Prevention and Control of Juvenile Delinquency by Expanding Opportunities* (New York: Mobilization for Youth, 1961), pp. 44-45. This theoretical perspective was developed by Richard A. Cloward and Lloyd Ohlin in *Delinquency and Opportunity* (Glencoe, Ill.: Free Press, 1961).

The employment problems of lower-class adolescents indicated a need for radical intervention. During MFY's planning phase, sensitive vocational counseling and aggressive seeking out of jobs in private industry were advanced as the means of remedying these problems. In view of the persistent marginality of lower-class youth, stemming from their lack of marketable skills coupled with restrictive practices based on color, "foreignness," language difficulty, and class mores, MFY planners emphasized instead the creation of new jobs in the public sector and new training opportunities. Mobilization's Urban Youth Service Corps, which provided subsidized work for disadvantaged youth, was the first such program since the New Deal's National Youth Administration. In concept, techniques, and structure, the programs of the Manpower Development and Training Act and the National Youth Corps owe much to this program.

In keeping with the "class consciousness" of the MFY approach, efforts were made to avoid an institutionalized atmosphere in the work program. Application blanks are filled out by clerical staff, so that youngsters who do not read or write can apply without embarrassment. Vocational counseling was made an integral part of the work operation itself, rather than, as is traditionally the case, a preliminary to job placement. Thus structured, counseling involves less talk than action and is therefore more congenial to lower-income youth.

Mobilization's education program is based upon an extension of the American concept of equality of opportunity. By and large, this has been taken to mean not only that all children have a right to a public-school education but also that individual differences in learning must be taken into account. In the view of MFY's planners, equality of opportunity implies, further, that cultural and economic (i.e., class) differences among children need to be similarly considered. Unless schools can gear their program meaningfully to the class and ethnic background of their pupils, equality of opportunity is more than half fiction.

Public-school programs must therefore take into account features of lower-class life that make it difficult for lower-income youngsters to do well in school: the inexperience of parents, their shyness and suspicion of the schools, the lack of intellectual stimulation, noisy crowded homes, and the like. At the same time, it is necessary to identify those features of the educational system that reduce the likelihood of academic success. In a school which is overcrowded and segregated, in which teacher turnover is high, equipment is inadequate, and insufficient time is devoted to actual teaching, and in which a disparity in social class and values exists between school and pupils, it is understandable that students do poorly. A more meaningful interrelationship of school and community is the major objective of the MFY education program. Emphasis is placed on greater involvement of parents through an indigenous-aide and community-organization program, the use of lower-income high-school students to tutor elementary-school youngsters, home visiting by teachers, and the development of more culturally meaningful curricular materials.

MFY's specialized services to individuals also reflect concern about lower-income patterns and needs. Neighborhood service centers—storefront helping stations—have been organized to make available under one roof the battery of skills and resources needed to deal with such practical problems as how to meet welfare eligibility requirements, how to use surplus foods to make pastelillos, the rights of a defendant to pretrial freedom, where to find a job for a youngster. A wide range of services is offered in an atmosphere that is highly visible, informal, and nonbureaucratic. The neighborhood service center program has become a cornerstone of the burgeoning community-action efforts organized under the Economic Opportunities Act.

The concept of the social worker as an advocate for the poor rather than a helper is a further contribution of the Mobilization program. MFY's legal division has focused on giving aid to impoverished persons acting as plaintiffs rather than as defendants, particularly vis-à-vis governmental agencies. While this is a departure from traditional legal-aid services, the role of the lawyer as advocate obviously is not. The legal model has been incorporated into social-work practice; its clearest manifestation is in the community-development program.

According to the Mobilization philosophy, broadly conceived, poverty may be viewed as the problem, and power, in the hands of those suffering the consequences of poverty, as the solution. Power, in the sense of the ability to affect one's life chances, can be provided to the individual through a network of services. However, a more substantive solution is to vest power in the group with the most at stake. A position within the power structure of the community enables the poor to press for additional

or improved services, to express and demand redress of grievances from public and private institutions, to develop leadership
skills, and to offer their youth some optimistic evidence of what
the future might hold. Helping a single family to deal with a
private slumlord, for example, may resolve their immediate
problem, but an effective tenants' organization can ultimately
change the housing policies and practices of an entire community. The development of programs and organizations by the
poor is a precondition of their assumption of power. The community-development program is regarded as the vehicle by
which services can be converted to systemic change and the
cycle of theory to program to goal completed.

Mobilization's proposal was published in December 1961, following a two-year planning period. The federal government, the
City of New York, and the Ford Foundation agreed to provide
thirteen million dollars for an initial three-year period, and the
inception of the program was announced in June 1962 by President Kennedy. Twenty-six months later, Mobilization was subjected to a widely publicized—and very nearly fatal—attack. On
August 16, 1964, immediately prior to the Johnson–Goldwater
presidential campaign, and during debate in Congress regarding
the passage of the Economic Opportunities Act, the New York
Daily News, a right-wing tabloid, accused Mobilization of having hired subversive personnel and of fomenting riots. (The
attack occurred one month after the riots in Harlem and Bedford-Stuyvesant.) The press onslaught continued through the
fall of 1964, encouraged by the public hostility of City Council
President Paul Screvane, who was also head of New York City's
antipoverty program and, for a time during this period, Acting
Mayor. The social-protest activities of the community-development program were clearly the central issue.

But the attack had its genesis four years earlier, during the
project's planning phase. Even then, the plan to muster the poor
to deal with their own problems provoked sharp disagreement.
Members of the local neighborhood association, representing the
conventional institutions of the area (settlements, churches,
schools, businesses, political clubs), insisted that community
organization take place under its auspices. Since many association
members were also members of Mobilization's board of directors,
theirs were powerful voices. Other board members and Mobili-

zation's planning staff insisted that neighborhood-association auspices would ensure middle-class domination of the community-organization effort, which would inevitably discourage lower-class engagement. This group carried the day, but critics on the Mobilization board and outside the agency were not reconciled to the program's "activist" objectives.

Not surprisingly, MFY's challenging social-action program met with frequent criticism. The project's encouragement of community participation in the March on Washington called forth anonymous complaints to the FBI. Its support of a group of Puerto Rican mothers who questioned a school's program contributed to the antagonism of the educational bureaucracy. Landlords complained to local political leaders about MFY's activities in regard to housing violations. Some local political leaders themselves looked askance at attempts to activate the minority community and complained about Mobilization's reformist coloration. Finally, there was the action of neighborhood groups and a statement of the Mobilization board calling for a civilian review board to investigate complaints against the police. During the beleaguered days following the Harlem riots, the police, with their channels to the local press, could perhaps not be expected to stand idly by. The *Daily News* was the recipient of undigested information, half-truths, and outright inaccuracies, and distorted the data further.

For a period of six months, Mobilization suffered intensive internal and external investigation. It acted and reacted under the buffeting of many of the most powerful groups in the city. And it survived. Indeed, it may be one of the first organizations in recent times to successfully withstand a sustained accusation of subversive infiltration without a single firing. This is not to say, of course, that the organization's scars are not deep and the consequences to it far-reaching.[4] The attack did have at least one salutary effect. It introduced a debate into the public arena regarding the role of publicly funded organizations in supporting the involvement of the poor in community social action. And it did garner support for such action from many prominent persons, notably the Attorney General of the United States, Nicholas Katzenbach, and the Secretary of Labor, Willard Wirtz, and from virtually all the New York newspapers other than the *News*.

[4] The consequences of the attack to the organization are the subject of current research study by one of the editors.

We believe that, with the completion of the two-year planning period and the initial three-year action grant, the end of an era arrived. Mobilization for Youth came into being before national attention turned to a "war on poverty." It stood alone in what has since become a pattern of community-action programs, and, as the forerunner of these programs, it made a significant contribution to their development. It had, in short, more than the capacity to innovate and chart directions. It was also provided by historic circumstance with the opportunity to do so.

This collection of articles is not a paean to Mobilization, and the articles do not reflect an institutional position. Many of them, in fact, are sharply critical, specifically or by implication, of the practices, policies, or theories of the agency. Some of the articles were written for publication; others, for oral delivery. Some are the work of action staff, closely concerned with the details of agency operation; some are the product of researchers, consultants, and others whose task it is to extract broad principles from day-to-day experience. Some articles, therefore, make frequent and specific references to MFY programs—the visiting homemakers, for example. Others mention Mobilization rarely or not at all but are clearly inspired by exposure to its theories and programs.

The collection is not a systematic exploration of aspects of the antipoverty crusade; nor is it a comprehensive survey of the history and achievements of Mobilization. As noted earlier, the articles were chosen because of their implications for today's antipoverty efforts. These implications are all the more meaningful because of the intimate and passionate involvement of the authors with an early and especially internecine phase of the battle.

The first section of the book sets the stage by identifying some of the participants in the war on poverty: its victims, the poor, and the public and private agencies that exist, ostensibly at least, to serve their needs. Thus Oscar Ornati offers a definition of poverty-in-an-age-of-affluence based on certain personal, social, and demographic characteristics that increasingly mark those who are excluded from full participation in the economy, either as producers or as consumers. Unless society is willing to "invest in human capital," making specific expenditures to alter these poverty-linked characteristics or their outcome, the aged, the nonwhite, the rural-farm or female-based family, the undereducated, and the underemployed are likely to be poor, to stay poor, and to get poorer.

The remaining articles in Part I document the failure of both private and public agencies to ameliorate some of the debilitating effects of poverty, much less to combat poverty itself. Cloward and Epstein show how and why the private agency is seeking out and serving an increasingly middle-class clientele and thus is abandoning its mandate to serve the poor. Charles Grosser's article reveals broad differences in the way in which a slum community is viewed by the low-income residents and by the middle-class social-agency staff who work there. The comparison is especially noteworthy since the agency in this case is Mobilization, whose staff members were chosen for—among other attributes—their sympathy with and, as far as possible, social proximity to their low-income clients. Finally, George Brager and Sherman Barr, drawing on the comments of MFY clients, show how the public agencies as well have failed to give adequate service to the poor by forcing welfare applicants and recipients to undergo countless indignities, humiliations, and injustices.

In Part II, articles by Brager and by Herman and Rosenberg consider the demonstration project as a way of reversing this situation, drawing on the experience of two Mobilization divisions. Mr. Brager, taking his illustration from MFY's "World of Education" program, is concerned in particular with the relationship between the success of certain MFY change objectives and the response of the schools to the substance of the proposed changes, the resources available to the agency, and its choice of strategies. Messrs. Herman and Rosenberg cite illustrations from MFY's youth-work program to show how a large demonstration project can contribute significantly to the solution of broad social problems by exploiting opportunities to influence the programs and policies of the organizations with which it deals. Frances Piven's article, which opens this section, examines the demonstration project as a means by which the federal government can influence social change on the local level.

Part III has to do with one of MFY's most important innovations in the area of community development: the concept that the poor themselves must be enabled, encouraged, persuaded, enticed—in short, mobilized—to join in attempts to better their situation. The result of organized social action by the poor, according to Brager and Specht, will be an improved self-image for the low-income participant and more effective pressure upon social institutions. There are, however, inherent problems—the practical difficulties of organizing the traditionally nonaffiliative poor; the ideological conflicts social action raises for the profession of social work, with its historic emphasis on cooperation and mediation; the dilemma posed for the public institutions which, in effect, would be sponsoring attacks on themselves. Frances Piven considers these and other problems with reference to urban-renewal and early community-action programs and then undertakes a critical examination of the strategies available for organizing the poor.

A second, and widely discussed, innovation by Mobilization is the employment of members of the client population to serve in various programmatic capacities. The articles by Brager and by Reissman explore the practical benefits to be derived—by the agency, the clients, the workers themselves, and society at large —as well as some of the drawbacks. Gertrude Goldberg's contribution is a detailed, analytical description of one such use of low-income residents: MFY's visiting homemaker program. Charles Grosser further illuminates the role of the untrained local worker by comparing MFY's indigenous staff on various measures with the professional staff and with a sampling of the community residents.

In part as a result of Mobilization's activity, the need for new roles for the social worker has become increasingly clear. Thus Purcell and Specht, using an MFY case as an illustration, argue in behalf of the social-work generalist, who focuses on the total problem rather than on aspects corresponding to traditional areas of professional specialization. Grosser contends that the social worker must abandon the goal of neutrality and the associated role of "enabler" to become an advocate and an activist in behalf of the poor. Cloward and Elman demonstrate the need for involvement by the social worker in their description of an MFY neighborhood service center and its clients. They then propose a way of institutionalizing the advocate's role, through the private welfare agency.

The final section considers the logical extension of the concept of social-worker-as-advocate: the enlistment of the legal profession in attempts to defend the poor man's interests in his interaction with administrative agencies, to compel recognition of his right to service, and ultimately to clarify and bring about needed changes in the policies and procedures of social institutions. Marvin Larson charges that certain welfare practices and policies violate the letter as well as the spirit of the Constitution and, particularly, of the 14th Amendment. Charles Grosser and Edward Sparer stress the need for cooperative efforts by lawyers and social workers to support the poor man's interests in his dealings with public social-welfare institutions. Sparer points out some of the many areas in which the poor urgently need the lawyer's services and discusses some of the problems posed for the lawyer by representation of the poor man vis-à-vis governmental agencies. Finally, Judge Marvin Frankel enters a plea for novel and creative approaches to the problem on the part of the legal profession and considers several possible plans for making legal services widely available to the indigent.

Part One

POVERTY AND SOCIAL WELFARE

CHAPTER ONE

Poverty, Affluence, and Opportunity*

by Oscar A. Ornati

The call to do away with poverty "here and now" is loud and clear. President Johnson's "declaration of war on poverty," the writings and speeches, the political discussions of the day, the very existence—albeit troubled—of Mobilization for Youth, all point to a burgeoning national awareness of poverty. This is in line with America's best and broadest values. Concern with the poor is not a new development. On the contrary, as a nation we have been more concerned with poverty—at least we have spoken and written more about the poor—than any other civilized country in the world.

At about the turn of the century, those concerned with poverty began to distinguish between the poor and the "pauper." "Paupers" were those who had given up the struggle, who could not be reclaimed. They were viewed as those "who are not unhappy: they are not ashamed; they are not keen to become independent; they are not bitter or discontented."[1] The *poor* worked hard, had self-respect, cherished their independence. They were the "toilers." Yet every day circumstances over which they had no control pushed the "worthy poor" into "pauperism." Once paupers, they were regarded as lost—at least by students of poverty in that era. The only way to keep the poor out of pauperism was by keeping them out of poverty. So it was that the fight against poverty became part of the tradition of social reform. The poverty-producing factors most commonly mentioned were low wages, sickness, industrial accidents, widowhood, unemployment, the flooding of

* Prepared for the Training Institute on "Urban Community Development Projects," Columbia University School of Social Work—Mobilization for Youth, April 27-May 1, 1964.

[1] Robert H. Bremmer, *Change and Continuity in Recent American Concepts of Poverty*, paper presented at the Faculty Seminar on Urban Poverty, New York, Hunter College, Oct. 25, 1962, pp. 3-4.

the market with immigrants, alcoholism, and poor housing. Individuals could not cope with these problems, but society could take steps to abolish some of them and alleviate the effects of others. The fight against poverty therefore became associated primarily with social reform and legislative action: tenement-housing legislation, abolition of child labor, maximum hours–minimum wages laws, compensation for industrial accidents, and the like.

In the New Deal era, the distinction between the poor and the pauper disappeared, and the problems of poverty were viewed primarily as problems of economics. Poverty was increasingly regarded as the result of the economy's working at less than full potential. The impact of governmental action in this period is difficult to assess. Clearly, no major inroads into poverty were apparent by the beginning of World War II. On the other hand, some slight improvements in income distribution which took place later must be ascribed to New Deal measures.

In the late 1950's we moved into affluence and became concerned with the poor of underdeveloped areas; yet poverty did not disappear. Today poverty is again a national problem and a major concern. There is, however, no consensus as to the definition of poverty, the scope of the problem, the steps that should be taken in order to do away with poverty, or the danger to society of not doing away with it. In Washington, in the state capitols, in the city halls, at the headquarters of foundations, debate is rampant as to meanings, priorities, and methods.

How can poverty be defined so as to clarify issues and develop meaningful policies?

Traditionally, poverty has been considered to be the condition of persons whose resources are insufficient to satisfy their basic needs and who therefore live below "minimum subsistence," not "adequately," or in "deprivation." But, having agreed that nobody should live below subsistence or be deprived, we seem, as a nation, unable to agree as to what minimum subsistence or adequacy means. Nor are the physical sciences of any help in determining minimum needs. Even "adequate nutrition" is not scientifically definable, for experts disagree about desirable intakes of calcium, iron, and various kinds of vitamins, and estimated protein requirements, according to Townsend, are little more than intelligent guesswork. "The problem," he adds, "is rather like that of trying to define 'adequate' individual height.

milies with the characteristics listed above would be re-
d as "poor."

 study for the Twentieth Century Fund,[5] we developed a
vely simple measure of the relation between possessing a
characteristic and having an income below certain specified
. This measures the risk of poverty and permits us to make
to-year comparisons for a given characteristic and among
cteristics which reflect changes in both composition and
ence. Conceptually, this measure of risk provides us with
quivalent of actuarial tables such as those used by insurance
anies.

 calculating the risk of poverty of different groups and at
rent times we have discovered three important things: First,
family has two or more of these characteristics, the prob-
ity of poverty is overwhelming. Thus families which have
following combinations of characteristics have *three out of*
 chances of earning less than $4,500 per year:

> nonwhite families (a) headed by a female (b);
> aged families (c) living on a farm (d);
> aged (c) Negro families (a);
> Negro families (a) living on a farm (d);
> farm families (d) headed by a female (b).

Secondly, except for the characteristic "male head of family
ver 65," the risk of being poor for all the characteristics men-
oned has *increased* since 1947.

 Thirdly, the risk of poverty has remained relatively unaffected
y the ups and downs of the economy. Expansion did not reduce
he risk of poverty, nor did contractions increase it by very
uch.

 A check on the validity of this approach and on the findings
eported for 1960 is provided by repeating the analysis of the
haracteristics for a population with nonpoverty-linked characteristics. This was done for families headed by a white male
aged 25–34, with two children under 18. The data showed that
in 1960 this constellation of attributes was much less frequent in
the low-income brackets. Thus individuals with these characteristics appear *not to have a high risk of poverty*, which for the

[5] Ornati, *op. cit.*

We know that a man must have some height but cannot say
whether it should be four feet or seven feet."[2]

 Furthermore, individuals differ with respect to their conceptions of need, their ideas about justice, their values. Their estimates of their own state of need will differ according to whether
they are themselves poor or not poor, thrifty or extravagant, interested in things or ideas, familiar with or ignorant of the lives
of the poor. Their explicit and, even more, their implicit notions
about the workings of the economy and the society become
crucially important. What levels of poverty they regard as unacceptable will depend on whether they have been trained as
economists, sociologists, or engineers; whether they received
their training at Harvard or Chicago; whether "survival of the
fittest" sums up their social outlook or they perceive themselves
as their "brother's keeper."

 Despite these differences, it is possible to group the various
estimates of national minimum needs in three clusters of dollar
equivalents. According to a survey of contemporary practices in
public and private agencies, "minimum subsistence" is generally
defined as an income of $2,500 per year for a family of four;
"minimum adequacy" requires an annual income of $3,500; "mini-
mum comfort," $5,500.[3]

 From such differences in judgment stem the many and varied
recent estimates of the number of poor in the United States. The
figure 30 million has been receiving increasing currency. Yet
statistical studies recently prepared for 1960, the last census year
with very detailed data, estimate the poor as between 20 and
70 million.

 There is also disagreement as to whether the population contains relatively more or fewer poor members today than in the
past. The differences stem from different judgments as to how
the comparisons should be made. Should the standards of the
past be taken as a guide and, having been corrected for changes
in the value of the dollar, applied to the present? Or should current standards be deflated and used to reappraise the extent of
poverty in the past? If we use standards that go back far enough,
we are bound to find that there are no poor today. The statement
of the President's Economic Report of 1964 that "since 1947,

[2] Peter Townsend, "The Meaning of Poverty," *British Journal of Sociology*
(September 1962), p. 220.

[3] For details on these calculations see Oscar A. Ornati, *Poverty in an
Affluent Society* (New York: Twentieth Century Fund, forthcoming).

prosperity and progress have reduced the incidence of substandard incomes from one-third to one-fifth" suffers from this very same bias. It is true only in terms of 1947 standards. Conversely, by taking present standards and projecting them backward in time we would find, for example, that Roosevelt's "one third of the nation" would be more like one half. Both exercises tell us more about changing standards than about changes in the percentage of the poor. If comparisons are to be made, they must be made in terms of contemporary standards. What needs to be compared are the proportion of people living "below adequacy" by 1947 standards and the percentage of those living below adequacy by the standards of 1960 or 1965. When this is done, we find that the proportion of the population living below levels of "minimum adequacy" and "minimum comfort" has not changed very much. In 1947, by 1947 standards, 27.5 per cent of the individuals living in households lived below "minimum adequacy"; in 1960, by 1960 standards of "minimum adequacy," they amounted to 26 per cent. The proportion living below "minimum comfort" was 39 per cent in 1947 and 40 per cent in 1960. The story is different where abject poverty is involved: the proportion of those living at or below "minimum subsistence" declined from 15 per cent in 1947 to 11 per cent in 1960.

It is also argued that the poor are still with us, so to speak, by definition. If we define the poor as making up the bottom of the income distribution, the lower fifth, eighth, tenth, or whatever fraction you will, their eternal permanence is guaranteed. To develop a strategy to fight against poverty the problems of income distribution must be separated from those of poverty. Not that policy concern with income distribution is unimportant, nor can we forget that income distribution has recently become even less egalitarian. But income distribution, it should be kept in mind, is a derived aspect of poverty rather than, so to speak, its definitional cause. The slope of the line tracing the income distribution becomes unimportant when throughout it is located above socially determined standards of sufficiency.[4]

[4] It is most unlikely that the whole line tracing the income distribution can be above socially determined standards of sufficiency since the standards themselves change in response to changes in income distribution. On the other hand, the situation is theoretically possible, particularly in a rich country. True social gains are achieved when reduction in income inequalities takes place faster than changes in the socially determined standards of sufficiency.

In studying poverty and in mobilizing action, what is important is not change To tell a poor man that for many in A have greatly improved since the pre-war than to tell a man working in a poorly l dred years ago even the very rich worked

Throughout most of the history of the was the fate of a large part of the popu men and women, farmers and city dwel North and South, all shared in the natio some the risk of poverty was greater, but present situation is quite another story. As poverty has lessened, poverty has become carried by select individuals. In the United is most usefully viewed as the problem of certain specific personal, social, and demogr In order to do away with poverty, then, we not engage in debate concerning the acceptab for a family. It is important, rather, to identif of individuals whose chances of being poor and to alter these characteristics in some way.

Available statistics on the incidence of pov States show that poverty is increasingly the s families with "poverty-linked characteristics." 1960 one out of eight families in the nation h below the extremely meager level of $2,000, th to one out of three in the case of

(a) nonwhite families
(b) families headed by a female
(c) families headed by an individual 65 y or over
(d) rural-farm families
(e) families whose head has had less tha education
(f) families whose head has had at most work experience.

If poverty is defined as having a family income $4,500—which is only a little more than what is garded as "minimally adequate"—more than *two ou*

1960's can be interpreted as meaning that such individuals are not poor. In 1948 the risk of poverty for such individuals was almost twice as great, even by 1948 standards.

The fact that in 1960, at incomes equivalent to those of 1948, poverty-linked demographic characteristics were more frequent is *not* due to increases in the number of persons at the low end of the income scale. Indeed, a modest decline has occurred in the total number of people in these groups. *The greater concentration of the population with poverty-linked characteristics at the low income levels of 1960 appears to be due, rather, to the fact that those who moved out of low income levels between 1948 and 1960 were predominantly lacking in the social and demographic characteristics which have been found to be associated with a high risk of poverty.* Thus the data indicate that individuals with poverty-linked characteristics, whoever they may be, have a greater risk of finding themselves in poverty, however it is defined.[6]

What follows from this redefinition of poverty is, first, that affluence and poverty coexist today in a fashion that was not characteristic of the past and is barely understood now. We can stipulate that we live in a rich society. The United States of the 1960's is rightly viewed, the world over, as the model of an affluent society. We also need to stipulate that an affluent society is *not* a full-employment society. It is not necessarily working at its full potential.

In the light of these facts, it is pointless to debate whether an aggressively pursued monetary and fiscal policy leading to full employment will contribute more to the "war on poverty" than will large expenditures on education, housing, health, welfare, etc. Obviously, both are required. It is useless to rely on the multiplier effect of even massive governmental spending if the current poverty cannot be blamed on the ineffective economy. Nor can the blame be placed on the fact that our potential is greater than our performance.

Thus, in spite of the very large number of poor, *poverty cannot be viewed as a "mass" phenomenon.* Policies which are aimed at the economic improvement of the total society and which are

[6] Since this paper was written, many more studies of poverty have been published. Recently the staff of the Council of Economic Advisers, using data from 1963 and a somewhat different methodology, have confirmed these findings.

believed, therefore, to help the poor are of very limited use in the fight against poverty.

Nor is a general restructuring of the labor market and of employment a sufficient answer, for the bulk of the poor are outside the labor market. Contrary to common belief, most of the underprivileged are not workers, and it is precisely this fact that creates the problem.

High levels of economic growth are a necessary but not a sufficient condition for the elimination of poverty. For the latter we need specific, focused action. What are the paths of such action? From recent work on poverty, our own and that of others, we know that the poor of today are the underendowed, those who are less able than the bulk of the population to participate in the mainstream of American life. The underprivileged are not *of*, even though they are *in*, the market society. They sit outside —Harrington calls them "invisible"—marginal sellers and not very good buyers.

The very poor are often physical and mental invalids. More generally, they are economic invalids, displaced by the market or never placed in it. At times the poor are exploited. Often, however, their income is greater than their marginal contribution. When the businessman argues that it is not worth his while to hire the poor, he is not necessarily espousing pseudo-Darwinistic prejudices. He may be making good economic sense. Indeed, the work of many of the poor is so ineffective that it does not contribute to their employer's income what he is paying out in wages. The lesser incomes of the poor, in short, are linked to their lesser endowments.

What makes the poor of the affluent society different from the poor of another time or place is, more than anything else, the fact that they lack the personal assets which produce income and thus make it possible for the possessor to emerge from poverty. This lack of personal assets has been much discussed in studies of deprivation and in environmental analyses of depressed neighborhoods. Such studies point to the peculiarities of the "culture of the poor" and to the lack of opportunities in the world of the poor.

That many poor communities have their own vitality, that their social structure and perception of life may in many aspects be even worthy of imitation, cannot be denied. From a policy point of view, however, the culture of the poor reveals not only a lack of elements central in the culture of the nonpoor but a desire to acquire the cultural traits of the rest of society. The poor, in other words, wish to become like the nonpoor.

Studies of the deprived and of deprived neighborhoods point to the existence of differential opportunities and to the notion of scarcity. "Perceivable" or, if you will, "subjective" opportunities are clearly in short supply. Indeed, in recent years, because of improvements in technology, perceivable legitimate opportunities have been shrinking. Automation has been displacing the poor and decreasing perceivable opportunities.

But automation, and this should be made clear, is not the major cause of the displacement of the poor from the market; nor has it—at least so far—brought about an actual decrease in the total number of available jobs. Changing social standards and a general upgrading in the requirements for participation in our society are much more the cause of poverty. Throughout society, making a living depends increasingly upon the possession of certain techniques. Filling out questionnaires, passing tests, using the proper words are more and more requirements for continuing participation in the economy. Many among the poor are poor because they do not meet these requirements. The affluent society is, at all levels, becoming more and more organized. It is a systematized and science-oriented society.

In such a society, a willingness "to do anything" is not enough to rescue a man from poverty, for jobs are available only for those who are able to do "something." And even for these people there is no great abundance of opportunities: they must be able to do "something" that is new! The changes are the result of the new educational requirements congruent to the systematization of personnel management rather than of technological innovations. They reflect a rise in managerial expectations as to the capabilities of their new work force. These expectations are moving faster than the actual improvement in the training and quality of the labor force or the actual changes in job content. They create new and additional shortages of perceivable opportunities with which no neighborhood reconstruction can cope.

The anomaly of poverty in an affluent society is thus underlined again: to the poor, the growth of the economy is visible in the new products that they are eager to buy, but not in new jobs. What is crucial is not the shortage of opportunities today but the fact that new opportunities are not perceivable by the poor.

What unfilled jobs and "objective opportunities" exist are located exclusively at the very frontiers of the society and at the very frontiers of economic development. The poor can reach for them only if they can be trained to bypass several steps of the existing social structure. We can save the potential juvenile delinquent, the potential poor young father, from poverty by helping them to skip the "manufacturing–automobile mechanic stage" and moving them to the level of the radiologist or the biophysicist. Intermediate stages can only be a palliative and lead to frustration. What we are proposing is that opportunities be recast, not by reconstruction of neighborhoods, but by reconstruction of the personal patrimony with which the poor face the labor market that lies outside the neighborhood.

Economists and other social scientists have been puzzled by rates of economic growth that were larger than observed increases in capital investment. The solution of the puzzle seems to be in the contribution to economic growth of individual human assets. The idea of investment in human capital is not new. What is new is the terminology and the econometric method applied. Since we have learned that the growth patterns of various societies reflect different rates of investment in human beings, we can conclude that in a high-income economy such as ours, different rates of investment in human beings determine who in that society is and who is not poor.

Why do the poor have an inadequate personal patrimony? Why does investment in human beings vary so much from group to group? What does it mean, and what are the implications of investing in human beings?

Central in answering this question must be the realization that services meant to strengthen the quality of men in our society have traditionally been provided by the public sector, and that as a nation we have starved our public sector. Because of our reliance on local taxation systems, we have tended as a nation to spend less on health, education, housing, and other forms of investment in human beings precisely where most is needed. Thus the poorest states and the poorest neighborhoods are also the states and the neighborhoods in which the least is spent precisely on those services most needed by the poor.

Poverty obviously has a geographic dimension: Southerners and those who live in Appalachia have a greater risk of being poor. But the notion of pockets of poverty is helpful only as it locates the area of action. The cause of poverty is rarely its location. Certain areas have a high proportion of poor because a high proportion of their population has those personal traits that link the individual to poverty.

The elimination of poverty in America requires the adoption by the community of the notion that human beings must be enriched by a series of specific expenditures intended to make them better able to participate in the workings of our society. Poverty in America can be eliminated only by intensified action along the lines of education, training and retraining, civil rights, a universal old age and survivors' insurance system, a national health insurance system, slum abatement, and the like. We are already working along most of these lines. Greater efforts still are needed.

These policies are economically right in that they are intended to prevent poverty in the future rather than merely to provide support for the poor of today. They are also morally right in striking at the source of the disease of poverty rather than merely ministering to the symptoms of its victims.

CHAPTER TWO

Private Social Welfare's Disengagement from the Poor: The Case of Family Adjustment Agencies*

by RICHARD A. CLOWARD and IRWIN EPSTEIN

In recent years, a general disengagement from the poor on the part of private social-welfare agencies of many types appears to have taken place. This development does not characterize all agencies, to be sure, but it is sufficiently pervasive to cause concern in a field which has traditionally awarded the giving of service to low-income people a high priority and at a time when poverty is once again a focus of national concern.

In an earlier version of this article, we summarized historical trends in the clientele of family-adjustment agencies from 1900 to the present, in order to document the shift of services away from low-income groups. Space limitations permit us to reprint here only the second part of that paper, which represents an effort to explain why the shift came about. It should be noted that the evolution and magnitude of the trend away from the poor can also be shown with respect to a number of other kinds of private agencies.[1]

---

* Abridged from *Proceedings of Annual Social Work Day Institute*, School of Social Welfare, New York State University at Buffalo, May 1965.

[1] In the field of group work and recreation, for example, see Elizabeth Douvan and Carol Kay, *Adolescent Girls* (Ann Arbor, Mich.: Survey Research Center, University of Michigan, n.d.); Elizabeth Douvan, *A Study of Adolescent Boys* (Ann Arbor, Mich.: Survey Research Center, University of Michigan, for the National Council, Boy Scouts of America, n.d.); Sidney G. Lutzin, "The Squeeze Out!—Recreation's Abdication of Responsibility," *Recreation*, LV, 8 (Oct. 1962), pp. 390-92; University of Maryland, Division of Social Sciences, *A Survey of Leisure Activities and Interests of Teen-Age Youth in the Washington Metropolitan Area*, Part I, Oct. 1960; *Program of the Girl Scouts of the U.S.A.* (Ann Arbor, Mich.: Survey Research Center, University of Michigan, Sept. 1958). By and large, these studies show a pronounced tendency among agencies to serve middle-income young people.

The Public–Private Allocation of Clientele

The movement of private family-adjustment agencies away from low-income people is nowhere better revealed than in an examination of their patterns of referral of clients to public-assistance programs.

Once publicly supported income-maintenance programs came into existence, following the depression, private agencies began to refer economically deprived clients, thus conserving their resources for other services. The extensive use of referral to public agencies as a way of closing out contact with the poor has been noted in a number of recent studies. Maas, for example, observes that "Proportionately more lower-occupational-status families terminate in consultation or referral."[2] Beck notes, "The proportion of cases closing on a planned basis at the end of the first intake interview increases rapidly as social class declines. To some extent," she goes on to say, "this probably reflects merely increased referrals to public agencies for financial assistance. Probably inappropriate requests for other types of direct service account for additional closings for these groups."[3]

The emergence of publicly supported income-maintenance agencies is sufficient to account for private-agency referrals of low-income people for relief. It is not sufficient, however, to explain the tendency of private agencies to act as if such referrals fulfilled their responsibility to poor people.

In 1934, Linton B. Swift described the developing relationship between private family agencies and public agencies. Because the Federal Relief Administration had eliminated subsidies to private agencies for cash relief, a huge proportion of the private-agency clientele was shifted to public relief rolls. The general public, however, was unwilling to support casework service as part of public relief administration. Hence, public agencies turned to the private sector for such services. Swift urged that this pattern of simultaneous service be more widely instituted, on the ground that private agencies should not duplicate but "supplement" public programs. He called for patterns of public–private services that were

[2] Henry S. Maas, "Sociocultural Factors in Psychiatric Clinic Services for Children," *Smith College Studies in Social Work*, XXV, 2 (Feb. 1955), p. 6.
[3] Dorothy Fahs Beck, *Patterns in the Use of Family Agency Service* (New York: Family Service Association of America, 1962), p. 34.

. . . not mutually exclusive, but . . . related: thus the adequate administration of relief requires [private agency] casework in some of its aspects: good casework in some situations requires relief resources, and so on. And all these elements in our community program grow out of two basic needs: (1) the necessities of life for individuals in distress, and (2) attention to other handicaps, within the individual or his environment, which hamper his capacity for social self-expression.[4]

This division of labor—that is, private-agency supplementation of public service—was, however, short-lived. As the pall of the depression lifted, many private-agency clients became economically independent, with the result that the private agency no longer felt constrained to integrate its program with that of the public agency. A new conception of private casework began to emerge —one heavily dominated by psychological conceptions of family problems. It tended to eschew environmental approaches (housing, employment, medical, and other concrete environmental services), leaving responsibility for them to public agencies, despite an awareness that the public programs were inadequate to the task. The private agency began to limit its responsibility for poor people to conducting studies and to giving expert testimony about the current needs of welfare recipients. Now, three decades later, even this "social reform" function often has little priority in the private agency. Jean Rubin, of the Public Issues Committee of the Family Service Association of America, recently commented on the difficulty of enlisting the interest of private-agency staff members in public welfare, equality of opportunity, and other matters which mostly affect the poor:

We hope these memoranda and materials [on problems of the poor] circulate among the staff . . . [of constituent agencies], but we have no control over what happens once they have left our mail room. I must confess that I sometimes feel as though I was putting a message in a bottle and launching it upon the high seas.[5]

[4] Linton B. Swift, *New Alignments Between Public and Private Agencies in a Community Family Welfare and Relief Program* (New York: Family Welfare Association of America, 1934), p. 18.

[5] Jean Rubin, "The Caseworker's Role in Public Issues," speech given at The Middle and North Atlantic Regional Institute, Pocono Pines, Penn., June 10, 1964, p. 7.

There is no question that it is appropriate for private agencies to help the poor make use of public services; only in the public sector are the necessary economic resources available to meet income-maintenance needs. However, many low-income people who have been referred have had a variety of problems extending beyond income maintenance (e.g., housing, health, employment). Who was to help with these problems? As we have noted, one possibility was that the private agency would define its role as giving continuing service *concurrent* with referral to a public-assistance program. But this happened only for a short time during the depression itself.

What is the evidence for the current lack of simultaneous service? First, we have noted that private agencies now refer a great many low-income clients to public agencies. This finding by itself might suggest merely a recognition that the public agency is far better able to meet the income-maintenance needs of the poor. However, it should be stressed that the early termination of contact does not occur because private agencies believe the poor to be without troubles beyond those of income maintenance. "Clearly," Beck observes, "lower-class clients are somewhat more likely than upper-class ones to have an overwhelmingly large number of problems."[6] Nevertheless, disengagement from the poor, as the FSAA study makes clear, "occurs *even though lower-class clients have somewhat more problems and cases with more problems generally receive more interviews.* It also occurs in a setting where inability to pay for service is no deterrent to treatment."[7]

Secondly, these early closings are not at the initiative of the poor. The wealthy are the clients most likely to decide when contact should be discontinued. Where the poor are concerned, it is the agency which planfully disengages from the relationship. Here again, the findings from the FSAA comprehensive survey should be pondered:

> Except for the top class, closings at client initiative dropped as social class declined. In the upper middle class, nearly six cases in ten took the initiative in terminating in contrast to only one in

---

[6] *Op. cit.*, p. 28.
[7] *Ibid.*, p. 33. Emphasis added.

three of the lowest group. Closings at worker initiative, while unusual at any level, were more than twice as frequent at the lowest
level than at any other.[8]

Referral to public agencies precludes the necessity for the private agencies to deal directly with the difficult reality problems
which the poor bring to their doors. In the private-agency sector,
closing a case after the first or second interview is one of the
chief ways in which the poor are disengaged. Such closings are
typically defined as "consultations" or "referrals." If the former,
the case record will usually show that the client was "inaccessible to treatment" or held "unrealistic expectations of the agency's
services." Of course, a more effective way of terminating service
is to pass the client on to another agency, for the client who is
being referred is likely to believe that he is being served rather
than simply disengaged, and potential resentment is thus drained
off. Such referrals, as we noted, are typically made to public
agencies, chiefly to public assistance agencies. As a consequence,
the public agencies frequently stagger under virtually unman-
ageable burdens. Private residential treatment institutions for
juvenile delinquents, having made "errors" in intake, "pass on"
their difficult cases to the public training schools; settlements
and community agencies arrange to have public detached street
workers assigned to the more difficult juvenile gangs; family
agencies abandon so-called multiproblem families to welfare departments; private hospitals shrug off the chronically ill patients
to the back wards of publicly supported custodial hospitals. Thus
the public programs have tended to become the repository for
the poor; private agencies have abandoned the neediest segment
of society as their chief target.

Why the Disengagement from the Poor?

How has this situation come to be? Why have private agencies
become, as we contend, disengaged from the poor?

The private agency, we suggest, did not respond to the development of public programs by defining a new role with respect to its traditional clientele, the poor; instead, it moved
toward a new clientele, economically more fortunate than the

[8] *Ibid.*, p. 35.

old. At the same time, a new conception of the private agency began to emerge.

Historically, the field of social welfare has been concerned with social problems arising from large-scale immigration, difficulties in the integration of age and sex roles, massive changes in the occupational structure, the unequal distribution of social and economic opportunities, and the like. Social-welfare institutions arose to ease the disturbances produced in the lives of people by these societal dislocations.

At a given time, of course, there are limitations in the resources to help people which the society makes available through agencies and other institutional systems. Hence choices must be made about which problems will be tackled and which will be shelved or ignored. The field of social welfare has generally been guided by the principle that its scarce resources should be allocated for the solution of problems that the people involved cannot be expected to solve for themselves, either because they lack the objective social resources—money, power, etc.—to overcome their problems, or because they have become incapable of resolving their difficulties without organized assistance as a result of their prolonged exposure to destructive social forces and their inability to purchase remedial help. These conditions obviously describe the poor, the powerless, and the dispossessed in the society.

The historic decision to give service to low-income people was not based on a belief that middle-income people could not use social services or had no problems. It was based on the conviction that help should be given where the problems are greatest and the capacity to overcome them least. The point is that the many problems common to all groups in an industrial society are considerably more severe when coupled with extreme and prolonged economic deprivation. Whether the problem in question arises from adolescence, aging, physical disabilities, or any other source, great material deprivation overshadows and worsens it.

In recent years, the profession of social work has been retreating from this position. The literature abounds in statements stressing the private agency's potential for service to all persons, regardless of class, and alluding to the "new mission of private-agency casework." To the extent that it is achieving a representative cross-section of clientele, it is said, the family agency is meeting its true purpose—to serve the community as a whole—

and thus is becoming a genuine "community agency." There is no discrimination in such an agency, against rich or poor. Those who question whether the field of social work ought to be serving the middle- and upper-income groups are told that these groups also have problems, that they too need help, and that social work needs to overcome its historic preoccupation with one class of clientele and give all those in need the benefit of its professional technology. Egalitarianism, in short, has become the guiding ideology of private agencies.

To account for changes such as these in private agencies—whether in ideology or in clientele—it is not sufficient to point to the emergence of massive public programs designed to deal with the problem of poverty. Great economic deprivation and associated problems remained then and remain now. The shift away from the poor has been concomitant, for example, with the migration to urban centers of extraordinary numbers of economically distressed rural Negroes. It hardly needs to be noted that such movements bring with them enormous problems of hardship and adjustment. There was, and still is, ample opportunity for private agencies to continue programs of financial assistance for many emergency situations, for supplementation of inadequate public-assistance grants, and for other purposes. There was, and is, ample opportunity for private agencies to concentrate their resources on problems experienced by the poor which are not dealt with adequately in public programs, especially in such spheres as medical care, homemaking, housing, and employment. Private agencies were dislocated by the emergence of public programs, to be sure; but they still had the option of developing new roles in work with their traditional clientele. The fact that these agencies have increasingly turned away from the poor and have attempted to persuade the public that their services should be used by *all* economic groups cannot, therefore, be explained on the basis of the development of broad public-welfare programs.

Professional Status and the Selection of Clientele

Strains in the occupational status of social work have doubtless exerted an influence on the intake policies of private agencies. The community has been niggardly in allocating professional status to social workers—a circumstance customarily attributed to the presumed lack of a coherent body of social-work knowledge, to the presumed lack of distinctive social-work technology, and to other presumed deficiencies in the field of social work.

But the status of any profession is to an important extent a function of the status of its clientele, whether that clientele is defined in terms of age, sex, socioeconomic level, or other factors. The dilemma of social workers, like that of, for example, criminal lawyers, is that there is little prestige to be derived from serving groups in the society which are generally defined as lacking moral virtue, ambition, self-reliance, and dignity—indeed, groups which are often viewed as being composed of "free-loaders" and "chiselers." In effect, the brush which tars social work's clients also tars social workers. The prestige of the public-welfare worker is probably lowest among social workers, only a notch above that of his clients on the dole. Thus the image lingers that social workers are soft-headed, sentimental, and "overhumanitarian"—and all this chiefly because of their ostensible concern with the poor.

The field has not been unresponsive to these occupational strains. They are a source of pressures toward private practice, toward "clinical" doctorates, and toward professional and legal certification. These same strains have led to marked status distinctions among types of casework and group-work practice—chiefly between traditional practices and the growing body of therapeutic practices, such as psychiatric social work and group therapy. One caseworker has commented on this tendency as follows:

> The high status in the casework hierarchy of the agency offering counseling services to clients with emotional problems as against the status of the agency supposedly geared to tangible [i.e., concrete] services should give us pause to reflect on the priorities which casework is setting for itself.[9]

Thus the search for prestige may have led social workers to upgrade their clientele by socioeconomic position. The price of prestige may well be abandonment of the poor.

[9] Ruth Ellen Lindenberg, "Hard to Reach: Client or Casework Agency?," *Social Work*, III, 4 (Oct. 1958), p. 25.

Social-Work Technology and Culture Conflict

Social-work technology arose from essentially middle-class conceptions of the universe and is generally practiced by persons identified with these conceptions. Among low-income groups, however, value patterns arise which are adaptive to poverty. Thus a situation of culture conflict exists, mainly along social-class lines, which permeates contacts between agencies and low-income people. Conflicting cultural values generate strains between client and worker, leading progressively to dissociation if not to estrangement. Culture conflict, in other words, is probably one of the chief mechanisms producing disengagement from the poor. This is not a new idea, although professional thinking has yet to feel its full force. Several years ago, a caseworker put the point as follows:

> The predominantly middle-class identification of the present-day social worker has . . . made him less able to appreciate the client different from himself, whether this difference is culturally based or lies in the different ego capacity of the client. . . . We look for and expect to find in the client's attitude and behavior those norms and deviations that are characteristic of the middle-class society we know, making surprisingly little allowance for different cultural and social orientation. . . . The increasing social and cultural distance between middle-class worker and "other class" clients fosters a communication problem which should be of genuine concern to social work.[10]

But the social agencies have always been dominated by middle-class values. How, then, can a force that has presumably remained constant be invoked to account for the changes in agency ideology and clientele which we have noted? The answer is that the current bases for determining the appropriateness of serving particular groups of clients and judging their receptivity to the services being offered differ substantially from those of earlier eras. Furthermore, the structuring of relationships between agency representatives and clientele has changed greatly. Together, these two changes have enormously intensified a long-standing culture conflict, making it more evident and more irritating. These changes, we contend, account in large measure for the current disengagement from the poor.

[10] *Ibid.*, pp. 24-25.

The chief manifestation of these changes is in the development of psychologically based, therapeutically oriented casework technology. If, in an earlier era, the field revealed its middle-class biases in its tendency to discriminate between the morally worthy and unworthy poor, it now exhibits these biases in its tendency to discriminate between the psychologically "accessible" and "inaccessible" poor. The field has substituted middle-class mental-hygiene bases of evaluation for the traditional middle-class moral bases.[11] Furthermore, the new technology calls for a strategy of help which requires intense interaction between caseworker and client. Concrete services, offered on a relatively routine basis, were once a sufficient attraction to overcome strains arising from a morally based culture conflict; now this inducement is largely gone. At the same time, the intimate, prolonged, and intensely personal character of the new therapeutic casework sharply reveals the differences between caseworkers and low-income people with respect to value orientations. The more deeply caseworkers and low-income people become engaged with one another, the more clearly are these differences revealed. Strains in relationships are the result.

Culture conflict and barriers to treatment. Strong evidence for the argument being made here can be found in the statistics on those selected for continuing treatment from among those who apply for service. If culture conflict is operating, we should find that lower-class clients are selectively screened out.

Coleman and his colleagues, for example, compared the selection of applicants for treatment in a clinic and in a family agency. They found

> . . . no significant differences in the distribution and severity of psychiatric diagnoses in the two agencies. It is important to note, however, that Class V [lowest] patients, regardless of diagnosis, tended to receive less favorable consideration for continued treatment in the clinic, and also in Family Service although to a smaller extent. A surprising, and at this point unexplained, finding was the high rejection rate of Class IV applicants in the family agency.[12]

[11] Kingsley Davis, "Mental Hygiene and the Class Structure," *Psychiatry*, I, 1 (Feb. 1938), pp. 55-65.

[12] J. Coleman, Ruth Janowicz, S. Fleck, and Nea Norton, "A Comparative Study of a Psychiatric Clinic and a Family Agency," *Social Casework*, XXXVIII, 2 (Feb. 1957), p. 79.

We might also expect to find that more lower-class applicants are assigned to waiting lists, as a means of disposing of them short of outright rejection. As it happens, the reverse is true, but this exception to our prediction—Beck to the contrary—unexpectedly serves to buttress the main argument. The FSAA study shows that upper-class persons are most likely to be assigned to waiting lists ("Thirty-two per cent of the highest class were placed on a waiting list, but only 11 per cent of the lowest"). Beck concludes from this finding that the poor are actually being given priority in service:

> The explanation for this seemingly odd finding lies first in the relatively high proportion of lower-class cases involving emergency situations where delay cannot be tolerated. In the second place, many more are referred immediately to public agencies because of their need for financial assistance. It is, therefore, the upper-class families with marital and parent—child problems in their early stages, when casework can be most effective, that most often have to wait for continued treatment. There is certainly no evidence that agencies are favoring upper-clients because they can pay fees.[13]

To infer that the rich are actually being discriminated against from the fact that they must frequently wait for continued treatment is a marvelous bit of social rationalization, because the truth is that low-income applicants are less likely to get continued treatment whether they wait or not. The FSAA report notes, "In general, the average number of interviews decreases as social-class status declines. . . . The drop is from an average of nearly eleven interviews per case in the top class to less than six for the lowest."[14] The poor, in other words, are not placed on waiting lists as often as the wealthy partly because they do not receive continued service as often or as long as the higher classes. Their cases are quickly disposed of without simultaneous continuation of treatment. Placing clients on waiting lists has the effect, whether intended or not, of favoring the wealthy over the poor in access to continued service.

Of 200 cases of continued service studied by the Milwaukee Family Service, "75 per cent were in the middle or lower-middle class. The former includes small proprietors, white-collar people

---

[13] *Op. cit.*, p. 32.
[14] *Ibid.*, p. 33.

and semiskilled workers. The remaining 25 per cent is split between . . . the upper-middle class and the lower class."[15] In
other words, only 12 per cent of the total cases in treatment was
drawn from the lower class.

That these selective tendencies are not accidental is suggested
by the Milwaukee study, for "the social class of the client seems
to affect casework evaluation, diagnosis and prognosis. The
worker's judgment of treatability becomes increasingly pessimistic as we move from upper-middle class clients to lower-class
clients."[16]

It should be pointed out that the tendency to select higher-
income people for continuing treatment is not limited to private
agencies. It has also been noted in public agencies in which the
decision to treat is discretionary with treatment personnel. In
1954, to take one illustration, a study was published by the Institute for Juvenile Research, a tax-supported child-guidance clinic
available at no cost to all residents of Illinois. Like many other
studies of intake, the IJR study shows that a representative cross-
section of the total population applies for service. However, the
characteristics of those who actually receive treatment are far
from representative (see Table I). On the basis of these data,

TABLE I

Distribution of Children Offered Treatment, by Family Income

Income Structure	Accepted for Treatment	Applicants
High	47.3%	29.5%
Middle	27.7	33.0
Low	25.0	37.5

Source: Sylvia Stevens, "An Ecological Study of Child Guidance Intake,"
Smith College Studies in Social Work, XXV, 1 (Oct. 1954), p. 82.

the IJR study concludes, "Even though income level . . . [does]
not affect intake, [it influences] the probability of entering treatment."[17] This evidence strongly suggests that the disengagement
from the poor by private agencies may be caused, not by the

[15] Family Service Association of Milwaukee, Wisc., *Study of Continued
Treatment Service Cases*, mimeo, Dec. 5, 1960, p. 2.

[16] *Ibid.*, p. 3.

[17] Sylvia Stevens, "An Ecological Study of Child Guidance Intake, *Smith
College Studies in Social Work*, XXV, 1 (Oct. 1954), p. 82.

division of labor between public and private agencies, but by
something in the nature of professional technology that exerts
pressure for disengagement *whatever the setting.*

Conflicting definitions of problems and solutions. The decision
to offer continued treatment probably depends upon a judgment
by the agency that the client is accessible, amenable, or otherwise suited to make use of a highly structured casework relationship. This decision appears to be greatly influenced by the class
of the client, as we have shown. The direct correlation between
social class and the likelihood of receiving continued treatment
can probably be explained, in turn, by class differences in socialization. In general, the higher his social class, the more likely
it is that the client will exhibit values which, in the judgment of
agencies, are congenial to a casework relationship. This decision
thus reflects a fundamental class-based culture conflict.

As might be expected, clients from different social classes
hold rather different definitions of their problems and the appropriate solutions to them. Maas, for example, concluded from
his studies that "the managerial and professional workers or
college-educated parents tended to expect the 'mother–father–
child' approach. The white-collar workers tended to expect the
'mother–and–child' approach. The skilled, semiskilled, and unskilled workers and 'high school and below'-educated parents
tended to expect a 'child-only' approach."[18] In these and other
respects, social classes have been found to differ in orientation.

The chief point to be made about such differences is that the
typical agency exhibits a point of view which accords more with
the view prevailing in the middle and upper classes than with
that characteristic of the lower classes. The lower-class emphasis
on a "child-only" approach is least congenial with current casework thinking. In this vein, Beck reports:

> Agreement on the principal problem in the first interview
> dropped from 64 per cent in the upper three class groups to 52
> per cent in the lowest. Agreement on the principal problem was
> relatively frequent when the problem was in the family relation-
> ship area or in such obvious situations as old age, physical illness
> or handicap, or unmarried parenthood. Worker agreement was
> low when the client saw the principal problem as one of employ-
> ment or the personality adjustment of a child.[19]

[18] Maas, *op. cit.*, p. 68.
[19] *Op. cit.*, p. 30.

The increasing tendency of private agencies to define client-problem priorities in heavily psychological terms has been accompanied by a reduction in the amount of agency resources allocated to the provision of concrete services. But low-income clients are buffeted by many environmental problems, they define their problems in concrete terms, and thus they seek concrete remedies. Hence a broad area of conflict exists which has been noted in several studies.

The FSAA study dramatically documents the lack of congruence between the expectations of agencies held by low-income clients and the actual services offered:

> In general, client requests do not match closely the services offered. Casework service, which is the core service of Family Agencies, is requested by 86 per cent of the top class but only 55 per cent of the lowest. Perhaps it is hard for a lower-class applicant to conceive of being helped merely by a talking process. Requests for financial assistance follow the reverse pattern and rise steeply as social class declines. Even though few agencies any longer give any substantial amount of financial assistance, 31 per cent of the applicants from the lower class still ask for such aid.[20]

Lower-class people also ask for more help in a variety of other reality areas, including "physical illness or handicap, substitute care of children, housing, old age, etc."[21] When Beck compared worker-client agreement levels on all problems, not just on the principal problem, the following results were obtained:

> Agreement on all problems dropped from 49 per cent to 34 per cent as social class declined. In the areas of family relationship and individual personality problems, workers reported one or more problems in many instances where no corresponding client concern was noted. As social class declined, discrepancies of this type became progressively more frequent. Apparently lower-class clients are less prone than others to define their problems in these terms. Instead they are accustomed to seek solutions through some type of environmental change or concrete service.[22]

[20] *Ibid.*, p. 31.
[21] *Ibid.*, p. 29.
[22] *Ibid.*, p. 30.

The FSAA report goes on to observe, "These marked differences between client expectations and the services actually provided pose a real problem for agencies, particularly in relation to services to the lower-class groups."[23]

These and similar statements in other research reports are extraordinary for several reasons. For one thing, they speak of social casework as a thing apart from concrete services; casework appears to have become a "talking process" in many agencies. Secondly, the very tentativeness of conclusions about the importance of concrete services in helping the poor bespeaks an unfamiliarity with the problems of people in poverty that is remarkable in a field which has made the elimination of poverty and its consequences one of its central aims.

The tendency of low-income clients to view their problems and the solutions to them in terms of concrete services appears to be an important basis for refusing continued service to them. In a study of 295 initial telephone contacts in 12 family service agencies (where there was no previous information about the callers), it was found that applications focused on problems of family relations were more likely to be made cases than any others (85 per cent). Applications centered on personality problems, old age or physical illness, or substitute care of children were also likely to be made cases. Of the sizable group of applications in which economic problems were central (and these are most likely to be lower-class persons), only 65 per cent were made intake cases.[24]

Ann Shyne, summarizing the results of a number of studies of continuing treatment, lists four factors associated with continuance and four associated with early termination:

Associated with continuance beyond a single interview were: (1) a request by the client for help with problems primarily of a psychological or interpersonal nature; (2) favorable response by the client to the worker's proposal for solution or treatment of the basic problem; (3) indication by the client that he saw the worker as a source of help in working through his own thoughts and feelings about the problem; and (4) movement forward during the interview in acceptance of the worker in a counseling role. Conversely, associated with termination after one interview

[23] *Ibid.*, p. 31.
[24] Family Service Association of America, *Study of Telephone Interviews: Part II*, 1955, p. 8.

were: (1) a request for help with problems of other than a psychological or interpersonal nature; (2) noncommittal or negative response to the worker's proposal for solution; (3) a conception of the worker as a source of concrete service; and (4) failure to move forward in accepting the worker in a counseling role.[25]

The chief point is that conflicting definitions of problems and solutions lead to strains in the relationship between social workers and low-income clients. As a consequence, disengagement occurs—disengagement by workers because they probably do not feel that clients can make effective use of service, and disengagement by clients because they probably do not feel that available services have a significant bearing upon the resolution of their problems.

The general conditions of life among the lower classes tend to produce modes of family structure, sex-role differentiation, values, language forms, ways of relating to one another, and the like which differ significantly from the more familiar and widely diffused patterns of middle-class life. In particular, the poor focus on the problem of survival, not because they are personally deficient, but because that is precisely the problem facing them. They often find incomprehensible the belief that natural and social forces can be harnessed and controlled, precisely because the experience of their lives—as contrasted with the lives of middle-class people—tells them that such pressures can only be endured. If their life conditions change—if their opportunities are enlarged—their values will change. But meanwhile they will adopt patterns of values and behavior which enable them to adjust, to accommodate in a reasonable fashion to their particular conditions of life. In this connection, Coleman notes:

> It is known to clinicians that psychological self-concern is in a sense a social luxury; that is, that it is dependent on the presence of a certain minimum of material and external security. In the presence of real, excessive deprivations and threats, the individual knows only one imperative, and that is to find ways of obtaining basic supplies and of escaping danger—of protecting himself against the bombardment of external stimuli.[26]

[25] Ann W. Shyne, "What Research Tells Us About Short-Term Cases in Family Agencies," *Social Casework*, XXXVIII, 5 (May 1957), p. 225.
[26] Coleman *et al., op. cit.*, p. 3.

In short, many low-income people probably regard as impractical the notion that a person in trouble can improve his circumstances through a better understanding of himself and the way in which he presumably contributes to his own problems. Members of this group value skills in coping with deprivation and uncertainty. They lack or do not value the personality attributes and skills required to make effective use of social-work technology—introspection, insight, verbal facility, and the capacity to use formalized, professional relationships. Such skills are much more likely to be the product of middle-class socialization. Thus, in many ways of which the field has not been sufficiently mindful, casework technology has become class-bound.

These are the terms, then, in which we account for the current disengagement from the poor by private agencies. In addition to status pressures, we suggest that the chief source of this disengagement is a culturally inflexible psychiatric technology. The private-agency field, having developed a new conception of casework, seeks out a clientele who can make use of it. Hence it moves toward those whose socialization is compatible with the new technology—the middle class. The field may know how to deal differentially with various types of small group or various types of personality dysfunction, but it does not know how to deal with people who have not been prepared in advance to use its technology. Coleman, commenting on the high percentage of cases in the lowest class group that were closed at intake, singles out as ". . . the most important factor . . . the attitudes of therapists toward their patients. . . ."

When a patient does not respond to the characteristic procedures that the therapist has learned to use in introducing him to the therapeutic situation, the tendency seems to be to react to the patient with indifference or veiled hostility and rejection, rather than to question the procedures. A person is apparently expected to meet certain requirements before he will receive approval as a patient. He must recognize that he has a problem relevant to the interest of the agency, that he is concerned about it and that he wants the kind of help the therapist is interested in giving him; furthermore, he must recognize the therapist's authority without its being explicitly imposed upon him. He must be prepared in a sense to do what the therapist wants him to do without having to be told what is expected. . . . In dealing with a great many patients, we shall be clearly at an impasse if we evaluate treatability by the extent to which a patient is able to comply with largely unverbalized requirements, derived from [middle class] sociocultural and educational experience.[27]

To help lower-class people, social work must construct a strategy of service which grows out of their patterned ways of understanding, perceiving, and grappling with the realities of their lives. A not-inconsiderable literature now exists which describes the life-styles of low-income people. In order to reverse the movement away from the poor by private casework agencies, these findings must be used systematically in the revision of problem classifications, the modification of service strategies, and the development of a different pattern of relations between the private and public sectors.

Conservative Explanations of the Disengagement from the Poor

It is characteristic of human societies that social problems of various kinds are defined as resulting, not from institutional inadequacies, but from the presumed moral, social, or psychological defects of the people implicated in those problems. To the extent that these definitions are successfully imposed, criticism is deflected from the social order and support is mobilized for the maintenance of the existing system of social arrangements. Hence such definitions are essentially conservative; they tend to preserve the institutional *status quo*. Social-welfare institutions are not exempt from this general tendency.

That a general disengagement from the poor has occurred in the private-welfare sector seems clear. If our analysis has any merit, at least some of the reasons for this disengagement are to be found in various agency practices, such as the decline in emphasis on concrete service and the increasing use of psychotherapeutic techniques, with all that this has meant for intensified culture conflict. But how is the problem of disengagement usually defined? How do agencies typically explain their failure to work effectively with the poor?

For the most part, the field has been content to assume that the sources of the problem reside with the poor themselves. It says that they are "hard to reach"—a definition of the situation

[27] *Ibid.*, p. 79.

which has become extremely popular in recent years. To illustrate this tendency, let us cite some common explanations for disengagement.

A frequently advanced explanation is that the poor generally lack awareness of their problems and of the ways in which professional help can be used to overcome them. For this reason, presumably, they do not seek help. In the Berkeley study, an effort was made to determine whether a relationship exists between social class and awareness of problems. Respondents from residential areas of varying economic characteristics were asked whether they knew of anyone who had problems in the following spheres: marital relationships, emotionally disturbed children, child care, well-baby care, medical care, and use of leisure time. The study findings indicate: "Although the lower socioeconomic tracts . . . appear to have the highest incidence of problems, there is no greater awareness of problems by persons of low socioeconomic status. . . ."[28] Wolins sees two possible conclusions that might be drawn "from the noncorrespondence of problem volume . . . and the population's awareness of problems."

> First, problem rates comprising the social breakdown index are taken from sources which may be more likely to register problems of persons of lower socio-economic status than of higher status. Higher status may, in other words, be a deterrent to an individual's having a problem or attaining recognition as a problem carrier. . . . Secondly, if the first conclusion is a false one and problems are fully reflected in the breakdown statistics, then the lower socio-economic person is less aware of the problems which surround him and/or less likely to express awareness.[29]

There is, of course, a further possibility. What people come to define as problems may have something to do with their life conditions. Had the classification of problems to which people were asked to respond included unemployment, inadequate housing, and the like, it is possible that low-income people would have expressed greater awareness than other people in their community. Indeed, the studies previously cited make it abundantly clear that the chief problem that the private agency encounters in dealing with low-income people stems from their

[28] Martin Wolins, *Welfare Problems and Services in Berkeley, Calif.*, Berkeley Council of Social Welfare and School of Social Welfare, Nov. 1954, p. 38.

[29] *Ibid.*, p. 39.

persistence in making, as the FSAA study puts it, "inappropriate requests . . . for direct service"—which is to say, requests for help with a multitude of concrete reality problems of which they are apparently very much aware.

Another common explanation is that the poor are so unsophisticated in regard to mental hygiene that they do not seek or effectively use casework services. The FSAA study suggests:

> Probably people who have had the advantage of extended education appreciate more than do those of limited background the importance of seeking professional help on personal and family problems. They may likewise find it a little easier to formulate and explain their problems verbally to a caseworker.[30]

The Institute of Juvenile Research study takes a similar view of the poor: among low-income groups, "the chief concern . . . is with economic well-being and, because of this 'practical-mindedness,' emotional problems are often overlooked."[31] But perhaps it is not so much that the poor tend to overlook emotional problems in their preoccupation with environmental problems as it is that practitioners tend inappropriately to define the environmental problems of the poor in psychological terms. Differing life conditions produce differing values and patterns of behavior. And such differences, when they are exhibited by people low in a system of social classes, tend to be regarded as moral or psychological or social defects. Low-income people, for example, often make external attributions of causality; that is, they appear to believe that the difficulties which afflict them are the consequence of outside forces and pressures. Middle-class people, by contrast, are more likely to attribute causality to inner forces. Persons who exhibit the latter value orientation are usually defined by agency workers as psychologically conforming. Agency workers define as "projecting" those who voice a belief that problems of living are generated by arbitrary and capricious external forces. Referring to clients who received only one interview, the bulk of whom were in the lower class, Ann Shyne writes:

> It was found that an overwhelming proportion phrased their problems in terms of the need of another family member or a tangible need, with little more than one in ten phrasing their re-

---

[30] Beck, *op. cit.*, p. 9.
[31] Stevens, *op. cit.*, p. 81.

quests in terms of difficulties in interpersonal relations, although most of the requests were considered [by caseworkers] to stem from problems in family living. This corroborates the [findings of other studies] of a predominance of attitudes of "projection" among one-interview cases.[32]

To say that lower-class clients "project" is in effect to call individual personality into question as an explanation of widespread disengagement. Thus the Milwaukee study reports "a continuous increase in the proportion of clients who are [defined by caseworkers as] rejecting, resistant, and evasive as we move from the upper-middle class to the lower class. Of those who are receptive, there is also a continuous increase in the number who are not strongly motivated [as defined by caseworkers]."[33]

Aside from the pervasive culture conflict to which we have pointed, and which is frequently misinterpreted as representing resistance and evasion, there may be other socially structured sources of strain between private-agency workers and low-income clients. For example, the way in which a person gets to a social agency—whether voluntarily or under duress—undoubtedly is an important determinant of his initial attitudes toward the agency. The individual's attitudes may therefore reveal less about his basic capacity to use agency services than about the processes by which he was led to the intake interview. We may ask, then, how clients are recruited and what consequences different recruitment patterns have for attitudes and expectations. In the FSAA study, the following class differences in recruitment were identified:

To the surprise of many, those coming because they had found the agency listed in the phone book were highest in social status. Those referred by private physicians and psychiatrists ranked second in this respect. Probably upper-class adults are more accustomed than others to locating help on their own initiative either through use of directories or through consultation with the medical profession. Clients coming because of what they had seen or heard through the mass media were predominantly from the middle or lower-middle-class groups. So also were those referred or steered to family agencies by other community organizations, such as schools, churches, and social and health agencies

---

[32] *Op. cit.*, p. 225.
[33] Family Service Association of Milwaukee, *op. cit.*, p. 3.

of other types. Over half of those coming on the informal advice of friends or relatives, on the other hand, were from the lower class. About three in four of those sent by lawyers, courts, police, and parole officers were from this same group.[34]

Concerning the relationship between occupational status and source of referral, the Maas study indicates that

Self-referrals [to the New York agencies studied] tend to be more frequent than expected in the two higher occupational statuses and less frequent in the two lower occupational statuses; upper-occupational-status families who are medically referred tend to come through a private physician, and lower-occupational-status families, through hospitals and clinics; and court referrals tend to be less frequent in the two higher occupational statuses and more frequent in the two lower occupational statuses. The San Francisco data on occupational status and referral source reveal a comparably significant relationship. Again one finds that self-referrals and referrals by private physicians, hospital clinics, and courts, as well as social agencies, offer families in different occupational statuses somewhat different routes for entry to the clinic.[35]

Sylvia Stevens, in her study of child-guidance intake in Chicago, also directs attention to this area:

. . . the lower-income group has a disproportionately higher number of referrals from the Juvenile Court, social agencies and the schools, while the upper groups have a disproportionately higher number from private doctors and self-referrals. This would tend to verify the prediction that the upper-class groups are more sophisticated in regard to mental hygiene and utilize available resources voluntarily, while the lower class tend to come to the clinic because of pressure from social institutions. It may therefore be concluded that referral source of the clinic's intake is influenced by income level of neighborhood residence.[36]

Two points should be made about such findings. First, the resistance and suspicion ostensibly felt by involuntary "lower-class" recruits may have a great deal of basis in reality, for the public agencies of social control (police, courts, etc.) are not

---

[34] Beck, *op. cit.*, p. 27.
[35] Maas, *op. cit.*, pp. 51-52.
[36] *Op. cit.*, p. 80.

TABLE II

Class Distribution of Intake, by Referral Source

| Referral Source | Class of Client | | | Total Referrals |
	Low	Middle	High	
Juvenile court	45.8%	33.4%	20.8%	12.0%
Social agencies	49.0	27.4	23.6	27.5
School	48.4	24.3	27.3	16.5
Private doctor	26.3	39.5	34.2	19.0
Self	22.0	40.0	38.0	25.0
All referrals	37.5	33.0	29.5	100.0

Source: Sylvia Stevens, "An Ecological Study of Child Guidance Intake," *Smith College Studies in Social Work*, XXV, 1 (Oct. 1954), p. 80.

noted for their humane and dignified treatment of low-income people. Failure to take the institutional sources of resistance and suspicion into account may lead to invidious definitions of the low-income client as "naturally" hostile. Secondly, it is methodologically inappropriate to draw conclusions about the lower-class client as such when we are obviously dealing with two rather different groups—those who are in difficulty with the agencies of social control, and those who are not. Findings about lower-class attitudes toward agencies would be much more useful if they were controlled by voluntary or involuntary character of referral.

These are some of the terms, then, in which the current disengagement from the poor is being defined in the private sector. As this disengagement has progressed, a category of persons has been created whom the field invidiously refers to as the "hard-to-reach." But we might also consider whether the problem is not, at least in part, one of "hard-to-reach services"—of a structured incapacity on the part of contemporary agencies to give effective service to the poor. It is all too easy to blame failures in service upon the apparent intractability, recalcitrance, apathy, resistance, or lack of sophistication of the low-income client, when in fact the poor are not necessarily any less capable of being helped than are other groups in the social structure. As one caseworker has said, we "have hidden too long behind the facade of 'client failure' in the problem cases where we have been unsuccessful. . . . We have assumed that our failures were inevitable and have excused ourselves from looking at our contributions to them."[37] The problem may be that the field has increasingly developed a strategy of help which is neither practicable for nor congenial to the needs and interests of the low-income person. It should be remembered that the so-called multiproblem family is fundamentally a multideprived family, and the difference in connotation is of no small consequence. Indeed, the multideprived family is all the more deprived because it is denied effective and meaningful service by those in the private sector who speak in its name. If this is so, and it appears to be, there is great cause for concern.

[37] Lindenberg, *op. cit.*, p. 29.

CHAPTER THREE

Middle-Class Professionals and Lower-Class Clients: Views of Slum Life*

by CHARLES F. GROSSER

Social work is gradually coming to recognize that in order to deal effectively with lower-class clients, we must understand that the life style of the poor man and his relationship to the social system are different from those of the middle-class social worker. Somewhat perversely, however, our national egalitarian tradition has encouraged the belief that, as a people, we share the same aspirations and ambitions and use the same means to attain them. It is largely from this perspective that social-work institutions offer helping services, in terms that are familiar to middle-class social workers and board members, directed toward facilitating the realization of goals which are like their own.

In other words, social workers at least appear to assume that the client's view of life is identical with their own; upon this basis, apparently, they diagnose needs and plan services. Yet the life style of the lower-class client has been molded by generations of poverty, and his existence is shaped around the social-structural parameters of giant welfare organizations. There is reason to believe that failure to recognize these cultural and structural differences between the professional and his client may lead to the development of a service pattern that the poor find alien. This article will offer some evidence of the similarities and differences between workers and clients. In seeking to qualify the assumption of a common view of life, we hope to derive some important insights which, when applied, will facilitate the provision of social-work services to the indigent. We will explore the validity of the assumption that social workers

---

* Abstracted from Grosser, "Perceptions of Professionals, Indigenous Workers, and Lower-Class Clients," unpublished doctoral dissertation, Columbia University School of Social Work, 1965.

and poor people are essentially similar by reporting on the ways in which a social-agency staff, on the one hand, and poor people, on the other, view the community in which the former practice and the latter reside. Specifically, we shall identify and compare their views on life chances, community institutions, employment, and community problems.

The area used for the study here reported comprises a large segment of the Lower East Side of New York City. Compared with the total community, the Lower East Side is underrepresented in the professions and skilled occupations, contains few well-educated persons, and falls in the bottom half of the national income distribution. It is, in short, a slum community. As is typical of the big-city slum, its population is disproportionately representative of various minority groups. Although the neighborhood is similar in many respects to all impoverished inner-city areas, it is also unique in several ways. It contains, for example, middle-income cooperatives as well as low-income public housing; the result is a somewhat peculiar pattern of ghettoization. We do not, therefore, attempt to make the case that we are reporting on a typical slum community—if, in fact, such a thing exists.

The populations of all communities are stratified along class lines, and there are distinct differences among social classes in many respects. Slum residents are overwhelmingly lower class. It is clear that professionals working in public and private social institutions are largely middle class. This class affiliation will be reflected in the attitudes and values they hold, and in their practice as well. We must point out, however, that the Mobilization for Youth staff group, which was used as our professional sample, feels an especially strong identification with the lower-class community. Mobilization staff would recognize the effect of social class on life chances, including access to and use of social services. They tend to see differences in behavior as the result of differences in social setting and structure. They are sympathetic with attempts to deal with the problem of delinquency among lower-class youth through a socially oriented program of promoting opportunities for conventional behavior. This disposition of staff was demonstrated by their having sought to participate in a project of this kind and further specified by the criteria used in their selection. There are, of course, many characteristics that are distinctive to the staff members of

MFY. Our point here is that ideological commitment of the type described is one of them.

The MFY staff is therefore a fitting sample against which to test the hypothesis that a discrepancy exists between staff and client groups. Our assumption is that if this group, given its ideological predilections, reflects middle-class bias, it is fair to generalize to all other groups of professionals dealing with low-income clients.

The study herein described exploits a unique opportunity to subject our hypothesis to empirical test. The opportunity grows out of the circumstances by which a group of agency staff members working in a low-income community was available to respond to a research instrument which was essentially identical to one administered to an excellent random sample of residents of the same community. The instrument is a questionnaire which explores, among other things, perceptions of life chances, the slum community, and its institutions. The use of a single questionnaire for both groups makes direct comparisons possible.

The Adult Survey Questionnaire[1] was administered to a proportionate stratified random sample of the Mobilization community during the planning period of the project. The instrument used for interviewing staff respondents during the early months of the action phase of the project was identical with the Adult Survey Questionnaire with three exceptions: the face sheet was altered in order to ascertain professional information which was not included in the community survey; the form was shortened to provide for its administration to groups rather than individuals and to eliminate questions with no relevance to this study; and the respondents were asked to indicate the response they believed various categories of local residents might make as well as their own.

Before staff and community responses can be compared, it is necessary to determine whether the perceptions of the various class and ethnic subgroups within the community are consistent. Determination of the degree to which community perception is homogeneous not only provides us with a series of benchmarks against which we can compare staff's perception but also permits us to test whether the differences we identify result from

[1] *A Proposal for the Prevention and Control of Delinquency* (New York: Mobilization for Youth, 1961), pp. 497-532. See also Appendix I.

class or ethnic factors. It also suggests a finding in and of itself; namely, which, if any, of the constellations within a slum-community sample tend to be alike in their attitudes and perceptions.

Apart from simply determining whether community agreement exists, we are also concerned with establishing the substantive areas in which it exists or fails to exist. Since most substantive areas are closely related to the professional duties of staff, the ability to analyze data along this variable is of relevance. Thus knowledge of the degree of agreement among the subgroups in the community and of the substantive areas in which this agreement occurs is an additional basis upon which staff response can be evaluated.

Our data indicate that the community itself is not a homogeneous unit, and its various subgroups do not necessarily hold the same views. Within the lower-class community sample, only the Negro and Puerto Rican subgroups were in substantial agreement. Comparisons of the responses of these two groups were statistically significant on 70 per cent of the items. The other subgroups—Jews, other whites, and all whites—when compared to one another and to Negroes and Puerto Ricans, were in statistically significant agreement on 40 to 45 per cent of the items.

When we examined the responses ascribed by staff to local groups, we found that staff made no distinction among Negro, Puerto Rican, middle-class, and lower-class residents. Staff sees the community as a homogeneous entity having the same attitudes regardless of ethnicity or social class. This perception, as we have noted, is contradicted by the responses of the residents themselves.

Social class is suggested as a factor that will affect perception. Since ethnic background is highly correlated with class status, a section of analysis has been directed to distinguishing between class and ethnicity in community response. Is the high degree of agreement between Negroes and Puerto Ricans a reflection of minority-group or lower-class status? By holding social class constant, it was possible to determine that middle-class respondents, regardless of ethnic background, showed a level of agreement so high as to border on unanimity. Among lower-class respondents, however, the same level of agreement was found as when class was not held constant. This result holds true regardless of lower-class ethnicity. Thus lower-class Negroes and Puerto Ricans were in 70-per-cent agreement. Similarly, the 40-

to 45-per-cent agreement found among other subgroups reflects comparisons of lower-class members of these subgroups. Middle-class members of these same subgroups show agreement on at least 95 per cent of the items.

Our major insights regarding the local population are that membership in either the middle class or, to a lesser degree, a minority group produces a high level of agreement in attitudes toward the community. All other community groups show diversity. Middle-class agreement is undoubtedly the result of the education of this group, their contact with the communications media, associational patterns, etc. They have been exceedingly well socialized in the dominant culture of the society. Objective class indices, such as education and income, obviously do not reflect the value preference of lower-class groups. The apparent diversity within the lower class may reflect our inability to draw sufficiently fine conceptual distinctions regarding this group. Recent attempts to distinguish between the lower class and the working class represent an effort in this direction. With regard to the Lower East Side population, we may deduce—and we are supported by clinical experience—that the new arrivals comprise the lowest level of the lower-class group, and that their views toward the community reflect a rural or small-town setting and hence are very different from those of older lower-class residents.

We turn now to a comparison of staff and community based on their responses to the same set of questions. Regarding the desirability of the Lower East Side as a place to live, staff responses can, in the main, be characterized as considerably more negative than the community's. Although 26 per cent of the community respondents rate the Lower East Side as a good or an excellent place to live, only 12 per cent of the professional staff would agree. On the other hand, the staff's view of the citizenry's ability to affect community issues tends toward greater optimism than the community's. Affirmative responses of 32, 59, 57, and 40 per cent were elicited from the professional staff regarding the possibility that "a great deal" could be done toward cutting graft in local government, improving schools, improving race relations, and eliminating juvenile delinquency. Affirmative community responses on these items were 26, 44, 38, and 38 per cent, respectively.

Staff's responses to questions pertaining to occupational choice differ from the community's in ways which have been identified as middle class: i.e., they prefer professional occupations, will relocate in order to get a desirable job, and will take risks, if necessary, for a better job.

Although a very high proportion of all respondents (95 per cent) agreed that a good education is essential for advancement, there were marked differences on other items dealing with education. Staff's responses generally reflect the negativism we saw in their view of the community. Professional staff believe that the Lower East Side schools are more inadequate and that fewer children are graduated from high school than does the community. Staff also feel more strongly than the community that teachers are poor, schools overcrowded, and poor children ignored and that the teachers don't know enough about Lower East Side children. In some instances these discrepancies are very marked; for example, only 16 per cent of the community respondents, but 50 per cent of the staff, feel that the schools are poor or very poor; 48 per cent of the community as compared with 83 per cent of the staff hold the view that teachers do not understand Lower East Side children.

Authoritarianism is tested in the survey instrument by six agree–disagree items. Our data, as might be expected, reveal a pattern of greater authoritarianism in the lower classes. Of all the substantive areas examined, this category reveals the greatest distance between staff and the community. On such statements as "People can't be trusted," "Prisons are too good for sex criminals," and "Will power overcomes weakness," 51, 50, and 78 per cent of the community respondents indicated agreement as contrasted with 10, 1, and 29 per cent of the staff.

The responses to items concerning aspirations and perception of life chances again indicate "pessimism" among staff respondents. Of the community respondents, 63 per cent believe the poor have an equal chance to get ahead as compared with 16 per cent of staff; 66 per cent of the community and 13 per cent of staff believe that all races and religions have an equal chance of getting ahead; only 8 per cent of the community and 30 per cent of staff believe that slum children have less chance to rise in the world.

Our view of staff and community responses shows that the community differs from the staff in several respects that have become associated with a life of deprivation. One might explain the differences between staff and community on the ground that staff is better informed and hence more pessimistic about the slim opportunities for slum children, discrimination in the schools, and the like. The staff's greater optimism regarding the potentialities of affecting social problems through social action is consistent with the traditional middle-class response to these questions. It may also reflect the bias of a group whose professional activity is based upon a belief in social change. One might also speculate that the relative pessimism of slum residents in this regard, as well as their optimistic responses in other areas, is a functional adjustive mechanism which enables them to cope with the problems of their daily lives. We think that both these explanations contain part of the answer. Our main concern, however, has been to point out that these differences do exist.

The fact that the responses of the staff sample more accurately reflect community conditions cannot be considered merely as an indication of more accurate perception per se. The staff survey questionnaire was administered shortly after staff arrived on the job. Responses, therefore, must have been determined before direct knowledge about the Lower East Side was available. Two factors are the likely determinants of this staff response—the ideology which was part of the recruitment criteria and indoctrination of staff, and the transposition of views of other slum communities with which staff was familiar. Agency ideology unquestionably created the parameters within which program was shaped. The views that staff brought to Mobilization for Youth were consistent with this ideology. In this context, the staff survey findings are something of a self-fulfilling prophecy.

The responses of the community sample, particularly in the areas of education and life chances, illustrate the misconceptions, false optimism, and illusory hopes of the poor. It is especially striking to consider these answers in the light of the current estimate that 20 to 25 per cent of our citizens comprise the nation's poor, for a high percentage of our community sample— 80 per cent of whom live in or hover around the edge of poverty —believes that they have an equal chance to get ahead and that any young man can earn $10,000 a year. Our community sample —80 per cent of whose children attend inadequate slum schools —also believes overwhelmingly that slum children are treated equally in school, that the schools are not poor or very poor, and that teachers understand slum children. Our staff respondents do not hold these favorable views of slum life.

These patterns of response probably reflect the fact that those fortunate enough to enjoy a semblance of privilege, the middle-class staff group, are able to recognize that inequality exists. For those whose lives are largely without hope, the articulation of the inequity, the acknowledgment that life is what it seems to be, is more than can be endured. One might say that staff, which have the "good life," can bear the knowledge that it is differentially available; community residents, who do not enjoy such a good life, must subsist on the myth that they do, or that they or their children will eventually attain it.

CHAPTER FOUR

Perceptions and Reality: The Poor Man's View of Social Services*

by GEORGE A. BRAGER and SHERMAN BARR

The terms used by social workers to designate persons who avoid or take minimal advantage of institutional services have a fleeting currency. Examples of those in recent vogue are "hard to reach," "multiproblem," and "dropout." To this list we may now add "the unmotivated client." Our inability to settle on one term or set of terms in part reflects the imprecision inherent in language. It may also reflect, however, an uneasy awareness of the underlying bias of the designations.

Each term suggests that the explanation for lack of service can be traced to some defect in the client. Thus the presumably eager agency cannot serve a client who is "hard to reach" or whose proliferating difficulties are beyond its powers to resolve; school nonattendance is a manifestation of the youngster's rebelliousness rather than of school pressures or inadequacies; a client who does not take advantage of available services does not wish to improve his situation. These words do not suggest a reciprocal relationship between client "defects" and institutional "defects." Yet these are two halves of a single equation.

The description of a client as unmotivated, for example, may be valid, or it may reflect distortion in the perception of the beholder (in this case, the service giver). There is, of course, a wide disparity between apparent disinterest and actual dis-

---

* This article is a revised version of a paper by George Brager originally entitled "Motivation—A Social Worker's Perspective," prepared for the Institute on Education for Social Work with "Unmotivated Clients," Brandeis University, Jan. 1965. The illustrative quotations used throughout and certain generalizations are drawn from a paper by Sherman Barr: "Poverty on the Lower East Side: A View from the Bottom," presented at the Training Institute, Columbia University School of Social Work—Mobilization for Youth, April 27-May 1, 1964. This paper reported on 200 taped interviews with low-income residents of the Mobilization area.

interest. Low-income parents are often charged with lack of concern for their youngsters' education; yet studies have shown the reverse to be true.[1] Some parents no doubt are disinterested, but others feel concern which is unexpressed because of family burdens, time factors, health problems, lack of knowledge, fear of the imposing school edifice and its more imposing personnel, or numerous other reasons. Their lack of participation in school affairs cannot be dismissed as an indication of lack of motivation.

The clients also have perceptions which may or may not be accurate. Thus welfare workers, according to one client, "make it hard for you," and they don't want to know from nothing. But *they* get a big salary every week. . . . One of these days I'll go up to the top of the Brooklyn Bridge, yell 'Here I go,' and then jump off. And you know what? Nobody will know! Nobody will care! Nobody will miss me. Maybe the Welfare would be happy because they wouldn't have to give me money any more." Obviously, the client's perception of the worker's motives, whether accurate or not, affects his own motivation to seek and accept services.

We might, had we the space, analyze the various perceived and real motivations of clients and service-givers in interaction with one another. We shall limit ourselves instead to consideration of two related questions: How are service institutions viewed by the poor? And to what extent are these perceptions valid?

Clients' Perceptions

Poor people see themselves as victimized by society and not themselves to blame for their predicaments. The community is loaded with "social booby traps" which are quick to snare depressed, desperate, and unaware people. Legal, law-making, and law-upholding institutions and personnel are essentially corrupt, and represent the self-protecting laws of the establishment. Most people can be "bought." A double standard of morality exists—one code for "uptown" and another for "downtown."

[1] According to a survey of Manhattan's Lower East Side, 95 per cent of the residents of that low-income community agree that "a good education is essential to getting ahead." Almost 80 per cent believe that high-school graduation or better is necessary. (*A Proposal for the Prevention and Control of Delinquency* [New York: Mobilization for Youth, 1961], Appendix I.)

Those in the lower strata have little understanding of bureaucratic problems and regard service systems as structured deliberately to intimidate and discourage them. Aid, they believe, is granted unwillingly, if at all. "You've got to have pull, and if you don't have it, it's no good." On the other hand, a client reports, "They're quick to cut you off, and slow to put you back on. When you're in need the department takes its time, but when it's to their advantage, they can work fast. In other words, they can be efficient when they want to be."

The poor are puzzled and resentful concerning certain public-welfare practices. One client, for example, had almost finished a television-repair course when illness forced him to stop work. Now well again, he is unable to find adequate employment and is largely supported by welfare. He comments bitterly, "Welfare won't pay for my schooling, and if I pay $10 a week from what they give me, they'll close my case. But actually they'd save money by sending me to school because then I could get a decent-paying job and we wouldn't have to be on Welfare. That's proof that they don't want you to get ahead. They want you to stay where you are."

To obtain adequate service, one must manipulate the system. Clients exchange information and rumors on which police station to go to for Christmas toys, which social agency for money, and which church offers members the most clothing. Almost all welfare recipients employ some "illegitimate" means to obtain additional funds or services. Thus an elderly blind man reports:

> Well, here's what I do with the surplus food. I'm Jewish so I don't use the lard, and they give you so much cheese that it's impossible to use. So I sell some things to my neighbors and with this money I buy myself an extra chicken. When I cook up the chicken I take off the fat first. I make good chicken fat and sell it back to the butcher. I make a few cents, my neighbors a few cents, and so does the butcher.

Says a young mother, reporting on the time of her pregnancy:

> I'd wear a girdle to the unemployment office and as soon as I'd sign for the check I'd run to the ladies room and take it off and thank God I had another check stacked away. What did I lie for? I'll tell you, to be able to buy my child's crib.

According to clients, the Department of Welfare and its personnel are the embodiment of society's injustice, callousness, insensitivity, and cruelty. "What can you do if you are not lucky enough in the richest city in the world? We've got to go on welfare," said one client, "and have the welfare worker come up to see us and tell us how to live and then she looks in the icebox at what we have. They want to know what kind of clothes you have and when they see a telephone they want to know who is paying for it and why that money isn't being used for food. They try every way to get you."

These impressions are supported by a more formal study of 159 social-agency clients living in two depressed areas of Chicago. Of these, "74 per cent complained that they were treated as inferiors; 69 per cent said they were kept waiting too long on their visits to the agencies; 58 per cent felt that they received insufficient funds from these organizations; and 81 per cent expressed unfavorable attitudes toward the caseworker."[2] Most are reluctant to complain, however, since this entails the risk of retaliation from the more powerful adversary. "I never complain about anything to Welfare," said a Lower East Side resident. "The more you complain, the more angry they get. And since the investigator gets $50 every time he closes a case, he's going to cut you off if you complain too much. I shut up and just take it." Obviously, the appeals procedures are unused for this reason as well as for lack of knowledge. Clients have little confidence that action by them can affect their access to scarce resources, or that they can participate in decisions which control their very lives.

Professional social workers are viewed as "welfare adjusters" —that is, as people who help the client "adjust" to welfare. Interviews are regarded as peculiar cultural rituals demanded by agency workers if services are to be given. The social worker is perceived as engaging in irrelevant activities, asking unnecessary questions in unneeded places at inappropriate times and after the horse has been let out of the barn.

This, then, is the view of at least some of the "unmotivated clients." For them, "unmotivated services" are the issue.

[2] Saul Borash *et al.*, "Conceptions of Social Agencies, Community Resources and the Problems of a Depressed Community." Unpublished M.S. thesis, cited in Peter M. Blau and W. Richard Scott, *Formal Organizations* (San Francisco, Calif.: Chandler, 1962), p. 76.

The underview of the client is undoubtedly subject to considerable distortion. People who have been chronically deprived, particularly if they are unemployed, tend to relate to their environment with passive resignation and pessimism. Lazarsfeld found that persons without jobs soon lost all time perspective; they arrived late, if at all, for appointments for job interviews or receipt of funds.[3] Komarovsky found that the sexual and authority aspects of marriage were severely disrupted when the male could not perform his socially defined role of breadwinner.[4] These empirical studies dramatically document the fact that inability to perform a social role (i.e., holding a job) can result in attitudes and behavior which are "self-defeating" in that they prevent the individual from effectively altering his situation. In such circumstances, factors which destroy a person's motivation are likely to distort his perspectives as well. Furthermore, in an individualistic society, one which often equates personal worthiness with material success, recipients of help may resent their dependence upon the helper because of the implication that they are worthless. Unmet demands, whether justified or not, can cause ire.

None of these qualifications, however, necessarily attacks the basic validity of the clients' perceptions.

Institutional Services

Even a cursory review of institutional services offers small support to those who would argue that client defects are the major cause of the estrangement of the poor from social agencies. The public-welfare system, which touches the lives of so many so deeply, is a dramatic but by no means unique case in point. By most accepted standards, the amounts provided do not constitute minimal subsistence. Dehumanizing policies and procedures prevail. The means-test framework, for example, necessitates extensive and often undignified investigation. Budgets are computed in minute detail. (In New York City, for example, an employed male is allowed funds for 90 razor blades and 12 haircuts per year, whereas an unemployed male gets only enough

[3] Paul Lazarsfeld and Morris Rosenberg, *The Language of Social Research* (New York: Free Press, 1955), p. 168.

[4] Mirra Komarovsky, *The Unemployed Man and His Family* (New York: Dryden Press, 1940), pp. 57-58.

for 50 blades and nine haircuts annually.) Arbitrary decision-making and restrictive regulations are inevitable concomitants. Perhaps the most debilitating of all activities that the poor engage in involve what is called "tail chasing"—that is, keeping up with the various appointments, visits, and the like required by agencies if service is to be obtained. The resulting stresses are financial as well as psychological.

The basic rights of the impoverished welfare client go largely unprotected. According to the director of the Kansas State Department of Social Welfare, certain practices, apparently intended to discourage clients from seeking service, constitute flagrant violations of their statutory and constitutional rights.[5] In the view of this expert, residence laws are clearly unconstitutional.[6] Whatever the validity of his position, it is little short of shocking that no attempt has been made to test their constitutionality.

Broad societal definitions of the poor are reflected in service-giving institutions. Keith-Lucas notes:

> Persons who find themselves impelled to receive governmental assistance are not in general, or at least always, considered to have the same political and social rights as those who can provide for themselves and their families from their own economic effort or resources. There is behind the present welfare picture a long tradition of English and American "Poor Law," of the equation of poverty with moral inferiority, and of fear of according rights to paupers who might thereby find some satisfaction in dependence on government aid.[7]

Welfare officials are, of course, not immune from these general societal attitudes; nor, we might add, are other professionals. More significantly, perhaps, public officials are subject to the pressures of powerful persons and organizations who strongly hold these beliefs. The imposition of higher moral standards on welfare clients than on the general population follows. An example are the "raids" upon the homes of welfare recipients at odd hours of the night and morning to gather evidence of im-

[5] Marvin E. Larson, "Public Welfare and Public Policy," *APWA Round Table*, December 5, 1963, p. 6. Reprinted below, pp. 283-91, as "Democracy and Public Policy."

[6] *Ibid.*, p. 3.

[7] Alan Keith-Lucas, *Decisions About People in Need* (Chapel Hill, N.C.: Univ. of North Carolina Press, 1957), p. vii.

moral conduct or unreported sources of income. These, too, may well constitute a violation of constitutional rights.[8]

A recent study comparing two agency divisions concluded that "the clients with the higher socioeconomic status and greater power enjoyed more attention from workers and more stable relations with them, and formally instituted procedures served to maintain these differential conditions. Moreover, the agency division serving the clients with superior status and power was more highly esteemed among workers. . . ."[9] Another study, this one of decision-making within welfare departments, "confirms the existence of a wide range of discretion, since normative guidelines and standards are often missing and the basis of decisions made by the public-welfare agencies is rarely questioned."[10] Taken together, these investigations illustrate a major problem for the poor in their institutional dealings: they are subject simultaneously to more capriciousness in decision-making and less attention than more fortunately situated clients.

These conditions are by no means confined to public-welfare and welfare workers. Illustrations may be drawn from the gamut of government services. The self-protectiveness and defensiveness of large-scale organizations has been well documented. In interaction with the poor, the least well-regarded segment of society, these strains are intensified. Policy challenges by impoverished persons, however weak and fleeting, call forth intense reaction. For example, high-level school officials referred to the nine Puerto Rican mothers comprising a parents organization as "sick and disturbed," "uncivilized" in expressing themselves, "simple," "primitive," and, finally, "not ready for freedom."[11]

The inadequacy of public programs serving the poor, their widespread violation of the legal rights of constituents, and their resistance to constituent influence and challenge are at least partly responsible for the perceptions of the "unmotivated" poor regarding institutional services. These perceptions are quickly learned by even the youngest members of the family. In many

[8] For further discussion of this point, see Charles F. Grosser and Edward V. Sparer, "Social Welfare and Social Justice," below, pp. 292-301.

[9] Blau and Scott, *op. cit.*, p. 79.

[10] Keith-Lucas, *op. cit.*

[11] Drawn from the records of Mobilization for Youth.

families, lack of motivation, anomie, alienation, and apathy can be traced to the duration and nature of involvement with the Department of Welfare. The role of the private agency in this context is suggested in the words of a client who sought help from one such agency in applying for public assistance.

> Miss K., the social worker, gave us a letter to take to Welfare. If she had gone with us instead of just writing a letter, it would have been different. If you go alone, they treat you one way. But if you go with somebody from an organization, they treat you another way. She's very nice, Miss K., but I don't know what she's going to do for me. She looks at me, smiles, and says, "Hm-um, hm-um!" Well, life just isn't that calm for us.

The dissociation of private social welfare from the poor has recently been documented.[12] With the acceptance of public responsibility for relief programs, private social agencies have come to emphasize psychological methods of helping. One need not question the importance of counseling to note that, for the poor, it must have lower priority than meeting their material needs or ensuring that these needs are met as the client's right, in a humane and dignified way. If, then, there are conflicting definitions of problems and solutions—for the low-income person in concrete terms, for the professional social worker in psychological terms—one can hardly ascribe all wisdom to the latter.

Even in the provision of mental-hygiene services, the poor are disadvantaged.

> Coleman and associates [found] that lower-class patients tend to receive less favorable consideration for continued treatment, regardless of diagnosis, in the psychiatric clinic and family service agency. They suggest that the attitude of workers toward patients who are from cultures of poverty may have something to do with this situation since these applicants may never meet certain requirements before receiving approval as "patients," i.e., recognition of their problems, concern about these problems, wanting help, and recognition of the authority of the workers.[13]

[12] Richard A. Cloward and Irwin Epstein, "Private Social Welfare's Disengagement from the Poor," above, pp. 40-63. See also Richard A. Mackey, "Professionalization and the Poor," *Social Work*, IX, 4 (Oct. 1964), p. 109.

[13] Mackey, *op. cit.*, p. 110.

The technology of social work, like that of other educative professions, is culture-bound and inflexible. The professions, inevitably owned and operated by middle-class persons, have failed to take into account, not only the differing needs, but the differing style of low-income persons. Thus, for example, although lower-income socialization does not ordinarily develop the verbal facility required in traditional psychotherapeutic processes, there have been few attempts to evolve treatment methods more relevant to these less verbal persons.

If there is any validity to the foregoing analysis, the "unmotivated" client may in fact have been "de-motivated."

Part Two

DEMONSTRATION PROJECTS AND SOCIAL CHANGE

CHAPTER FIVE

The Demonstration Project: A Federal Strategy for Local Change

by FRANCES PIVEN

Federal action in local communities under "demonstration" program auspices seems to be acquiring increasing importance. Demonstration projects have been initiated in the field of housing by the Housing and Home Finance Agency, in education by the U.S. Office of Education, in manpower training by the Department of Labor, and now in antipoverty measures by the Office of Economic Opportunities. In the field of delinquency prevention and control, 16 such projects were launched during the early 1960's, under the auspices of the President's Committee on Juvenile Delinquency and Youth Crime.

The demonstrations are typically small-scale "pilot" programs of an intensive and developmental character; we have not ordinarily attempted to "demonstrate" the more diffuse ramifications of changes in regulatory policies, for example. Demonstration projects usually include some form of research evaluation. They are generally put forward as serving long-term social-policy formation by developing knowledge, by fostering experiment and innovation, and by activating or stimulating change. Such projects are generally heralded as promising major advances toward the solution of some social problem. They connote a mobilization of resources and expertise toward a "scientific break through."

The rationale for the demonstration as a pilot program which will develop new knowledge attributes to the federal government a pioneering and inspirational role in social policy, a role which in the past has been associated more with foundations and universities. It is in this role that the federal government has also been active in sponsoring research studies and in exploring and publicizing social issues through commissions, conferences, and publications. These activities are consistent with the view that there is a federal responsibility to promote intelligent reform in local government and community institutions. According to this view, local institutions are more limited in outlook than the federal government and more responsible to considerations of immediate political and organizational expedience. The demonstration program, as one means of federal intervention in urban communities, is an expression of federal responsibility. Under the demonstration auspice, federal funds are used to undertake relatively intensive and localized developmental programs through the instrumentality of local organizations. The strategy of "demonstration," of deliberately launching a program in order to examine its outcome, is hardly unique to contemporary social policy. What increasingly distinguishes these projects, however, is the involvement of different levels of government and different organizations, usually under the initiative and guidance of the federal agencies.

Since the demonstration program is typically of an intensive and developmental character, it requires new and expanded investments from federal and local government and from other organizations which may be involved, either because of prior jurisdiction or potential contribution. Support must be mustered for the programs, and opposition deflected. These are the requirements of political functioning, which do not merely parallel or underlie the public purposes of the demonstration program but are closely intertwined with them. This article undertakes to examine the significance of the "demonstration" auspice as a strategy of federal influence in the formation of these relationships between levels of government and between government and voluntary organizations, taking as our illustrative "case" Mobilization for Youth, a demonstration project in delinquency prevention. We will proceed by detailing the public purposes of Mobilization for Youth and some of the organizational and political requirements which the implementation of these purposes would entail. We will then consider some of the tactics by which support was mustered for the demonstration and opposition deflected, as these tactics served to implement or to divert the pursuit of public purposes. Finally, we will consider some of the organizational and political factors which account for the emergence of the demonstration.

A Federal Demonstration in Delinquency Prevention

In May 1961 an executive order from the White House established the President's Committee on Juvenile Delinquency and Youth Crime.[1] The Committee was charged to coordinate the activities of the Departments of Justice, Labor, and Health, Education and Welfare in a national attack on the problem of delinquency.[2] Not long afterward Congress enacted legislation permitting this committee to develop pilot delinquency programs in local communities.

In its own words, the President's Committee set out to develop programs which would "demonstrate effectiveness in the prevention and control of juvenile delinquency . . . [and] offer the greatest national potential for learning and action."[3] To this end, the committee would initiate or encourage programs in those communities which showed "an immediate potential for local change."[4] Thus an arm of the federal government would reach directly into the core of our cities and attempt to reshape local welfare functions which had been the traditional jurisdiction of city government and voluntary social agencies. The first and largest of the President's Committee demonstration grants was to the Mobilization for Youth project on New York's Lower East Side. It was announced by President Kennedy and Mayor Wagner at the White House on May 31, 1962, and was for its time a major event in the field of social welfare. Over thirteen million dollars was granted to the project, contributed by the President's Committee, the National Institute of Mental Health, the City of New York, and the Ford Foundation.[5] The local corporation, Mobilization for Youth, to which the funds were

[1] The preceding years had seen considerable activity anticipating more aggressive federal action, in the form of congressional hearings, conferences, and agency reports. In 1960 a White House conference on children and youth provided a stage on which to dramatize federal concern and mobilize professional support.

[2] See *Report to the President,* transmitted by President's Committee on Juvenile Delinquency and Youth Crime, May 31, 1962, mimeo.

[3] *Policy Guides to Presentation Proposals for Funding under Public Law 87-274,* Department of Health, Education and Welfare Administration, Office of Juvenile Delinquency and Youth Development, Sept. 5, 1963, mimeo.

[4] *Ibid.*

[5] New York City contributed $4.8 million, N.I.M.H. $5.2 million, the President's Committee $1.9 million, and the Ford Foundation $1.8 million.

channeled was itself formed by representatives of both local voluntary agencies and city-wide public agencies.

Mobilization for Youth was the first project sponsored by the President's Committee on Juvenile Delinquency and Youth Crime. It served as a major source of inspiration and legitimation in the development of the President's Committee itself,[6] and as a model in the development of other demonstrations. In its *Report to the President,* the committee described Mobilization as

> . . . the most advanced program yet devised to combat delinquency on a broad scale. Never before have neighborhood workers, the city government, the federal government, private agencies and a great university of the stature of Columbia University joined together for a planned coordinated attack on the sources of delinquency. Mobilization for Youth is the first concrete example of the comprehensive local action we believe necessary to meet the complex problems facing today's youth . . . this project promises to be of the greatest national importance.[7]

Because of its influential role, Mobilization seems an important case through which to examine some of the organizational and political aspects of the demonstration strategy.

The Public Purposes of the Case Demonstration

The formal structure of Mobilization was designed in part to reflect the various organizational compacts through which it was formed. It consisted of a board of 65 directors and a large, diversified staff. The board was composed of local agency leaders, a number of city-wide notables in social welfare, representatives of city government agencies, faculty of Columbia University, and a scattering of "indigenous" representatives from the neighborhood. The funding sources, federal, city, and foundation, remained related to the project by periodic review procedures. The city was not only a funding source but, through various city agencies, a partner in many of the programs.

The Mobilization for Youth plan laid out five program areas:

[6] Mobilization for Youth was initiated by a group of local social agencies on the Lower East Side of New York. In 1959 they received a planning grant from the National Institute of Mental Health. The project therefore preceded the President's Committee in time, and many of its ideas and even its personnel were influential in forming the legislation under which the President's Committee operated.

[7] *Op. cit.,* p. 20.

work training, education, group work and community organization, services to individuals and families, and training and personnel. Each of these program areas included several different activities, to be implemented by different organizational subunits and frequently staffed by different professions. And, since specific program activities might involve other agencies, public or private, as collaborating partners, external liaisons proliferated throughout the Mobilization structure.

In examining the various public purposes attributed to the Mobilization project we are interested in the implications of the project's structure and its external organizational relationships. Our object, as we have noted, is to illuminate the tactical significance of the demonstration auspice in resolving problems of organizational structure and relationship, and to indicate also some of the problems in the pursuit of public purposes which are generated by the tactical employment of the demonstration auspice. We are not, however, counterposing public purpose to organizational and political interest as if these were manifested at different times by different actors, or even as ideals of public action as against mere expediencies. Public purposes acquire political life out of organizational and political interest, and it is the interrelationships of these interests and public purposes which finally determine whether ideals of public action are carried forward or corrupted. It is these interrelationships that we are trying to illuminate.

It is always difficult, and finally somewhat arbitrary, to assign purposes or goals to a very complex organizational structure, which includes a proliferation of subunits, on the one hand, and a multitude of external commitments, on the other hand. A complete treatment of organizational purposes would require consideration of the range of attitudes toward the joint endeavor operative in different parts of the organization and among different supporters. We undertake here to examine organizational purposes only insofar as these have been formulated in public statements and documents, thus acquiring the character of a public mandate for the organization.

The Demonstration as a Delinquency-Prevention Project

Mobilization for Youth was funded principally from delinquency appropriations designated by Congress. The National

Institute of Mental Health had been given a considerably increased allocation for work in delinquency only a short time before its grant to Mobilization.[8] The President's Committee on Juvenile Delinquency and Youth Crime was mandated by the President and Congress to address delinquency. The early local impetus for the project also had its sources in concern with delinquency, particularly the rising incidence of gang conflict on the Lower East Side.[9]

The federal agencies made their respective grants to Mobilization presumably on the basis of *Mobilization for Youth: A Proposal for the Prevention and Control of Delinquency by Expanding Opportunities.*[10] This was understood to be a plan of action to combat delinquency on the Lower East Side, distinguished by a theoretical perspective known as "opportunity theory."[11] In brief, this theory relates delinquent behavior to social structure, specifically to the availability of opportunities for alternatives to deviant behavior. Thus, to the extent that major social institutions can be modified so as to provide slum youth with access to and opportunity for achievement, delinquency will be reduced. This theoretical perspective indicated that changes were required particularly in the schools, as community socializing institutions, and in the structure of opportunities for employment and occupational achievement.

Since this viewpoint associated delinquency with conditions of social and economic deprivation generated by inequities in opportunities, over time, the original focus on delinquency expanded to the broader goal of altering these general conditions of poverty. Thus, in a statement of goals adopted by the board in June 1963, a year after the project had entered its action

[8] A report on delinquency prepared for Congress by N.I.M.H. and the Children's Bureau in 1959 reflected most of the purposes subsequently attached to the Mobilization for Youth project. (See *Report to the Congress on Juvenile Delinquency*, U.S. Department of Health, Education and Welfare, 1960, 54 pp.) The Mobilization for Youth group was influential in procuring initial increases in appropriations for N.I.M.H. and provided supportive testimony for increases in subsequent years.

[9] It should be noted that this early concern with delinquency was not formulated in the terms presented here but was conceived rather more simply as helping children and their families by meeting self-evident needs.

[10] New York: Mobilization for Youth, Inc., Dec. 9, 1961, 617 pp., mimeo.

[11] See Richard A. Cloward and Lloyd E. Ohlin, *Delinquency and Opportunity: A Theory of Delinquent Gangs* (Glencoe. Ill.: Free Press, 1960), 220 pp.

phase, reducing poverty was given first priority "in order to prevent and control delinquency." This expansion in goals was accompanied by a shift in program approach to "total community development." The very early impetus for the project had been largely a bid for support for traditional services in casework, group work, and recreation, reflecting a strategy of psychological remediation. Under the forceful influence of the federal agencies, the "opportunity theory" perspective became predominant. The very process of specifying this new perspective into program activities tended to push the boundaries of concern from delinquency to poverty. The structural sources of deprivation identified as preconditions of delinquency were no less relevant to the more general problem of poverty. Thus the original Mobilization proposal was *For the Prevention and Control of Delinquency by Expanding Opportunities*, while a report submitted to N.I.M.H. two years later was more sweepingly called *Action on the Lower East Side*.[12]

"Community development" to eliminate poverty depended most importantly, according to the project's own statements, on the development of employment opportunities. As staff scrutinized the strategies available to a neighborhood-based project, with no jurisdiction over other public institutions, it became apparent to them that a local demonstration could alter employment conditions only in rather divisive ways. Even the local school system was largely inaccessible to the project, except insofar as the schools could be induced to join in programs largely auxiliary to the regular curriculum. The project was therefore thrown back on such approaches to community development as work training for out-of-school youth and the exploration of programs for adult employment which could be generated out of the project's own resources. Such measures were sharp accommodations from the project's general perspective, but they were all that could be mustered out of the limited political and physical resources of the demonstration.

[12] Mobilization was not, of course, alone in this shift but in consonance with a national move from concern with delinquency to concern with poverty. Thus, the HARYOU project in Harlem also began as a delinquency program, locating delinquency in the "powerless" community, and then found itself a poverty project, drawing funds from the poverty program. Nor is the association between delinquency and poverty peculiar to opportunity theory. It is, rather, a historically recurrent association, which seems to find particular favor during periods of reform.

In short, "community development" was conceived as requiring major changes in the structure of employment opportunities, in the schools, in the range of the major institutions which affected the life of the poor community, and finally in the structure of political influence. These changes were largely outside the jurisdictional reach or organizational capability of the demonstration project.

The Demonstration as Scientific Investigation of Social Policy

Perhaps the principal interest of N.I.M.H. in originally encouraging and funding the Mobilization group was in scientific evaluation of social-action approaches to delinquency.[13] This view of Mobilization was a reflection of the character of N.I.M.H. itself as an organization mandated to promote research on mental-health problems.[14] The Mobilization project, according to this view, was a scientific instrument for the evaluation of action techniques, and the Lower East Side area designated by the Mobilization boundaries was, in effect, a 67-block laboratory. The President's Committee on Juvenile Delinquency and Youth Crime shared this view, as did, although perhaps less wholeheartedly, the Ford Foundation.[15] Scientific research was itself understood in terms of several purposes. First, the Mobilization programs had presumably been designed with reference to community surveys conducted during an earlier research and plan-

[13] Scientific evaluation of these approaches could logically be regarded as a means to the end of reducing delinquency and poverty. To ascribe this relationship to views of the Mobilization for Youth participants is to read an order into their different purposes and to miss the significance of diverse priorities for the development of the project. For some participants the principal purpose of the project lay in the means or strategies which would be used, one of which was the scientific development and evaluation of social policy.

[14] The N.I.M.H. report to Congress in 1959 emphasized knowledge and research needs in the delinquency area. Indeed, that report was so convincing in its emphasis on how little is known that no basis seemed to remain for the further argument in the report criticizing current treatment arrangements and recommending reforms.

[15] The concern of the federal agencies for a scientific research component in Mobilization led them to require university participation in the project. Although the apparent impetus for university participation was the concern for research evaluation, the university group and the federal agencies shared the same "opportunity structure" perspective for an action program and therefore served to reinforce each other in influencing the direction of the project.

ning period. Research thus formed the groundwork of the action program. Secondly, the outcomes of the program would be evaluated by scientific research. And thirdly, the location of Mobilization in a slum community provided an opportunity to test basic theoretical formulations regarding delinquency, particularly the formulations of "delinquency and opportunity" theory.

Some of the problems entailed by these research purposes are apparent. In order for community surveys to serve in formulating action programs, the surveys would have to be addressed to service questions regarding conditions of need and other factors pertinent to strategies of change. This suggests an extended interaction between program formulations and research information and assumes also that it is feasible to examine the pertinent empirical factors by community surveys. In fact, the scheduling of research surveys and action programming did not allow for extended research-action interchange. Most of the local organizational participants in Mobilization for Youth, as well as the professionals who staffed the project, were practitioners and hence action-oriented. They were also expected by the groups which supported them to produce visible activities addressed to the problems of delinquency and poverty. If scientific data were made a prerequisite of program formulation, then the action programs and the goals of reducing delinquency and poverty would have been considerably delayed.

Just as most of the local organizational participants and the professional staff were principally interested in producing action programs, so were the research staff principally interested in producing research studies. Thus, community surveys were not entirely appropriate to the action perspective. Many of the factors suggested as pertinent by the opportunity-theory perspective—the distribution of employment opportunities, for example, or of institutional barriers to educational achievement or to occupational mobility—were not revealed by the community surveys. Research methods, however, were well suited to conducting surveys. Pertinent research on institutional structures was far more difficult to develop methodologically and would in any event require the cooperation of outside organizations which were probably not willing to submit themselves to research scrutiny.

If evaluation of action programs is a dominant purpose, the programs must be staged so that the operations and service populations of each are discrete; i.e., the activities engaged in by each program must not overlap and so contaminate any other program. The programs should also be clearly structured and stable, so that the research is evaluating some definable method and not a fluid and changing process of uncertain character. And finally, the intended outcomes of the programs must be described in terms of researchable indices, preferably subject to quantifiable measurement.[16] In fact, however, neither research concerns nor research personnel were so authoritative as to determine the structure and operations of programs, or the intended outcomes of these programs. Nor were the research staff intent only on studies to evaluate programs, since these were seldom entirely appropriate to their own theoretical interests or methodological skills. Mobilization was, however, a collaborative endeavor, joining research to social-welfare concerns, and joining research and social-welfare personnel.

The basic theory of delinquency and opportunity could not be "tested" by research into action programs. To the extent that such testing was possible at all, it required extremely elaborate development and extension of the theory into the concrete terms of an action program. Not only was the development of such a theoretical structure a formidable intellectual task, but the research evaluations of programs based on it would "test" only the specific propositions describing the action strategies. This inherent gap between basic theory and action programs seemed not to be recognized by the federal agencies, which, after all, sought authority from this theoretical perspective in promoting certain action approaches.

The Demonstration as a Strategy for Institutional Change

In the view of the sponsoring federal agencies and the Ford Foundation, Mobilization for Youth was a strategy for "institutional change." The targets of this change included both the local voluntary agencies and major city bureaucracies but, consistent with the expanding focus of the project on "community

---

[16] This problem should not be underestimated. Most social-welfare services are associated with valued outcomes of a very diffuse and qualitative nature. It is not only the practitioner's conviction of the value of a service that leads to reluctance in specifying desired outcomes. Specification and quantification do in fact put in focus outcomes different from and fewer than those pertinent to the practitioner.

development" and poverty, there was, over time, a shift in emphasis from the local voluntary agencies to the public institutions.[17] The neighborhood social agencies had traditionally been a major locus of social-welfare action in delinquency, and even a project dedicated to new approaches began within the framework of this tradition.[18] The logic of the "opportunity theory" perspective, however, placed the public institutions in focus, complementing the developing federal interest in local reform.

The principal strategy which the federal agencies appeared to rely on in pursuing institutional change was institutional collaboration and coöptation. Formal participation in the demonstration would presumably impel organizations to support it and might even lead them to adopt the changes which it initiated. Thus, its early concern with change in local social-agency practice led N.I.M.H. to require collaboration among the local voluntary agencies in the Mobilization area. A similar strategy with reference to the public sector led the President's Committee on Juvenile Delinquency and Youth Crime subsequently to require the involvement of the city government. The demonstration involved its collaborators as joint sponsors of programs, as contracting agents, as representatives on the Boards of Directors, and through the liaison provided by the City Administrator.

Demonstration funds were, of course, the principal incentive for inducing collaboration. Once they were collaborators, the agencies would be exposed to the demonstration program and accessible to continuing negotiation and persuasion. Demonstration funds could not, however, ensure subsequent adoption of pilot programs or susceptibility to negotiation and persuasion. Moreover, the strategy of collaboration was pursued on all levels of organizational structure. The fact that the agencies which were the targets of institutional change were participants, not

[17] The early N.I.M.H. committee had given considerable emphasis to local social agencies and the importance of innovation in their practice. As the project developed, however, public institutions in education, public welfare, and housing assumed more importance and were more usually the reference for "institutional change."

[18] The voluntary agencies were also major competitors of M.F.Y. for professional authority and political support, a position only slightly obscured by their coexistence with Mobilization within the formal boundaries of a "collaborative" effort. For this reason also they were an important target of criticism and change in the Mobilization project, particularly during the early period, when the governing ideas and controlling groups were unsettled.

only in programs, but also in the governing board of the demonstration project meant that the direction of influence was by no means unilateral.

Institutional change was also pursued by the alternate strategy of criticism and protest. This strategy was emphasized particularly by the project staff, who, being in constant confrontation with discordant collaborators, were impatient with the uncertain and diffuse outcomes of negotiation and persuasion. Thus institutional change came to be interpreted in terms of two principal strategies: influence through negotiation and persuasion, and influence through criticism and protest. Each of these strategies tended to strain the other; criticism and protest damaged the informal relations through which negotiation was facilitated, whereas a concern with persuasive efforts weakened the force of protests.

The Demonstration as a Strategy for Comprehensive Planning

Mobilization for Youth was regarded by most of the principal organizational participants as a "comprehensive" and "coordinated" approach to the problems of delinquency and poverty. This purpose received particular emphasis from the President's Committee on Juvenile Delinquency and Youth Crime, and from the City Administrator. A "comprehensive" approach seemed to mean, on the one hand, simultaneously addressing all or many of the social conditions considered to underlie delinquency or poverty and, on the other hand, simultaneously emphasizing the various action strategies pertinent to these problems. A "comprehensive" approach suggested the employment of a wide range of programs. Just what programs depended, however, upon assumptions regarding pertinent social problem conditions and the appropriate means for altering these conditions. "Coordination" referred not so much to the scope of social conditions and action strategies as to the interrelations of these strategies. It had to do with efficiency, with the arrangement of various program activities so as to rationalize their joint operations and to maximize their joint outcomes.[19]

---

[19] Thus the purpose of "coordination" of project activities indicated that a strong central unit should be established within the project to plan and administer a "comprehensive" range of programs, each charged with a somewhat different problem, manned by different professions, and involved in different external liaisons.

The goal of a "comprehensive" and "coordinated" program was in effect a specification of "institutional change." That is, the specific changes that the Mobilization project should seek to induce in social-welfare institutions had to do with the reorganization of services to procure rational, planned collaboration. According to this view, Mobilization was presumably engaged in an administrative experiment with, or for, the public services, an experiment which would presumably mark the path for future reorganization. Mobilization was an experiment in two ways: (1) within the boundaries of its own programmatic activity Mobilization was "comprehensive" and "coordinated," thus demonstrating the organizational means for such programming; and (2) Mobilization would initiate "comprehensive" and "coordinated" services by the liaisons it formed with the regular agencies, both public and private, which ordinarily performed the relevant welfare functions. If Mobilization was in fact to be instrumental in developing public planning on the community level in this latter sense, the project would have to stand in a relationship of considerable influence with the public services. If it were only to demonstrate such planning within its own boundaries, it would fall far short of addressing the social conditions considered to underlie delinquency or poverty and the various action strategies pertinent to these problems.[20]

Demonstration for Experimentation and Innovation

A final theme repeatedly sounded by various participants as a purpose of the Mobilization project was experimentation and innovation. By itself, this purpose did not go far in governing the substance of any program. It did, however, establish the imperative of distinctiveness; Mobilization was enjoined to develop forms of service which were different from those generally being offered by social-welfare agencies. Program descriptions and proposals were riddled through with the terms "experimental," "new approaches," and "innovation."

[20] In advocating this public-planning variant of institutional change, Mobilization was put in an abrasive relationship with the public and private agencies which were viewed as requiring change, and a kind of change that would subordinate them to some overhead planning agency. The project also, however, found a strong ally through this goal in the City Administrator's office, which saw comprehensive and coordinated planning as its own proper function and Mobilization for Youth as a means of beginning to implement it.

The purpose of experimentation and innovation was loosely related to scientific research. It was the prevalent notion that these innovations would be evaluated by research. Innovations in service were not, however, made conditional upon the feasibility of research evaluations of the outcomes. Similarly, scientific evaluation of programs did not require innovations, since most traditional practices were also quite innocent of research scrutiny. Experimentation and innovation constituted a distinctive purpose, valued in its own right. Considered apart from any requirement of scientific evaluation and apart from any perspective regarding the etiology of delinquency and poverty or of the institutional changes required for their remission, experimentation and innovation comprised a mandate which suggested extraordinary latitude and discretion in the formulation and management of public programs.

Interrelations of Purposes

In a general way, these different purposes were related. Juvenile delinquency was located in the poor community. Both delinquency and poverty had their sources in major institutional structures, to be addressed by strategies for "community development," for "institutional change," and for "comprehensive and coordinated" planning of services. An attack on delinquency might therefore reasonably be joined with an attack on poverty. And scientific research was a method governing policy formation for each of these strategies, as well as a tactic in the pursuit of these policies.

When, however, these different views of purpose are examined in terms of the actions required to implement them, conflicts become apparent. Thus, while delinquency might be located in the poor community, it referred to a highly selected group from that community. A primary focus on delinquency, therefore, led to a different target population, which seemed to be more accessible by direct services than by the more diffuse institutional strategies.

When some of the requirements of scientific research were specified, they also strained other purposes. First, to require a scientific-information basis for the formulation of programs would mean to considerably delay these programs, and consequently to delay efforts in delinquency and poverty, institutional change, etc. Secondly, only some kinds of question could readily be answered by research, given the limitations of scientific technique and available data. To require a scientific-information basis would therefore severely curtail the directions of the project. Finally, research evaluation of programs required discrete and insulated program organization, directly conflicting with the alternate purpose of demonstrating a comprehensive and coordinated approach.

Experimentation and innovation as a purpose also strained scientific requirements of evaluation. An experimental priority tended to lead to continuous program changes and inventions, making research evaluation of some final outcome rather meaningless.

With regard to the purpose of institutional change, the rather weak negotiating position of the demonstration tended to propel it into tactics of criticism. The resulting strained relations with other organizations made it difficult, not only to pursue the alternate tactic of negotiating change, but also to conduct research which required institutional access and to develop those programs which required joint organizational auspices. Strained relations also cast into doubt the purpose of a demonstration in comprehensive planning, on which the public services, now antagonized, would eventually model themselves.

The Tactics of Mustering and Sustaining Support

We have indicated here only some of the organizational and political dilemmas following from the different mandates with which the project was charged. In brief, the demonstration was lodged in a collaborative structure with a closely limited jurisdiction and closely limited tenure. Yet it was charged with purposes which required formidable and far-reaching power and resources. The problems initiated by these purposes marked the demonstration efforts from the outset, vastly increasing professional difficulties in spelling out the specifics of the program.

The question presents itself of why a better accommodation was not developed between the structure and purposes of the demonstration. Why was not a strenuous intelligence applied to relate and order purposes, to establish priorities, and then to pursue the structural and political problems of implementation? Why did these purposes persist and yet remain vague and fragmented? It is our contention that whatever organizational and political support the project was able to muster depended on a collaborative structure with closely delimited jurisdiction and on a rationale which was loose but authoritative. It was by exacting very limited commitments and permitting diverse interpretations that the project won the professional and organizational allegiances which were necessary even to make gestures in the direction indicated by the demonstration purposes.

The Local Level

In moving into local communities, the federal agencies were entering a complex political terrain. They had neither the political power nor the organizational resources for unilateral action. Any regular social policies consistent with the views of public purpose detailed earlier would have required a very improbable centralization of political power and organizational resources, including provision for massive expenditures. General solutions of the employment problem, for example, would seem to require a full-scale national program. And whatever exercise of political power or organizational resources might alter and improve the policies and practices of local boards of education, these were surely formidable. Moreover, even among the federal initiators, the expert solutions which would fill in the specifics of program and method for these broad purposes were often not agreed upon or even apparent. Federal policy had to be carefully negotiated and accommodated, mustering local support and deflecting opposition while preserving the federal consensus.

In order for the Mobilization demonstration to be mounted, agreement had to be obtained not only from the several federal agencies that were involved and the congressional groups upon which they were dependent, but also from the city government, the Ford Foundation, Columbia University, and a range of voluntary social agencies. Not only did the city act through the Mayor's Office and the City Administrator, but a variety of city agencies were directly concerned and involved, either because they saw implications in the project for their existing jurisdictions or because of explicit commitments which the new program would exact from them. In the local neighborhood, the project brought together the settlement houses, churches, and a scattering of local political leaders, all with local territorial and functional jurisdictions pertinent to the project. Finally, the staff itself, presumably employed to carry out the terms of the various organizational sponsors, were in fact influential agents in developing and interpreting these terms.

The problem is to secure commitments for a joint endeavor, under federal leadership, from such diverse groups. In meeting this problem, the distinctive structural characteristics and the distinctive public rationale of the demonstration provide important bases for inducing collaboration.

The demonstration has designated limits of time, area, and population. It is therefore an essential aspect of the "demonstration" that it is not a commitment to some general public policy. Commitments need only be exacted from the various organizational and political collaborators for a limited time, to apply to a limited area or population. Jurisdictional antagonisms to the new organization and its new programs can therefore be more readily appeased: on the one hand there is the immediate promise of new funds; on the other hand long-term implications for existing organizational jurisdictions are at least unclear.

The public purposes under which the demonstration project is put forward also serve in mustering support and deflecting opposition. The mandates of experimentation, inquiry, and change reflect in a general way the jurisdictional claims of the professions and the professionalized bureaucracies. At the same time, the malleability and diffuseness of these mandates permit the accommodation of diverse professional views and of different organizational mandates, federal as well as local. This latitude enables the various organizational and professional collaborators to answer and appease their different public mandates and diverse constituencies by reference to the demonstration effort. This is not simply a matter of manipulating public images; generality of purpose and an emphasis on experimentation also facilitate the actual consolidation in programs of an assortment of organizational and professional practices.

These public purposes of inquiry, experiment, and change also serve the project and its collaborators in confronting public arenas of legislative and electoral politics. The demonstration project is typically put forward as a major effort toward the solution of some social problem; it is partly in response to a political climate that seems to require such improvements that the federal bureaucracies initiate action, and it is in this context that they bargain for local cooperation.[21] The over-all demonstration rationale also, by its professional and scientific aura, commands considerable prestige and authority in public presentation. Moreover, under this rationale of innovation and inquiry, policy accountability is somewhat suspended, creating a protected environment in which to struggle with professional and organizational dilemmas lodged in the broad visions of purpose.

In short, the demonstration project typically requires new kinds of political and organizational cooperation, particularly on the local level. The capacity to bargain for this cooperation may be enhanced simply because the demonstration auspice requires only limited cooperation. Furthermore, this cooperation may be elicited because the demonstration rationale carries the impress of authority and promise of accomplishment while providing latitude for varying interpretations of policy goals and procedures and for a variety of implementing tactics.

The Federal Level

We turn now to the questions of why these purposes emerged as guides for federal action, and how the organizational and political problems which they initiated federally were resolved.

The federal government was represented in the Mobilization coalition by the National Institute of Mental Health and the President's Committee on Juvenile Delinquency and Youth Crime, and subsequently also by the Department of Labor. The President's Committee in turn was formally designated as the coordinating body for the Departments of Justice and Labor and the Department of Health, Education and Welfare. These agencies and the professional groups by which they are staffed are major influences in the arena of social-welfare policy. Much of the activity through which social-welfare policy is formed is played out within the institutional and administrative spheres shared by these bureaucracies and the professional groups which form their constituencies. Only at certain junctures in the history of any policy proposal is it exposed directly to the larger and

[21] This tendency to present the demonstration as a policy solution when, according to its own rationale of inquiry and experiment, it is an acknowledgment of a problem has given rise to criticism of these projects as merely a tactic to deflect discontent, providing short-term concessions in order to avoid substantial and enduring improvements.

more public arenas of legislative and electoral politics. Large bureaucratic organizations, staffed by professionals and watched over by various professional constituencies, represent a latent force for social-welfare policies which serve to nurture these organizations. These professionalized bureaucracies and the professional groups with which they are closely interrelated act first to protect their existing jurisdictions and sources of support. They inform and direct federal action so as to ward off any threats to their own sustenance; they respond to any disequilibrium in their political environment. The issues which are formed, for example, by public concern over the delinquency problem, or by disturbances among minorities, may become threats to organizational jurisdiction and bases of support or propitious opportunities for the initiation and funding of policies which expand jurisdiction and support.[22]

That the demonstration project had undertaken to address formidable problems with such broadly sweeping strategies was not an indication of idiosyncratic zealousness. At times when new governmental action is impelled by events in legislative or public arenas, it may be that organizational jurisdiction and support can be conserved only by aggressive and expansive proposals. At such times the professionalized bureaucracies will act to reinforce symbolic claims which legitimate their jurisdiction, consisting largely in scientific and professional claims to expertise and public-spiritedness, and well represented in purposes of inquiry, innovation, and change. And symbolic bases for authority should not be underestimated in the political sphere of vast organizations, where real actions and outcomes are so obscure. The public agencies, and the professionals who staff them, thus reassert their mandate to address such problems and begin to explore the organizational and political requirements of new and expanded policies.

When new action is impelled on the national level, the political tasks of mustering support for policies to expand or conserve organizational jurisdictions and to preserve sources of support must take place first among the national organizations. It is

---

[22] According to a federal agency report, the national rate of reported juvenile-court delinquency doubled in the decade prior to the establishment of the President's Committee on Juvenile Delinquency and Youth Crime. (See *Report to the Congress on Juvenile Delinquency, op. cit.,* p. 5.)

partly in terms of this task that the political function of conferences, commissions, studies, and reports, which also tend to emphasize purposes of inquiry, innovation, and change, can be
understood. These activities serve in part to explore the reactions
of relevant groups and also to establish a climate of opinion
legitimating new policies.

The main drift in these federal developments seems to be toward a national, cosmopolitan predominance among the professions and social-welfare organizations. In this process, the federal
agencies are leaders more than symbiotic partners. The White
House Conference, for example, is often the platform from which
new perspectives in various fields of social welfare are launched.
And these perspectives are promoted by the federal agencies and
those groups in each profession which federal funds have already
nurtured.[23] In this process, purposes which are vague but with a
scientifically authoritative cast serve as an umbrella under which
to consolidate the support of diverse organizational and professional groups.

Conclusion

The demonstration seems in a way a big blast for a toy engine.
It attempts to initiate policies only in a limited area under protected auspices. At the same time it employs as a strategy for
this limited endeavor the opportunity for various collaborators
to lay claim to comprehensive efforts in addressing major social
problems. But to dismiss the demonstration because it falls far
short of its public claims may be to take only a surface reading.

The demonstration and its sister strategies of commissions, research studies, and reports are frequently criticized as mere
tactics to deflect pressures for thoroughgoing policy changes.
Alternatively, they are defended as a means of initiating and
promoting new social policies. This duality suggests of itself the
functions of the demonstration as a strategy for organizational
and political exploration and innovation. It provides a means
for entering a federal option for reform into local affairs and for

[23] In the recent White House Conference on Education, for example, the
educators put forward as professional leaders were men whose work had
for some years been funded by the federal agencies and also by the foundations. A conference sponsored by the Department of Health, Education and
Welfare on the extension of legal services to the poor was also preceded
by federal support of the lawyers who dominated it.

exploring the organizational and political requirements of such reform. The case may rest, not on the virtues of the demonstration tactics, but on the energy and astuteness with which the federal option is put forward and finally also on the extent to which local political pressures make it opportune for agencies to take up the demonstration option. The political agitation in our major cities today among the poor and the minorities may be a precondition for federal influence in local communities. Strategies like the demonstration may be used to "cool out" such agitation, as critics have been saying, but they may also provide a form guiding agitation into coherent pressure for reform.

CHAPTER SIX

Effecting Organizational Change Through a Demonstration Project: The Case of the Schools

by GEORGE A. BRAGER

The prospects for any advocate of change are intense opposition, lengthy, costly, wearing maneuvering and negotiation, and uncertainty about results until the last battle is won. If the anticipation of such a struggle, with all its costs in money, time, energy, and the possible disruption of long-standing friendships and alliances, is not enough to discourage campaigns in support of many proposed innovations, the strain and the drain of the actual fight may well exhaust the supporters and induce them to abandon their causes before they have come near their goals.[1]

These remarks, although written about city government, apply as well to the educational system. This paper reviews specifically the problems and probabilities of influencing change within an urban school system, drawing on the experience of Mobilization for Youth.

The success of any planned attempt to influence organizational change depends, in general, upon three factors. The first is the substance of the proposed change. Some proposed changes violate cherished beliefs or firmly established patterns of the target. In other instances, change agent and target share basic objectives. Between these two extremes are situations in which agent and target share objectives but disagree regarding subgoals, or in which differences in objectives exist but are relatively minor. The scope of the proposed change also affects the amount of resistance it calls forth.

The second factor relates to the resources available to the change agent (e.g., money, prestige). These affect not only the

---

[1] Wallace S. Sayre and Herbert Kaufman, *Governing New York City* (New York: Russell Sage Foundation, 1960), pp. 716-17.

agent's ability to exert influence over the target but to some extent the substance of the changes being urged. The third factor has to do with the strategies used by the change agent—i.e., its skill in choosing methods and in manipulating the available resources so as to capitalize upon the vulnerability of the change target. The choice of strategies will be influenced by the type of change proposed, the reaction of the target group, and the resources which can be called upon. Thus, there is significant interdependence among these three change factors.

The Substance of the Changes

Mobilization for Youth has identified three broad substantive areas in which change is needed if the public schools are to serve low-income minority-group children adequately.

The first of these concerns educational technology, particularly in reading. Because the school program has a high verbal content, scholastic accomplishment relates directly to reading comprehension, writing, speech fluency, and the like. School failure, conversely, springs primarily from difficulties in the basic skill subjects.[2]

Mobilization and the schools together have developed a significant number of experimental programs designed primarily to improve instruction in reading. Intensive study of the reading interests of low-income children has been initiated; language arts in preschool and kindergarten have been emphasized; and self-directing, self-correcting reading materials have been developed to make individualization of instruction possible.

In all these programs, the schools share the general objective of the Mobilization staff—i.e., the improvement of instruction in reading. Apart from the difficulties inherent in the rivalry of two organizations vying for credit and control—albeit politely, indirectly, and even unconsciously—the pursuit of these objectives results in only minor strains. Substantive resistance by school officials, when it occurs, stems primarily from their reluctance to risk innovation and from their greater interest in expanded services than in study and experimentation. (This greater interest in services supports a generic institutional defense: failure is

---

[2] In slum communities such as the Lower East Side of New York, the average rate of reading retardation for the six elementary grades is one and a half years.

ascribed to lack of funds rather than to lack of knowledge.) For the most part, however, the subgoals necessary to improve reading instruction are not the cause of significant disagreement. What differing orientations and organizational irritants do exist impede change in relatively minor (if exasperating) ways.

Another goal of Mobilization is reduction of the gap which exists between the educational system and its low-income minority-group clientele. The failure of such persons to achieve in school is widely ascribed to their "inadequacies." Although it is undoubtedly true that lower-income socialization gives a youngster poor preparation for managing the classroom environment, insufficient attention has been paid to that environment itself. Most teachers are middle class in orientation, and those who teach in slum schools are often alien to the neighborhood in which they work. Slum schools tend to have high teacher turnover, hence less experienced instructors and reduced instructional time. The curriculum reflects middle-class concerns. Further, as studies have shown, teachers have a generally low expectation of deprived children, even when their school achievements are good.[3] The youngster who is defined by his society as inferior will behave in such a way as to confirm that definition, for we tend to achieve, in part at least, in proportion to what is expected of us. Education must break this vicious cycle.

Many low-income persons feel, with some justification in fact, a sense of powerlessness. As a result, they have little motivation to learn. If fate, luck, or chance controls one's destiny, attempts to improve one's lot are a waste of time. A recent study in a reformatory supports the view that an individual's expectancy for control governs his subsequent learning. Inmates who believed that they could not affect their environment showed little interest in the parole possibilities and did not learn the procedures.[4] The implication for educators is that the schools must be prepared to teach minority-group members and persons with low income the ways in which they can achieve power and use

[3] Helen H. Davidson and Gerhard Lang, "Children's Perception of Their Teachers' Feelings Toward Them Related to Self-Perception, School Achievement and Behavior," *Journal of Experimental Education*, Dec. 6, 1960, pp. 107-18.

[4] Melvin Seeman, "Alienation and Social Learning in a Reformatory," *American Journal of Sociology*, LXIX, 3 (Nov. 1963), pp. 270-84.

it responsibly to affect their own destinies.[5] Obviously, since the school system itself is a major institution of the society, this means that low-income persons must be taught how to influence the schools as well as other institutions.

As might be expected, the schools do not accept the premise that there is a gap between the system and its low-income clientele. Obviously, they cannot share the objective of remedying a problem whose existence they deny. The system itself subscribes to the prevailing definition of the low-income adult as inadequate and a failure. School officials, like other professionals, jealously guard the prerogatives of their craft and find it easy, particularly with low-income parents, to deflect criticism onto the critics themselves. To bring the schools closer to their lower-class clients, then, is a change which so violates the norms and patterns of the system that it inevitably results in strongly defensive resistance. The target's relation to this change objective obviously affects the resources which can be brought to bear and the strategies to be pursued by the change agent.

A further impediment to adequate educational opportunity is the strict hierarchical ordering and rigidity of the system. A school official of high rank, for example, assured the superintendent of schools: "I am a soldier—just tell me exactly what you want me to do and I'll do it." Similarly, a principal insisted that his supervisor "*cannot* be disputed" on any grounds. The teachers—we might say "the troops"—complain that they are infantilized and that school-system communication is a one-way street.

The rigidity of the system impedes required changes. Strict hierarchical ordering operates to select the "good soldier" for promotion, rather than the more imaginative educator. Mechanisms to avoid responsibility are the rewarded learnings. Administrative arrangements, such as strict accountability and centralization of decision-making, discourage innovation. With tasks as complex as educational ones are, flexibility at all levels is required to ensure sufficient creativity.

"Unfreezing" the system, encouraging creativity in its various parts, is a change not readily amenable to outside intervention. Nor does the neighborhood base of the demonstration project lend itself to city-wide administrative change. Thus this task is beyond the resources of Mobilization for Youth.

[5] See Dan W. Dodson, "Power as a Dimension of Education," *Journal of Educational Sociology,* XXXV, 5, pp. 203-15.

In summary, three broad objectives have been identified by Mobilization as required. Where there has been prior acceptance of the goal, as in the case of the need for technological change, it has been possible, in spite of minor and ongoing controversy, to launch an extensive series of cooperative programs. If the organizational stability of the change agent were to be the primary consideration, the change effort would be limited to this category of objective. There is serious question, however, whether technological innovation alone can reverse the educational retardation of the disadvantaged child in the slum school. What is required, rather, is sweeping systemic change of the schools to establish the preconditions necessary for both creative technology and responsiveness to the consumer of educational services. This objective, however, is beyond the resources of Mobilization. Even the more limited and immediate goal of reducing the gap between the schools and the poor is barely possible of achievement—indeed, may not be possible at all—given the change resources available to MFY and the strategies which must inevitably flow from them.

Resources for Change

It has been suggested that Ghandi's use of nonviolent disobedience as a change strategy stemmed at least in part from a scarcity of other weapons. Although moral sentiment may have supported his choice of method, it is possible that the unlikelihood of success by force encouraged the moral sentiment. The strategies employed to promote change inevitably depend upon the resources available to the change agent, as well as on the substance of the proposed change.

The various resources available to Mobilization and similar projects are listed separately here for analytical purposes, but clearly they are interrelated.

Money

The concept of money as a source of power is so firmly established that it hardly needs exposition here. As is often noted, "He who pays the piper calls the tune." But money is effective as a change resource only if the recipient needs or wants it badly.

Furthermore, there must be an actual or implied threat of sanction in the event that the donor's wishes are ignored.

Mobilization for Youth makes available more than one and a quarter million dollars a year for programs of an educational nature. Most of these funds are spent within the school system by contracted school personnel. As a change resource, however, this money has had little effect.

In the planning period and the early phases of its operation, the project needed public-school participation in order to obtain its funds. Mobilization was at least as eager to grant the money to the local schools as the schools themselves were to receive it. Patterns of relationships were established which continue to inhibit the use of funds as a major sanction.

The source of the funds may also limit the effectiveness of money as a resource. MFY's school program is supported by the City of New York. The influence of the schools with city officials is undoubtedly greater than the project's. And in any case, city officials would hardly encourage the disruption which would be caused by a withdrawal of MFY funds, however justifiable this would be from the project's point of view. Moreover, even if MFY were able to do so, school personnel would not view the decision to withdraw funds as of intrinsically serious consequence. The services purchased by the Mobilization funds are neither crucial to the stability of the system nor a sufficient carrot to promote Mobilization-desired changes. Mobilization's contribution represents less than 5 per cent of what is expended in the local area's public schools.

As we have implied, the extent to which the use of money or any other resource will accomplish a change objective depends in part upon the intensity with which the change is resisted by the target, as well as upon the amount of funds involved—i.e., the size and succulence of the carrot. Money can serve a subtly intimidating function even when there is relatively little dependence upon the largesse of the change agent, but only if resistance to the change is proportionately minor. For example, the schools accepted home visiting by teachers, although they qualified it by a plethora of restrictive rules, when the Ford Foundation expressed interest in supporting such an MFY program. The following year, when withdrawal of funds was threatened as a result of the limited teacher response to the program, the schools hastily rescinded earlier prohibitions so as to encourage teacher participation. (There is question, however, whether the school system's apparent change was due primarily to the promise of funds or to the prestige of the foundation's interest in the program.)

Prestige

The greater the prestige of the change agent, the less vulnerable it is to the eddies and currents of the political scene, the more likely to risk direct action, and the better able to withstand counterattack. If the major functionaries of the change target ascribe prestige to the change agent, they cannot comfortably ignore its position.

In its early years, Mobilization attracted primarily favorable attention throughout the country. (Indeed, the first public criticism of the project came from the local schools.) Its prestige undoubtedly served to postpone and to blunt attack by the schools.

The Mobilization program has not, however, managed to engage prestigeful education professionals.[6] (Even Robert Kennedy, U.S. Senator and former Attorney General, is an insufficient prestige resource since he is not part of the education profession.) School officials can therefore dismiss project recommendations as reflecting a lack of understanding of education prerequisites. The position of those professional educators who are supportive of the change effort may be deprecated in any case since, as academicians, they lack classroom experience. To the system's practitioners, they are, by definition, impractical.

Influentials

The use of influentials as a change resource is closely related to the use of prestige. Persons who are in a position to employ sanction can obviously exert considerable pressure for change. Mobilization's close relationship to the Deputy Mayor's Office provides it with such a resource. Because of its political independence, however, the NYC school system is able to be less

[6] There is nothing inherent in the MFY structure which precludes the involvement of academicians prestigeful in educational circles. While attempts have been made, the failure to assiduously court and win their favor may be as much the result of project inadequacy as of project structure.

responsive to the Deputy Mayor than, in this instance, is desirable. The political independence of the schools is highly valued by social reformers, but accountability to an electorate is also desirable. Much ultimately depends on the farsightedness of municipal as compared with school officials. Furthermore, since the authority of the Deputy Mayor's Office is limited and at times unclear, its support in school matters tends to provide prestige without political influence.

Legitimation and Communication

The relationship between the change agent and the change target, particularly as it affects legitimation of the agent's role, can be a further resource. If the agent is located within the system, it has legitimation as an "insider." Although it may be hampered by the strictures of the system,[7] its position within the organization gives the agent access to certain tools and strategies in a change effort. The outsider, on the other hand, is viewed with suspicion by the "experts" who stand guard against his efforts. Free-wheeling activity is more possible for an outsider, but legitimation as a change agent is not.

Clark has noted that a proposed change is unlikely to be adopted if it represents "precarious values."[8] Values are precarious (1) when they are inadequately defined, (2) when the position of the proponents is not fully legitimized, and (3) when the values are unacceptable to the "host" population. The change objectives of Mobilization, compared to those of most action proposals, are well defined. Essentially, however, they are the standards of a group external to the system, embodying values unacceptable to the "host" population. Furthermore, since they are outsiders, the position of Mobilization functionaries can never be fully legitimized.

The location of the change agent affects both the quantity and the quality of its interaction with the change target. The insider, if well placed in the hierarchy, has the opportunity for

[7] For a cogent analysis of the intellectual (for present purposes, read innovator) in a bureaucracy, see Robert Merton, "Role of the Intellectual in Public Bureaucracy," *Social Theory and Social Structure* (Glencoe, Ill.: Free Press, 1957), pp. 207-24.

[8] Burton R. Clark, "Organizational Adaptation and Precarious Values," in Amitai Etzioni (ed.), *Complex Organization: A Sociological Reader* (New York: Holt, Rinehart and Winston, 1961), p. 160.

extensive communication, for "chipping away" at values or programs he believes need to be changed. His words carry the weight of his position, with all the sanction (or lack of it) his role implies. A place at the "communication center" of an organization affords him considerable power to effect change. This may be less than is often assumed, however, since as an insider he is bound by all the constraints of organizational role. Thus there are advantages and disadvantages in both positions which contribute to the determination of appropriate strategy. The integrative strategy, for example (described later in this article), is undoubtedly preferred organizationally but it can probably not be employed successfully by an outsider agency in efforts as radical as reducing the gap between the system and its low-income clientele. For Mobilization even to attempt this strategy would require systematic channels to the Board of Education, the local Lower East Side Board, educators of repute who serve as referents for the superintendent of schools, the superintendent himself, some of his deputies, and the local administrator, principals, supervisors, and teachers. Such widespread communication has not been possible. Although through training programs and other services Mobilization has established communication channels with three or four hundred of the area's 1,200 teachers, the value of even this limited interaction is compromised by Mobilization's position outside the system. For example, teachers who had been highly negative about their principal closed ranks and became his staunch supporters when a group of parents (i.e., outsiders) demanded his ouster.

Community Support: Institutional and Indigenous

An institution located within a network of community agencies is likely to be responsive to those other institutions. The support of other agencies working with the change agent therefore represents another change resource.

If the concurrence of other institutions is to generate sufficient pressure for resisted change, it must be made public. Most institutions, however, avoid taking a public stand on controversial matters. This is particularly true in the case of value issues which threaten organizational self-interest or status, since the American norm is that organizational interest supersedes any humanitarian or other interest when the two are in conflict. It is true even for organizations with professed humanitarian objectives, as witness the reluctance of social-work organizations to participate fully in civil-rights efforts. A humanitarian or "principled" stance tends to be taken when it converges with organizational interests—for example, when it is necessary to satisfy particular constituencies.

Thus Mobilization's ability to develop a coalition of agencies to promote school change is sharply limited, even despite private assurances of agreement with the agency's position. The project's best strategy, then, may be to neutralize the participation of other institutions.

A more potent resource for community change—particularly given the substance of the proposed changes under discussion in this article—is the support of large numbers of residents. School officials are strongly sensitive to criticism and will go to great lengths to silence public argument. Their eagerness to achieve "cooperation" in the face of militant action leads to accommodation, and in this exists the seeds of change. But we should not be highly sanguine even here. Institutions, when responding to pressures, act to protect familiar patterns of operation. Criticism of the New York City school system and Mobilization's own efforts in the Lower East Side have led not to integration or even to basic changes in curriculum or method, but to a vast expansion of early-childhood programming. Nevertheless, while this does not represent a departure from traditional educational form, it should not be deprecated.

In an area of low-income concentration, such as the Lower East Side, organization of the community holds further significance as a resource. It ensures that decision makers, if they accommodate, will accommodate to the needs of low-income persons as *they* define the needs. Without the involvement of slum residents, programs of community change represent "professional colonialism," and there is extensive evidence that community-development efforts in the underdeveloped countries of the world fail unless indigenous (not necessarily formal) leaders are actively engaged in the change process.

To harness this resource, Mobilization has tried to develop ties with middle-income residents who are ideologically oriented to low-income minority-group problems, as well as to seek out low-income leaders. The project is potentially well equipped to perform this task. It has come upon the scene at a time of militance in civil rights, with significant community disposition to action. Further, the change issue reflects a major community concern, since parental dissatisfaction is widespread. Finally, through its many programs and other resources, Mobilization has extensive contact with low-income persons.

Knowledge

Knowledge is hardly power, and it alone cannot be expected to induce change. In combination with other resources, however, it is a useful tool. The ability of a change agent to collect information, marshal documentation, and provide analysis obviously affects its ability to persuade significant persons or generate widespread community support.

Mobilization's position as an outsider agency is advantageous in this regard. Its direct program participation within the schools enables it to observe with an independent eye the functioning of the system and the effects its policies and practices have upon its clientele. The agency can be both objective and unencumbered by organizational restraints. Illuminating anecdotal material and systematic data are available to Mobilization's staff of educators, social scientists, and researchers.

Publicity

Access to news media is another change resource. Prestige is enhanced by an image of responsibility, knowledge, and competence. An effective public-relations program can thus decrease the vulnerability of the agent. It may, in addition, be used as a weapon, to focus upon institutional abuses.

Mobilization has frequent contact with a wide range of reporters and writers to whom it supplies information that, indirectly at least, supports change attempts. However, the project must avoid becoming identified as the source of data critical of a school system with which it has a working relationship.

To summarize, we have identified seven resources that can be used by Mobilization for Youth in attempts to change the school system. Each is available to the project, to greater or lesser degree, in its efforts to develop increased public responsiveness and accountability to lower-income minority-group persons. *In the context of the substantive changes proposed*, however, the most promising resource is the large number of indigenous community persons who may be organized to act in coalition with the agency.

Strategies for Change

It is not possible in this presentation to devote the attention they deserve to the various strategies for effecting institutional change. We shall broadly indicate and briefly comment upon three of the most common ones.

Demonstration Methods

Demonstration shows the way by example. It is an assumption of this method that a proposed change in practice can be demonstrated definitively and proved effective. There is the further assumption that, once proved, the new practice can or will be adapted to other settings. Knowledge and research are the primary resources required for this approach.

This strategy is, of course, basic to much of the technological innovation of the Mobilization program. The homework-helper unit, for example, is attempting to demonstrate that low-income high-school students can effectively teach elementary-school students of similar background.

The location of program and change agent is an important consideration of the demonstration method. In order that a program may become adopted by an ongoing structure, it has been assumed by MFY and others that the demonstration should be established within the target institution. Thus, it is believed, the virtues of the change are made clear to institutional officialdom and their commitment is ensured. The result, however, may be to dilute the impact of the experiment or to transform it to the traditional (in which case, who is the change agent and who the target?). The desirability of organizing a demonstration to compete with an existent institution has not been sufficiently appraised, although the improvement of a product through competition, as espoused by the free-enterprise system, is no less sound conceptually for the educational or welfare task than for commercial endeavors.

One obvious limitation of the cooperative demonstration is that it is not applicable to issues about which prior agreement does not exist. A proposal to use Spanish as a second language in the teaching of reading could not be demonstrated, for example, because of the school system's disapproval of the idea. But whether the demonstration is cooperatively or competitively organized, the transferability of even a highly effective demonstration program is by no means automatic. Other resources and strategies are required as well.

Integrative Methods

With an integrative strategy, the agent works with the change target, solving problems, educating, and negotiating. It is an assumption of this strategy that good relationships and heightened communication will promote change.

The feasibility of an integrative strategy depends largely on the substance of the change in question. When objectives are shared, problem solving is the integrative method of choice. Information is assembled and alternatives examined so that a mutually satisfying solution can be evolved. When there are shared objectives but differences regarding subgoals, education or persuasion is employed. Differences are then mediated by reference to the common goals. Negotiation or bargaining is an integrative strategy often employed without agreement over basic goals. For example, a program may be included which is significant to the change agent's basic plan in return for its consent to include other programs which are favored by the target.[9]

The technological educational programs of Mobilization for Youth were developed, and have been continuously refined, by such integrative strategy. Because the objective of improving reading instruction is shared by Mobilization and the school system, a problem-solving approach has been feasible, with project and school personnel sharing knowledge and exploring alternate arrangements. The use of high-school students in the teaching of reading was resisted by the schools on the basis of methodological differences. Because the over-all objective was shared, however, persuasion was possible. Bargaining, too, plays a significant part in Mobilization–school-system interaction. Because the schools have reluctantly accepted a teacher home-visiting program, Mobilization buys a guidance-counseling

[9] These strategies have been suggested by a discussion of the processes by which organizations react to conflict. See James O. March and Herbert A. Simon, *Organizations* (New York: John Wiley, 1958), pp. 129-31.

package—with a notable lack of enthusiasm. Settlement by negotiation often involves a continuing bargaining process, for agreement is never actually reached and terms are usually insufficiently defined. Thus, while Mobilization devotes much effort to shaping the guidance program in directions it regards as more congenial, the schools are busy subverting the home-visiting program.

Integrative strategies are limited to changes of the type previously described. These strategies are not possible with issues which violate cherished beliefs or firmly established patterns, and which call forth heightened defensive reactions.

Political or Pressure Methods

The use of politics or pressure methods in a change attempt assumes basic disagreement between contending parties. Unlike the "horse trading" of bargaining, this strategy implies that forces must be aligned and power brought to bear. It assumes that the other strategies are ineffectual or too "soft" to result in meaningful alteration of things-as-they-are, unless the resources available for the contest are much beyond Mobilization's present capacity. Changes that are "not politically palatable and relatively easy to accomplish require great amounts of influence brought to bear with great skill and efficiency."[10]

The schools' strong resistance to Mobilization's objective of increasing their responsiveness to low-income persons, combined with the project's limited strategic maneuverability, clearly suggests the necessity of employing pressure methods. Prestige, the participation of influentials, conclusive documentation, skillful publicity, and the support (or neutralization) of other institutions must be effectively marshalled to exert pressure.

More promise, however, rests with the engagement of low-income persons in an insistent demand for change. To organize them inevitably results in conflict. It is inconceivable that low-income residents can direct attention to school issues without such conflict—they see the world differently from the middle-class institutional representatives, their very challenge of "what is" is taken as a provocation, and to involve community residents

[10] Nathan Polsby, *Community Power and Political Theory* (New Haven: Yale University Press, 1963), p. 135.

requires a dramatization of issues, which further inflames ill feeling.

Paradoxically for Mobilization, the community conflict which is a result of the successful attempt to organize residents endangers the project's efforts for educational technological change. It also threatens the project's maintenance requirements, since its funding sources, like social agencies, eschew public controversy. In pursuing this strategy, Mobilization inevitably becomes vulnerable to charges of political naiveté. A large staff will make mistakes, of protocol and otherwise, which will reflect adversely upon Mobilization. The project will also be attacked for the ways in which it goes about this task, even if no mistakes are made. When there are substantive positions which cannot easily be assailed, disagreement is ascribed to the process—how things are done—rather than to the issue.

In balance, however, these are risks which must be taken. There is comfort in the fact that conflict itself tends to enlarge the extent of community participation, which, in turn, enhances the possibility of change. There is a further resource, heretofore uncited, in the very impermanence of Mobilization for Youth. It may act upon a strategy which the organizational requirements of a "permanent" agency would prohibit. A temporary project can risk dissolution for principle. Oriented to change, as it is, it ought to do this if nothing more.

CHAPTER SEVEN

Effecting Organizational Change Through a Demonstration Project: The Case of a Youth-Work Program*

by MELVIN HERMAN and BERNARD ROSENBERG

America has changed greatly since the 1950's. Today we feel less reason for self-congratulation about our society's seemingly unlimited abundance of spiritual and material goods. The cultural cornucopia is not so brimful as it appeared to be a few short years ago. Pockets of poverty—whose existence was always admitted—turn out not to be isolated eyesores which could be eliminated with a little effort; in the perspective of this decade, they loom very large indeed. A new urgency animates those who are concerned with stemming the tide of misery that suddenly threatens to engulf more than a fifth of the nation.

The total social system is characterized by change of such unparalleled velocity and ubiquity that it approaches permanent revolution. Static models of society, conceptualized around "equilibrium" and "stability," were never so wide of the mark. A kind of headlong, pell-mell, unplanned process seems to be at work, loosening and transforming institutions that were once assumed to be securely established. Furthermore, there is now a merited disposition to acknowledge all this flux, even in official quarters, as "natural," perhaps regrettable, but also inevitable.

Professionals are encouraged to tinker with a system, but are rarely if ever allowed to go beyond it. Yet at this moment, commitment to the American way of life can only mean commitment to a new way of life. When the national administration sets out to join those who would reverse centuries-old racist social patterns and thereby to abolish the poverty which has always been

* Prepared for the Training Institute on "Urban Community Development Projects," Columbia University School of Social Work—Mobilization for Youth, April 27–May 1, 1964.

with us, professional intervention is no longer designed to stem the tide of wholesale change. Most of the change will occur willy-nilly in response to global pressure over which neither politicians nor other experts have much control. They have their hands full maintaining a semblance of stability while "waves are made" and the boat is rocked by great impersonal forces.

None of this is to say that all obstacles have been overcome. Far from it. Conflict, too often violent and irrational, continues. It may even continue to accelerate. There is perhaps no other way to resolve the fundamental contradictions by which we are threatened. In this conflict, we as citizens feel morally obligated to take a stand. Professionally the task is different, more restricted, less ambitious—and yet not without its uses.

What, in this situation, is the role of the social worker? Confronted with immense problems that require drastic action, given his peculiarly marginal position, does he have any role at all? Unfriendly critics may always be expected to pose such questions; today they are likely to emanate from within the profession itself.

It is the burden of this article that the social worker has effective means at his disposal by which he can further the solution of broad social problems. These means flow from his practice and are rooted in a view of social change which the social psychologist Robert Chin has accurately described as lying dynamically in the structural stresses and strains of any system, whether externally induced or internally created.

Consider the theoretical and methodological orientation of Mobilization for Youth. The angle of vision is broad, attempting to encompass the whole picture, not focused upon only small parts of it. Implicit in this approach is the motto: stop swatting flies and start draining swamps! If our approach to a social problem is holistic, political patchwork or individually oriented social work will not do. We must look to basic institutional change, which is, after all, our shared cultural context. In point of fact, this is our mandate.

Given widespread agreement that the present social structure is faulty in its operation, our aim must be to remedy those faults. The time is long past for urging "adjustment" upon the millions of people who live in painful wretchedness or dumb despair. A society insufficiently responsive to human needs has to be altered. Our professional point of entry in pursuit of such broad-based social change must be the organizations with which we regularly deal. By our impact on them we may bring about significant change in the structure of welfare services that reach large numbers of people. It is only a step, albeit a long one, from this kind of organizational change to sweeping social change.

Whatever the change (and no matter how widely or demonstrably beneficial it may be), we have every reason to anticipate resistance. Anyone who has ever attempted to initiate a new procedure, let alone a new policy, knows that he will encounter powerful opposition from those who, out of malice, vested interest, or ignorance, oppose any social advance, any alleviation of human suffering other than their own. If, however, the innovator is prepared for nothing but conflict, he imposes an unnecessary handicap upon himself. For the social worker, organizational change is less an arena than a forum. We will try to indicate why this should be so.

As has been pointed out, "The cooperative effort to achieve innovation is crucially affected by the number of objectives shared by those involved in it."[1] Our immediate objective may not be exactly the same as that of trade-union leaders, for example, or worse, it may be antipathetic. If so, there is little use in seeking their support, however much we need and want it in the struggle to attain other values which they share with us. We found at Mobilization for Youth that most labor leaders are reluctant to join vigorously in a campaign to widen their ranks. Given the onslaught of automation and a steadily shrinking job market, this attitude struck us as understandable, although fatally short-sighted. At the moment, labor leaders by and large are satisfied if they can hold their own. Although we think our interest in the long run is wholly compatible with theirs, in the short run it is not. Therefore, we needed to look elsewhere for partners in our effort to find jobs and train young people for them.

As part of the MFY work programs, which are designed to increase the employability of youth, it seemed to us that on-the-job training in private industry would be exceedingly valuable. Here, however, Congress had inadvertently created difficulties

---

[1] George Brager, "Effecting Organizational Change: The Case of the Schools," above, pp. 104-18.

by passing legislation that was ambiguously worded. The Manpower and Development Training Act provided inadequate guidelines for us. Lacking a fixed policy, the Bureau of Apprenticeship Training (BAT) assumed that it would implement the law by acting on the basis of an old long-term apprenticeship model. That model is largely founded upon preparation for the crafts associated with the building trades, and it is geared to slow, traditional training. Furthermore, precedent required a minimum of ten trainees in a single location—which effectively excluded small employers and left little flexibility in training assignments. We were faced with a law about whose implementation Congress had been vague and with administrative machinery that was inappropriate for our purposes.

We might have gone off on our own, since we had funds sufficient for our own small on-the-job training program and we could have fashioned it to our particular ends. Alternatively, there was the possibility of making an impact beyond the customary narrow precincts. We decided, after consultation with officials in Washington, to try to modify public policy. We therefore submitted an application to the Office of Manpower, Automation and Training (OMAT) proposing that Mobilization for Youth be established as the prime contractor and thus be permitted to subcontract on-the-job training to a variety of employers, using a minimum of one, rather than ten, trainees. All this took considerable negotiation with OMAT as well as with the Bureau of Apprenticeship Training and their legal counsel. The investment of time and ingenuity yielded results which so far include a redefinition of apprenticeship to encompass preapprenticeship; re-invigoration of the program of a federal agency (BAT) so that it might function more usefully in a new setting; the facilitation of training, which for too long had been unnecessarily slow and cumbersome; and, perhaps most important, the involvement of many more employers than could previously be reached. A fresh interpretation of the law, leading to a formal change, has given us something better suited to our purposes. The case did not go unnoticed. So far, contracts similar to ours have been negotiated with the Department of Labor in ten other cities, with prospects for many more.

Another example: early in our work program, we learned that the average trainee under the age of 19 functioned quite responsibly. Here the federal program offered no ambiguities: the

Manpower and Development Training Act prohibited payment of training allowances to youth below the age of 19, presumably because it was feared that youngsters might be tempted by the training allowance to abandon their studies. Our experience with youth both in and out of school contradicted that expectation, and we so reported it in testimony before Congress. Our recommendations, coupled with those of other specialists, contributed to a modification in the law: 17 is now the lower age limit. Here was no spectacular shift but a slight change, which will nevertheless be advantageous to many more youngsters than those who come directly under our purview. First we had to develop a service; then we learned by doing; finally, we could argue, with reason, for a general change. Others, with power, paid attention. We had made our point and demonstrated it.

If social work can provide services for a specific community, it will meet traditional needs and fulfill professional demands. If we want to extend our reach, however, it will not do just to provide services. Wherever possible, others should be drawn in. We must cultivate a kind of dual vision which enables us to keep one eye on the welfare of our clients and another on the general welfare. In a demonstration project we want results to spread by a kind of "planned" contagion, not just to stand as a possible object of emulation. Close association is obviously the prerequisite for such contagion.

Once again, Mobilization's experience with on-the-job training supplies a case in point. We sought and, in a modest way, developed a new kind of on-the-job training by starting our own gasoline station and our own auto-repair shop. A contract for youth training in these facilities was negotiated with OMAT. For the station, we signed a dealer's lease with Shell Oil Company, whose decision has encouraged several other oil companies to follow suit elsewhere in the country. Shell itself, which had been donating large sums of money to colleges and universities, became actively interested for the first time in lower levels of education. An enthusiastic account in *Business Week* described the "spanking new gas station" located on "New York City's notorious East Side, where boys universally regarded as unemployable were hard at work." Shell took pride in being the first to lease to such a group, and its president, Monroe E. Spaght, declared that Shell would henceforth turn more and more to problems of "hardcore unemployment and delinquency among young people." Approaching a giant corporation with the aim of involving it in a community program paid off at the local level—and far beyond that. By the exercise of our demonstration function, we had caused a good thing to spread. Instead of helping just a few selected boys at home, we had had an impact across the land—and it is through repeated impacts of this nature that institutions can be refashioned. In this instance, a corporate giant and a federal agency were helped to see something in a new light.

Our task is to identify a social need and develop a program to meet it. If the program promises to work but for a bottleneck that effectively stymies us, we may be said to have pinpointed the need for a change. There remains the task of capitalizing on our access to policymakers and recommending the change to them. This does not necessarily produce the change, but failure to make the effort obviates any possibility of change. Lower-echelon personnel are always accessible to us. Those occupying upper echelons may become more accessible through the medium of our own program innovations.

Locally, for example, the New York City Department of Welfare's policy on family income proved to be a serious obstacle in our path. We were not the first to be frustrated by that policy, which actually tends to discourage youngsters from working if they belong to families on relief. Since the amounts they earn are deducted from family allotments, they feel, with some justification, that they are in effect working for the welfare department, and that there is really no incentive to work at all. The policy, insofar as it was meant to reduce dependency, could be accurately described as self-defeating, a fact that has long been known to many agencies.

With access provided by our own work program and our payment of training allowances, Mobilization for Youth was able to initiate discussions with the Commissioner of Welfare. We suggested possible policy changes and found him amenable to the idea of arranging an experimental exception for us. The Commissioner could not act entirely on his own; he sought and obtained state approval. Our position was reinforced by our meeting with the United States Commissioner of Welfare, who informed us that such changes were indeed in the spirit of recently revised legislation. We had touched a number of bases: removing an obstruction in a demonstration program indicated how it might be removed in the city, state, and nation—that is to say, wherever welfare policy clashed with work-training programs. In managing a demonstration project, our value is directly proportionate, not to what we do for a small number of individuals in one neighborhood, but to how alert we are to the world beyond that neighborhood—a whole world of implications and ramifications.[2]

Out in the field, a vigorous and intelligent social worker learns how to do many things; he also learns how and why it is impossible for him to do certain other things. Running up against barriers, he may decide that they are insurmountable, and often they are. If so, he must resign himself to inaction. If not, he searches for a way around, over, or through the barriers. Finding the way, he learns that something must be altered, maybe only a little, maybe quite a bit. Later, he finds himself proposing an innovation and thus grasps an opportunity for professional leadership. Whether it means persuading department-store executives to reduce their hiring qualifications experimentally (as MFY recently did, with good results) or cutting through red tape in government, the opportunity must be detected—and taken.

As Cloward and Ohlin point out, the expansion of opportunity is a way of solving the dilemma of slum children; so also it is a welcome answer to the social worker's problem. We enlarge our scope precisely by creating opportunities and taking advantage of them. Nevertheless, there are limits to the direct services to clients that a demonstration project can provide, and it is essential to be mindful of those limits. To illustrate: Mobilization for Youth has some reason to be pleased with itself for the successful initiation of a program in sewing-machine operation. For one thing, both organized labor and management cooperated—the International Ladies Garment Workers Union contributed power machines to our shop, and Indian Head Fabrics contributed cloth. These were solid but subsidiary achievements. Our principal purpose was to demonstrate that youth in a deprived environment constituted an untapped human resource for the production of needed goods. Our trainees were able to perform a public service by producing clothes for poverty-stricken people who live nearby and for children of migrant workers in

[2] It was gratifying to us that under the Economic Opportunity Act, passed somewhat later, most of the payments made to youth are excluded from consideration as earnings in computing a family's welfare budget.

southern New Jersey. The program is so popular among girls in Mobilization that there is a large waiting list. Nevertheless, we have refused to increase the size of the shop to accommodate them, for we recognize that our sewing program can never be enlarged to the point where it will clothe an appreciable segment of the needy. Serving ten more youngsters in the shop would serve no significant demonstration purpose; our job must consist largely in inciting others to do much, much more of the same. Then we will have made an impact—and thereafter things will not be quite the same.

Instead of duplicating a modest success, we cast about for another, searching here and there for what looks propitious at any given moment. Hence, we are now planning to move on from children's clothes to children's shoes. Large numbers of our children are badly shod, and many stay away from school for no other reason. Coincidentally, the leather industry is in crisis as synthetics threaten to deal it a severe economic blow. Neither shoe workers nor tanners care particularly about our goals, but, like everyone else, they are vulnerable to an appeal to their self-interest, which in this instance coincides with our plan to make leather shoes. We believe that a program such as we project, if undertaken widely, might well result in the federal government's becoming a large purchaser of leather, which in turn could be used to fill the unmet need of the large number of families living in poverty. Consequently, we anticipate no opposition from labor or management. Indeed, industry leaders look with favor on what we have set out to do, and we confidently expect that they will contribute the necessary leather to our pilot program. We infer from this kind of experience that an identity of objectives between any two forces in society seldom exists, and that for fruitful collaboration it is necessary only to have a harmony of objectives. Demonstration projects should be tirelessly engaged in the quest for such harmony.

Let us illustrate our general thesis with one more example. In our community, there is a public housing project constructed in the 1930's, still sturdy but in need of substantial exterior renovation to make it more usable by its large proportion of aged tenants. That job the New York City Housing Authority would ordinarily contract out to a private builder. However, lacking the funds, it was forced to pigeonhole this project for several years. Not since WPA days had such a project come under the heading of Public Works—until the Housing Authority agreed to let Mobilization boys do the job. Thus, we introduced a new resource to a public agency, which, at the same time, armed us with new experience, additional knowledge, and a fresh supply of ideas.

As we gained increasing knowledge and experience, doors began to open. We had a chance to offer testimony before congressional committees on the youth-employment bill and to propose changes in MDTA legislation; to meet with the Secretary of Labor, and then with the Secretary of HEW, to discuss problems at the federal level which related to implementation of Manpower legislation; to consult with key officials, not only in Washington, but at the state and city levels as well; and to be summoned by other cities for help in planning programs. We were propelled, and we propelled ourselves, into the thick of things. Once there, we attempted to get our bearings and help others with much more formal authority to get theirs.

Our theoretical assumptions are not very complex. We recognize that change in society is inevitable. Lest we be overwhelmed by that change and lapse into a state of alienation based on a feeling of impotence (so characteristic of the delinquents we have set out to help), we must channel, direct, influence, and plan change as intelligently as we can. We can anticipate at least that there will be some unanticipated consequences of purposive social action. A few of these will be negative, but, by the same token, a few will be positive. (For example, it had not occurred to us that the Area Redevelopment Administration would be interested—as it has been, to our delight—in the gas station and the luncheonette which we have set up and staffed with teenagers. In combating juvenile delinquency, we have unintentionally aroused the interest of others concerned with the stimulation of small business.)

The experiences described herein are, of course, unique and, as such, unrepeatable. Yet it would be surprising if similar situations did not arise as aspects of social work in many other settings where similar principles might be suitably applied.

Our business of problem-solving, today more than ever, requires us to tackle familiar problems by unfamiliar methods. We may wonder whether or not these activities are included within narrow descriptions of social-work practice. This concern must be set aside if we expect to have significant impact upon social issues. Social workers will increasingly be involved in activities new to most of us; yet the net effect, we think, will be to enlarge our traditional function without disrupting it.

As we feel our way by pragmatic trial and error we will meet many obstacles, some so formidable that we are ill-advised to dissipate our energies in a vain effort to overcome them by direct attack. At the same time, one cannot always take their measure beforehand: some apparently insuperable obstacles turn out to be illusory, while others are just what they appear to be, serious or petty as the case may be. Obstructions are generally matched by opportunities. It is to the avoidance of massive obstructions and the exploitation of available opportunities that we must address ourselves.

Whatever little we have learned about organizational change is potentially valuable, not only to ourselves, but to others engaged in related tasks. Pooling our experiences with others in social-work practice may make it possible ultimately to develop a body of systematic knowledge around the frontier we are all at present rather haphazardly exploring. To that end, certain assumptions are in order:

Planned social change is necessary and, within limits, it is possible. We should demonstrate our common commitment to such change by any means at hand, but most especially by the influence we can exert on public and private organizations. In touching many organizations, we can sometimes affect the network existing between one and another. Eventually a new configuration may emerge.

To take our place in promoting organizational change will not damage our hard-won standing as professionals; on the contrary, it promises to give us a greater fulfillment than we have previously known. More and more, administrators will call upon us for advice. We may help to initiate programs which will generate friction. Some conflict we take for granted, but an excess of conflict can only defeat our purposes—which are more often won by probing for, and adroitly exploiting, relatively friction-less areas where the self-interest of organizations operates in our favor. In our fluid social system, there is no reason for social work to feel permanently blocked if it meets with indifference or outright hostility from any one quarter. With resourcefulness, we may find other quarters, and they may yield up precisely what has previously been denied. With appropriate allocation of resources, careful selection of targets, and judicious innovation, much can be done.

Our examples here are drawn for the most part from moderately successful attempts to win policy changes. If such changes are considerable in number or highly significant, an organizational change takes place. Organizations affect and are affected by other organizations. Such change causes realignment of institutional relations, of the norms governing entire classes of behavior; sooner or later, a structural or deep-going social change will materialize. For this to happen by any process other than by aimless drift, someone must realistically apprehend possibilities and take full advantage of them. That someone can very often be a social worker, acting as a catalyst for desperately needed change.

Part Three

MOBILIZING THE POOR FOR SOCIAL ACTION

Social Action by the Poor: Prospects, Problems, and Strategies*

by GEORGE A. BRAGER and HARRY SPECHT

Sentiment in social work, especially in community organization, supports the notion that "all the people" and "every group" must participate in community efforts to deal with social problems.[1] The increased participation of low-income people in particular is sought, both because of its value as a resource for social change and because of its effects upon the participants in the change effort. Both objectives conform to the valued norms of the profession.

Yet the disadvantaged have been virtually excluded from community-action and planning efforts.[2] Attempts to involve low-income people are not common, and successful attempts are dramatically rare. There appears to be a greater propensity for giving lip service to the desired ends than for making wholehearted efforts to achieve them. Thus municipal officials publicly champion the right of low-income groups to "fight City Hall" while privately searching for ways of preventing such activities without appearing to do so.

Among professionals, there are doubts that the poor can be effectively mobilized, or that their participation makes signifi-

* This article is an amalgam of "Mobilizing the Poor," a paper prepared by George Brager and Harry Specht for the National Conference of Social Work, 1964, and George Brager's "Organizing the Unaffiliated in a Low-Income Area," *Social Work*, VIII, 2 (April 1963), reproduced with permission of the National Association of Social Workers.

[1] See, for example, "Community Organization for Social Welfare," *Social Work Year Book, 1954* (New York: National Association of Social Workers, 1954), p. 123; and Ray Johns and David F. DeMarche, *Community Organization and Agency Responsibility* (New York: Association Press, 1951), p. 237.

[2] See, for example, Morris Axelrod, "Urban Structure and Social Participation," *American Sociological Review*, XXI, 1 (Feb. 1956), pp. 13-18; and Floyd Gibson Hunter, *Community Power Structure: A Study of Decision Makers* (Chapel Hill: University of North Carolina Press, 1953).

cant contribution to community change. The barriers to low-income involvement are undoubtedly formidable. We shall discuss some of them later in this article. It is our over-all intent, however, to explore the potential as well as the problems, the feasibility as well as the difficulty, of involving the poor in organized social action to bring about social change. We shall also review alternative strategies for organizing the poor, drawing heavily upon the first two years' experience of the Mobilization for Youth community-development program.

The Potential of Social Action as a Resource for Change

It has been noted that social change is least likely to be generated by the lower strata of society:

> Those who have nothing to lose but their chains are too closely chained, psychologically, to the desperation of their lot to generalize their predicament, face the consequences of a malcontent position, or otherwise add to their suffering by striving for social change.[3]

This contention is supported by a study comparing the attitudes and perceptions of community residents and professional social workers in New York's Lower East Side. The residents, who were overwhelmingly low-income, expressed less dissatisfaction with community conditions than the professionals had anticipated, yet were more pessimistic about the possibility of changing these conditions than was the social-work staff.[4] The community reaction—relatively uncomplaining acceptance of depressed conditions coupled with a disbelief in the likelihood of improving them—may be interpreted as a realistic adjustment to the facts of low-income status. However, the civil-rights movement attests to the fact that low-income social action can lead to social change.

The political revolution of the Negro minority has had far-reaching effects upon public and private programs and policies.

[3] Seymour M. Lipset and Juan J. Linz, "The Social Bases of Political Diversity," reported in Bernard Berelson and Gary Steiner (eds.), *Human Behavior* (New York: Harcourt, Brace and World, 1964), p. 617.

[4] Charles F. Grosser, *Perceptions of Professionals, Indigenous Workers and Lower Class Clients*, unpublished dissertation, Columbia University School of Social Work, 1965. See also Grosser, "Middle-Class Professionals and Lower-Class Clients," above, pp. 64-71.

It has led to changes involving education, public accommodations, voting practices, and employment policies on national, state, and local levels. Thus the Negro revolution presents a dramatic example of the achievements that can be won by an aroused minority. Although it is not specifically a low-income movement, scores of poor Negroes *have* been involved and have made gains in scores of local communities across the land.

The national character of the movement has heightened the visibility of the problem and the means of its solution. It has also contributed to the success of the movement by drawing on national Negro political power as a resource. Nevertheless, the movement began in a *local* community with *limited* objectives. It thus can reasonably serve as an example of the possible community impact of organized groups of disadvantaged citizens.

Neighborhood efforts, more modest in outlook and accomplishment, can also be cited. The Woodlawn Organization in Chicago and the early experiences of the Mobilization for Youth community-development program represent fruitful attempts by low-income persons to alter their social conditions.

Both the observers and the organizers of social action have noted that the underlying issues are really political. Thus the problems of the poor require political action, and political action requires power. According to Rossi, the major sources of power with which to induce social change are: wealth and other physical resources; control over prestigeful interaction (i.e., board memberships); control of communications systems (i.e., the mass media); control over values (a resource which is available to the church, for example); threats to property, such as take place in civil-disobedience demonstrations; and the backing of solidary interest groups, either as voting blocs or as potential votes.[5]

The resources available to low-income groups are sharply circumscribed by their social location. However, their primary source of power—the manipulation of solidary groups—is formidable. Since the major social changes of interest to the poor fall within the domain of the public-welfare structure, the marshalling of group support is an effective spur to institutional response. Politicians and public officials are attuned to the interests

[5] Peter H. Rossi, "Theory, Research and Practice in Community Organization," in Charles R. Adrian, ed., *Social Science and Community Action* (East Lansing: Michigan State University, 1960), p. 13.

of organized constituencies representing potential voters,[6] and thus are sensitive to the demands of participants in large-scale social-action efforts.

The support of social agencies and political-action groups reinforces the potential for institutional change inherent in organized social action. So, too, does the aid of prominent and powerful persons who are sympathetic to the struggles of the poor. By drawing on such support, Dahl suggests, impoverished communities can "pyramid" their resources for gaining the power to improve their life chances.[7] One resource attracts another. Thus leaders of low-income organizations formed with the assistance of Mobilization for Youth were invited to participate in community-planning groups which had previously ignored them. When organized groups of the poor capture public attention, decision-makers are more likely to accommodate to their needs as the poor themselves define them.

The Problematic Aspects of Social Action for Social Work

Organized social action has problematic aspects for social work, which may account for the field's minimal involvement. The problems, broadly conceptualized, are two-fold: ideological and institutional.

Ideological Problems

Although social workers have become increasingly aware of the fact that political power is required in order to effect change,[8] the notion is discomforting, and its consequences for practice have been largely ignored. The concept implies inequality in access to power. Yet the traditional techniques of community organization are integrative in function, with the implicit assumption that, given the opportunity to do so, all will participate on an equal footing. Ross suggests, for example, that organizations dealing with community problems must involve

[6] Wallace S. Sayre and Herbert Kaufman, *Governing New York City* (New York: Russell Sage Foundation, 1960), pp. 717-18.

[7] Robert A. Dahl, "The Analysis of Influence in Local Communities," in Adrian (ed.), *op. cit.*, p. 36.

[8] Robert Morris and Martin Rein, "Emerging Patterns in Community Planning," *Social Work Practice, 1963* (New York: Columbia University Press, 1963).

leaders who are identified with and accepted by all the major subgroups of the community.[9]

The life view of the professional logically places considerable emphasis upon education and reason. There is an awareness of the complexity of societal problems and a belief in the ability of technology to provide solutions. Thus, social workers are instructed to rely "principally on facts and interpretations as the source of their influence rather than on the mobilization of political and economic power."[10] This perspective leads to a predisposition to depend upon the persuasion and education of policy makers as the preferred method of change.

Some professionals, of course, do take power into account and believe that policy makers are, to some extent at least, motivated by self-interest and responsive to pressure. Yet these professionals are often unaware of the scarcity of resources available to low-income people. They propose negotiation without sufficiently taking into account the fact that successful negotiation requires certain strengths at the bargaining table. The differential results of strike threats by steel workers and by welfare workers are related, of course, not to the former's greater persuasive powers, but to the differential consequences of their actions. Low-income people, as we have mentioned, have only their numbers and the disconcerting effect of public attention to contribute to the outcome of the contest. Negotiation and bargaining must therefore follow either the threat or the reality of bringing these resources to bear upon the change effort. Both run counter to the professional belief that it is unwise to antagonize people in power.

Successfully engaging a defeated and alienated population is a formidable task. In the words of a novelist:

> How can a man be made to struggle for freedom without an appeal to his deepest instincts? Hatred, hunger, thirst, and revenge are tremendous powers that must be mobilized. The virtues, bourgeois or not, are insufficient to shake off man's torpor.[11]

[9] Murray G. Ross, *Community Organization: Theory and Principles* (New York: Harper, 1955), pp. 155-58.
[10] "Social Action," *Social Work Year Book, 1960* (New York: National Association of Social Workers, 1960), p. 531.
[11] Nicos Kozantakis, *The Rock Garden* (New York: Simon and Schuster, 1963).

Invoking issues of deep meaning or passionate concern is not within the sanctioned scope of professional practice. Traditionally we have concentrated upon process to the discouragement of interest in substantive outcome. We are likely to be not entirely unsympathetic to the position of the school official who claimed that members of a low-income parents' group were not ready to participate in school affairs until they had been educated in the workings of the institution and had formulated "positive proposals."

The value placed by social work upon neutrality, the "enabling" role of the worker, also runs counter to the necessity of converting to action on their own behalf the anger felt but often unexpressed by low-income people. The worker's offer of consultation instead of commitment is often perceived by the client as temporizing; the traditional claim of neutrality sounds like an expression of fear to individuals who risk much to protest. Fortunately, an exposition of the advocate role of the social worker, akin to that of the lawyer, is beginning to emerge in the literature.[12]

Coleman has demonstrated that previously nonparticipating citizens are most likely to be drawn to political action when they have objections to register.[13] According to this study, community conflict is likely to result if the precipitating situations have three major features: (1) They touch upon an important aspect of people's lives, such as the education of their children or their means of livelihood. (2) They affect people differentially. Proposals for correcting school imbalance, for example, affect various parts of the community in different ways. Proposed changes which strike deeply at the gains and privileges of established groups are potentially more conflict-laden than changes which affect everyone in the same way. (3) They involve issues about which people feel action is possible and may result in a desired outcome.[14] Social-work professionals tend to prefer cooperation,

[12] Charles F. Grosser, "Neighborhood Community Development Programs Serving the Urban Poor," below, pp. 243-52. See also Morris and Rein, *op cit.*, p. 174.

[13] James S. Coleman, *Community Conflict* (Glencoe, Ill.: Free Press. 1957), p. 19.

[14] *Ibid.*, p. 4.

no matter how spurious, to conflict, no matter how necessary.[15] If, however, these situations are avoided in an attempt to avoid conflict, the consequences must inevitably be the failure of a community-development effort.

Conflict for its own sake is of dubious morality and may be strategically unwise. Nevertheless, controversy can serve positive as well as negative functions. For example, it closely correlates with membership participation;[16] one consequence of the civil-rights struggle has been the reawakening of interest in the institutions of local communities throughout the country.

Institutional Problems

Established institutions tend to respond to criticism with self-protectiveness and defensiveness. In interaction with the poor, the least well-regarded segment of the society, these strains are heightened. Policy challenges from the very people who are the recipients of help, and who are therefore expected to be grateful, call forth a shock reaction. When autonomous action by the poor is encouraged by professional community organizers, insult is added to injury. In such instances, the institution can be expected to turn on the community organizer or the service agency which employs him and to charge them with manipulating the "simple" poor. Certain school officials in the Mobilization area, for example, went so far as to accuse Mobilization of hiring "full-time paid agitators and organizers for extremist groups."[17]

Most voluntary associations tend to limit their activities in social-change projects to noncontroversial issues, those seen as a benefit to all and a detriment to none.[18] As Banfield and Wilson note:

[15] A similar trend has been described in American sociology. As increasing numbers of professionals have worked for large bureaucracies, they have become increasingly concerned with the problems of preserving the existing institutional arrangements, for conflict within and around these structures is seen as dysfunctional. Lewis Coser, *The Functions of Social Conflict* (Glencoe, Ill.: Free Press), p. 27.

[16] Coleman, *op. cit.*, p. 3.

[17] *New York Times*, January 31, 1964.

[18] Rossi, *op. cit.*, p. 14.

If a point is reached where some substantial achievement in terms of the association's ends can be made only at the cost of losing some membership support, he [the professional] is likely to forego the achievement. Not to do so, he would say, would destroy the "effectiveness" of the organization in the long run.[19]

Interlocking board directorates also discourage service institutions from aligning themselves with protests against another community organization. Social obligations, mutual favors, and minor accommodations among the personnel of various institutions further reduce the likelihood that any agency will adopt a critical position with regard to another organization. Furthermore, when low-income groups force contention, there may be a greater degree of commonality between the two institutions than between the sponsoring agency and its contending clientele.

A major, and often overlooked, source of strain in a social agency's support of organized social action is the likelihood that the social-change objective of the program will impede the agency's service functions. Necessarily, the service-oriented agency and practitioner focus upon the singular interests of the client or group. Concern about broad issues of policy, administrative rulings, and categories of clients is secondary. In negotiating his client's needs with another institution, the professional depends upon his rapport with other professionals to obtain special favors. His agency's support of a community challenge of that institution's policies endangers his power to obtain dispensations for his clients. This danger is often exploited by institutions seeking to avoid change. Thus large bureaucracies often make concessions to individual clients to avoid a challenge of administrative rulings which affect many people.

Even when social change is an objective of the agency, organized social action may produce strain. The resources available to the agency to pursue its change objectives are different from those available to low-income groups. Its strategies are therefore different also. The agency depends upon essentially persuasive methods, drawing on its reputation for expertise, its access to prestigeful figures, and its relationship with the change target. The public offensive and the strength of numbers upon which low-income groups rely may be incompatible with the

---

[19] Edward C. Banfield and James Q. Wilson, *City Politics* (Cambridge, Mass.: Harvard University Press, 1963), pp. 253-54.

agency's strategy. This is not always the case, however; the two strategies may at times be mutually supportive or reinforcing.

It is primarily the maintenance requirements and service functions of social agencies that discourage their support of organized social action by the poor. Commitment to the involvement of the poor in attempts to affect their environment, an understanding of the resources available to them, and a primary concern with solutions to broad social issues will impel some agencies to take the required risk.

Barriers to Low-Income Participation[20]

If community-oriented organizations are to be successful in their efforts to combat social ills, they must involve significant numbers of representative lower-class persons.[21] However, as we have noted, membership in community organizations is not very common among the lower class. A considerable number of studies indicate that formal group membership is closely related to income, status, and education; the lower one's income status and educational level, the less likely one is to participate in formal community groups.[22]

Furthermore, those members of the lower class who do participate are likely to be representative of a minority among slum dwellers: i.e., the upwardly mobile. In every slum neighborhood there are adults who, in attitudes, strivings, verbal skills, and know-how, are oriented toward the middle class. Although their children are less likely to experience strains toward deviance, these are precisely the parents who tend to join formal community organizations and to have faith and competence in the collective solution of such social problems as juvenile delinquency. Because lower-class persons tend to eschew formal organizations, organizers who set out to reach the effective community of the delinquent frequently settle for those slum dwellers who are

[20] This section is excerpted from George Brager, "Organizing the Unaffiliated in a Low-Income Area," *Social Work*, VIII, 2 (April 1963).

[21] The word "representative" is used here in the sense of "typical of their group, i.e., class" rather than in the political sense of "functioning or acting in behalf of others." Elsewhere in the literature it has been restricted to the latter use. See Chauncey A. Alexander and Charles McCann, "The Concept of Representativeness in Community Organization," *Social Work*, I, 1 (Jan. 1956), pp. 48-52.

[22] Axelrod, *op. cit.*

easiest to enlist. Why are representative lower-income adults less likely to become closely involved in community affairs? The source of the barriers to their effective participation rests with all three elements of the interaction: the characteristics of community life, the nature of lower-income adults, and the structure of the community-organization effort.

Characteristics of Community Life

One such community characteristic is residential mobility. Local communities have been inundated by new migrants, many of them unfamiliar with the demands and opportunities of urban life. Although public housing mitigates some of the problematic aspects of slum life, the recruitment of single-family units from widely dispersed parts of the metropolitan area collects in one place thousands of deprived families, strangers to one another and to local community resources. Physical-redevelopment programs and the consequent exodus of old residents have in many instances shattered existing institutions, so that they are unable to help in assimilation of the newcomers into the urban system. For example, the diminishing vitality of some local political machines, with their attentive political leaders, eliminates an important interpretive link to the new world.

Intergroup tensions are also a barrier to community integration, as are the bewildering operations of massive bureaucratic systems. The size, impersonality, concentrated power, and inflexibility of these large organizations makes them seem to local residents hardly amenable to their influence.

The community characteristic that may act as the major deterrent to involvement of lower-income people in community affairs, however, is the opposition of already entrenched organizations. New groups in a community—especially new minority groups—are often confronted with hostility from established groups whose positions of power are threatened by the possibility of forceful action by the newcomers. There is evidence, for example, that some political machines will avoid registering minority-group members, even under the impetus of national campaigns. This is so even though the minority-group member is assumed to support the machine's national candidates. It is recognized that the new group will inevitably challenge the dominance of incumbent leadership.

This resistance of political parties, governmental agencies, and private organizations is never directly specified. Ordinarily it takes the form of statements such as "the minority groups are not really interested," they are "not ready," "they'll take positions we don't agree with," or they will be "controlled by the left-wing agitators." Whatever its form, the opposition of established community groups is a formidable obstacle to indigenous community participation.

Characteristics of Lower-Income Life

The circumstances of lower-income life and the nature of lower-income persons constitute another set of obstacles. The realities of lower-class life—i.e., the necessary preoccupation with the day-to-day problems of survival—hardly encourage attention to broad community matters. Furthermore, lower-class persons lack the verbal or literary requisites for organizational skills; neither do they tend to be comfortable with the formal methods of doing business in organizations. Their general pessimism and self-defeating attitudes, as we have noted, also interfere with community integration. As one observer has pointed out, "Seeing his chances for improvement as slim produces in the slum-dweller a psychology of listlessness, of passivity, and acceptance, which . . . reduces his chances still further."[23] Such defeatism, resulting in lack of participation, produces a loss of interest in changing their conditions.

Structure of Community Organization

The community organization itself, while purportedly seeking the involvement of lower-income persons, offers certain obstacles, whether inevitable or otherwise. Most community activities, for example, are staffed by middle-class personnel. To the extent that lower-class people feel that they are being dominated, they are likely to withdraw from collective activities. The predominance of the middle class in community organizations has a number of sources. When community problems become so severe that people are motivated to act, it is generally the middle-class element (or at least those who are oriented toward the middle

---

[23] Michael Harrington, "Slums, Old and New," *Commentary*, XXX, 2 (Aug. 1960), p. 121.

class) that reacts first. Although lower-class persons may affiliate with the organization, its predominantly middle-class style soon becomes a subtle source of intimidation. Its leaders are likely to be businessmen, professionals, social-welfare personnel, ministers, and other members of the middle class. The formality of the organization meetings, with predetermined agendas, concern with rules of procedure, and the like, tends to make the lower-class participant, unfamiliar with these matters, feel insecure and inferior.

Furthermore, organizers who insist on maintaining control of the activities and policies of the organization, subtly or otherwise, inevitably encourage the participation of lower-class persons whose values and skills are congenial to those of the middle-class organizer. Those whose values and skills differ, however, will gradually sense that such differences matter and that the organization exists to serve middle-class ends. They may, therefore, disassociate themselves.

It may be that, because of the disparity between lower- and middle-class "life styles," significant numbers of both groups cannot even be expected to participate together within the same organization. For example, a study conducted by the Girl Scouts, focused upon recruiting volunteers from working-class communities, was forced to conclude that the agency could offer no program suitable to both middle- and lower-class groups. As noted by the authors, lower-income adults are less interested in "the joys of fully integrated personality in a democratic society" than in the need to better their standard of living. They do not even object to their children's being handled authoritatively if it serves such an end.[24]

We have indicated that the tendency of social workers to emphasize the amelioration of conflict and the reduction of tension may also, in effect, discourage lower-income participation. If issues are flattened rather than sharpened, differences minimized rather than faced, there may be little to arouse the interest of a group that already lacks the predisposition to participate.

The sponsorship of the community-organization effort will also affect the character of participation. The primary interests of a sponsoring group will tend to determine membership criteria, organizational form, objectives, and activities. Organizational-

[24] Catherine V. Richards and Norman A. Polansky, "Reaching Working-class Youth Leaders," *Social Work*, IV, 4 (Oct. 1959), p. 38.

maintenance requirements of the sponsor will inevitably limit the independence of an action-oriented affiliate. Further, its responsibility to a board of directors with widely variant views and connections to numerous community interest groups will limit a sponsor's freedom to encourage a free-wheeling community-action program. When the sponsoring group is an already established community organization, it is likely to contain significant representation from groups that actively oppose the effective participation of lower-income and minority-group people.

Strategies of Increasing Participation in Social Action

With the foregoing pitfalls in mind, it is possible to develop a specific strategy for a specific area. The techniques employed to increase the social participation of the poor depend on the goals of organized social action. Three different but related strategies characterized the first two years of the Mobilization community-development program. Although they can be used to reinforce one another, they are oriented to different types of persons, require different kinds of organization and resources, and result in different outcomes. They include (1) social brokerage to increase participation, (2) integrative mechanisms to strengthen organizations, and (3) social protest to support social movements.

Social Brokerage to Increase Participation

Increased participation in social action may be encouraged by recruiting previously unaffiliated individuals for group membership. These are individuals attracted by the offer of services to meet their immediate needs. Thus groups have been organized to deal with such problems as lack of heat and hot water in tenements, rent overcharges, language barriers between parents and teachers which hamper discussion of children's work, fraudulent installment plans, and inadequate welfare allowances. The organizer's function in his initial contact is to serve as broker between the clients and the appropriate person or institution.

The groups that are shaped by such social brokerage tend to be primary groups that serve as liaison between their members and public or private agencies. Although this is the most personalized form of social action, it affords greater access to agency resources and a more efficient utilization of available services than any one client could achieve.

It is assumed that action of this sort will encourage clients to participate in action of less individualized and immediate consequences. A shared problem leads to the formation of an informal group, and in the cooperative attempt to solve the problem, the members learn how to meet some of their needs through group processes. Ultimately, other group activities are suggested.

The expectation that informal groups which emerge out of individual needs will develop an interest in community problems assumes that community organization results in social maturation—that is, that successful experience in informal groups will lead to a willingness to experiment with other forms of group life. The use of social brokerage in MFY's community-development program suggests, however, that there is neither an inevitable evolution of forms of group life nor any necessary transferability of social experience. Many of the informal groups succeeded in gaining greater access to agencies, and the resources made available to them did "pyramid" as predicted. For example, when the mothers in a condemned building became involved in a controversy with city agencies, other organizations offered assistance, and some local activists and politicians entered the fray on the side of the mothers. By and large, however, the informal groups did not move from the immediate solution of shared individual problems to a common concern with larger social issues and action. It appears that, rather than small groups creating issues for institutions, issues created by institutions are imposed on small groups. Formal groups and organizations, leaders and politicians, select the salient problems and seek out small groups with grievances that present opportunities for confronting the underlying issues. Thus issues representing deep cleavages in the social structure move from general to specific forms of conflict.[25] Local housing organizations, for example, saw the tenement situation as an opportunity to dramatize the ways in which landlords harass tenants in order to have them relocated at city expense so that their buildings can be renovated for middle-income occupancy.

To the extent that social brokerage does stimulate social ac-

[25] Coleman, *op. cit.*, p. 10.

tion, that action is often not commensurate with the resources required to bring it about. It seems unreasonable to expect a group that has found a meaningful *modus vivendi* to change its form and purpose. Although the small-scale social action encouraged by social brokerage does give the participants an educational experience in the utilization of existing institutions, such utilization presupposes acceptance of the *status quo* and the belief that the established social structure permits the solution of individual problems. When shared needs cannot be met by existing institutions, an orientation to issues is prerequisite to an orientation to change. But such orientation is alien to the informal group.

Although social brokerage attracts a wide variety of unaffiliated individuals, it serves as a source of social organization only for those who share similar social characteristics and live in a geographically circumscribed area—e.g., Puerto Rican mothers of children in the same school, the tenants of a single apartment building, the Negro tenants of a housing project. The structure of groups formed by social brokerage bears more resemblance to that of an extended family than to the goal-directed organizations of the middle class. Interpersonal relationships, rather than abstract issues, are the source of social cohesion.[26] To meet the challenge of social change, therefore, other kinds of organization must be employed.

Integrative Mechanisms to Strengthen Organizations

The informal groups and organizations in low-income communities are not part of the established institutional structure.[27] Indeed, they maintain little or no relationship with one another. Moreover, they lack the organizational skills and resources for effective participation in social action.

Mobilization's community-development program assisted and strengthened such groups as the Council of Puerto Rican Organizations, consisting of hometown clubs, athletic groups, social clubs, and block associations. Struggling and disorganized, the Council was assigned advisors, the financial resources to set up a headquarters, and other agency services. As a result, it was

[26] *Ibid.*, pp. 18-19.
[27] H. H. Doddy, *Informal Groups and the Community* (New York: Teachers College, Columbia University, 1952).

able to operate a housing clinic, and several of its committees dealt with public-school problems, police brutality, housing, and civil rights. Similarly, the Negro Action Group, organized by Mobilization, became the focal point for the organization of Negroes in the area and ultimately enrolled several hundred members. Once again, staff headquarters and program expenses were made available to the organization. Through an extensive committee structure, it became actively involved in issues similar to those which engaged the Council.

From these organizational efforts and effects are forged new political pressure groups. Smaller groups, once voices in an institutional wilderness, are heard—and heeded—as their respective and representative organizations give new voice to their demands.

To the extent that organizations representing the poor take on the characteristics of all other organizations, they acquire defects as well as virtues. The majority of members may be members in name only, content to leave organizational policy to a small core of leaders. There is as wide a variety of leaders in low-income organizations as in any other type; indigenous leaders, whether paid or volunteer, range from militant activists to organization men. Low-income organizations experience the same problems of organizational maintenance as do established organizations. It is difficult for any organization to achieve its goals when there is more affiliation than participation, more vested interests than shared concerns. Such organizational difficulties may create special problems for organizations engaged in social action, keeping them from confronting significant issues. Issues may be selected to serve the needs of organizational maintenance rather than to meet the needs of members. This tendency is reinforced by the disproportionate number of organizationally oriented leaders attracted to these groups.

Many of these problems simply reflect the fact that the new organization has begun to develop interests and investments in the community. Involvement in the institutional structure, however, has special risks for low-income organizations. Established organizations make overtures to the leaders of new groups, and these overtures, if successful, can deprive the members of organizational autonomy and strength. Co-optation of indigenous leaders not only undermines the collective-bargaining power of the poor but also abuses the confidence of the membership. Among people accustomed to being ignored or even exploited by vested interests, suspicions of a "sell-out" are easily aroused by cooperation between their leaders and established organizations.

Significant issues must be confronted in spite of, as well as through, the organizational structure. This requires strategies that do not rely wholly on organizations as a source of social action and change.

Social Protest to Support Social Movements

Social protest is a militant and dramatic form of social action involving large numbers of people; as such, it draws public attention to social problems. Social protest thus requires issues capable of attracting wide support. Large numbers of low-income people from the Mobilization area were included, for example, in the March on Washington, the Puerto Rican Silent Prayer March in New York, and the March to Albany for a $1.50 state minimum wage. Other protests included picketing of public-housing construction sites to demand the employment of more Negroes and Puerto Ricans, participation in school boycotts, and a campaign to withhold rents from the owners of buildings with code violations.

In contrast to other strategies of social action, in the organization of social protest, the development of indigenous organizations and leaders is secondary to the expression of protest. It does, however, have important, if unintended, consequences for organizational life. The *ad hoc* groups that emerge out of such movements are a source of increased social participation. Although formed for the specific purpose and duration of the protest, these groups, which attract issue-oriented and activist persons, do not always disband after the period of protest.

Ad hoc groups forged in community conflict are also a vital source of militant leadership. Coleman observes, "New leaders tend to take over the dispute; often they are men who have not been community leaders in the past.[28] These are independent leaders who are relatively free of ordinary organizational constraints; their followers enjoy similar independence. "Because it either has no staff or has one that has been recruited for tem-

[28] Coleman, *op. cit.*, p. 12.

porary services, the *ad hoc* association is less likely than the permanent association to fall under staff control."[29]

The advantages of social protest for social action may constitute disadvantages for sponsoring agencies. The activities involved in social protest are difficult for an agency to supervise. When the participants in protest challenge repressive statutes, it is not always possible to predict or control the outcome of their action.

Organizational autonomy is thus most problematic in the protest strategy. A sponsoring agency is held responsible and often criticized for the activities of an indigenous organization which is not accountable to the agency. One defense is to articulate the need for low-income involvement and independence prior to the expected criticism. It is also possible to specify the nature and limits of the sponsoring agency's commitment to social protest in its relationship with new organizations. Communication may be diffused and strain reduced by contracting with new organizations, or with old ones which will subcontract, in order to dilute the sponsoring agency's role. These methods help to protect the agency from public involvement which may be embarrassing or identification with action which it considers unwise, but they can be only partially effective. No method of escaping criticism fails to pose its own undesirable consequences.

Nevertheless, social protest, in the Mobilization experience, is the most effective strategy for increasing the participation of the poor. It can succeed—in fact, has succeeded—in bringing about change in institutions and individuals. The social gains are reflected in an enhanced sense of achievement, achievement made all the more exhilarating by its relevance to life in the low-income community.

Whatever strategy is adopted, plans for indigenous community organization must assess community conditions realistically, including the sources, both direct and subtle, which oppose such organization. They must take into account the life styles, feelings, and needs of lower-income persons. Rather than hope to change people to fit predetermined structures, we must be willing to revise the structures to suit the people we wish to attract. Unless we come to terms with these issues directly and honestly, our much-vaunted desire to organize lower-income groups will inevitably seem more lip service than commitment.

[29] Banfield and Wilson, *op. cit.*, p. 251.

CHAPTER NINE

Resident Participation in Community-Action Programs: An Overview*

by FRANCES PIVEN

Conceptions of Resident Participation in Developmental Public Programs

The widespread advocacy of the participation of residents of local communities in public programs by no means reflects agreement regarding the goals of such participation, the forms it should take, or the means of effectuating it. Some of the different concepts comprehended by "resident participation," and the problems these entail, are suggested by a review of recent experiences with urban renewal and the early community-action projects, predecessors of the antipoverty program.

Both urban renewal and the antipoverty program can be viewed as underdeveloped-areas policies. They represent a new move forward in the developmental functions of government, as distinguished from more traditional regulatory functions. It follows from the developmental tasks of these programs that they have extraordinary—and differential—impact on selected local communities.

Resident participation became a major issue in local areas earmarked for rebuilding under urban-renewal programs. The dilemmas regarding resident participation followed in part from the fact that local areas were selected as targets for redevelopment, but these areas were to be redeveloped in terms of assumptions regarding the welfare of "the city as a whole." Whatever diffuse benefits such a program might come to have for the

* Reprinted from *Social Work*, January 1966.

larger community,[1] an immediately disruptive impact was felt by groups residing in the target area. It was these groups that were most sharply hit by the costs of renewal, but it was not necessarily these groups that were to be benefited by the new development. Economic and cultural revitalization of central city areas was spelled out for slum residents by clearance and dislocation. The new developments included chiefly high-rental housing. Existing residents in areas scheduled for renewal were confronted with the distress of upheaval and the loss of neighborhood, and also with the prospect of greatly increased rentals.[2] In consequence, adamant local protests came to be an earmark of renewal programs, often spelling political turmoil for the projects.[3] These experiences resulted in a growing concern with resident participation in renewal, and also influenced the kinds of participation which were advocated and solicited by those responsible for the programs. In order to avoid local protests which often rocked the projects when they were already well under way, steps were taken to initiate resident groups at an early stage in order to educate and win them to the plans.

Efforts to bring about resident participation in urban renewal were thus marked by an irony reflecting the dilemmas of renewal policy: programs for resident participation were developed to offset the spontaneous—but disruptive—participation of local protest groups. Critics came to describe such programs cynically, as a mere "cooling out" tactic. However, as long as renewal plans were oriented to the welfare of "the city as a whole" they would almost surely generate acute protest and conflict in local areas. Only the most blithe and happy faith in the democratic consensus could permit a program geared to "the community as a whole" to promote participation *and influence* by local resi-

[1] Considerable outrage has been occasioned among the advocates of government action in housing and renewal by the recent publication of an extremely critical study of urban renewal by a conservative economist. See Martin Anderson, *The Federal Bulldozer* (Cambridge: MIT Press, 1964), 272 pp. For a very general but more judicious review of urban-renewal policies and problems, see Herbert J. Gans, "The Failure of Urban Renewal," *Commentary*, April 1965, pp. 29-37.

[2] For a review of problems in relocation, see Chester Hartman, "The Housing of Relocated Families," *Journal of the American Institute of Planners*, November 1964, pp. 266-86.

[3] For a discussion of the political dilemmas created by renewal programs, see James Q. Wilson, "Planning and Politics: Citizen Participation in Urban Renewal," *Journal of the American Institute of Planners*, November 1963.

dents in renewal areas. It was virtually inevitable that educational forms of participation would be emphasized in renewal programs.

The community-based poverty projects which are already under way also emphasize the place of resident participation. These projects have, however, been given a different public mandate than renewal programs in that they are oriented to the problems of the poor in the project community, rather than to the larger urban community. Moreover, they have developed at a time when the civil-rights movement has lent new force and meaning to political and organizational activity among the minority groups which form a large bulk of the urban poor.

The new concern with resident participation reflects a characterization of the low-income urban community as disorganized and politically ineffective. Low-income people tend not to belong to organizations, and they do not participate in community affairs. They are relatively uninfluential in the formation of policies and practices of major institutions which affect the course of their lives. This kind of social and political inactivity is viewed as an aspect of social disorganization, and closely linked, therefore, with many of the problems of the low-income community having to do particularly with socialization of the young and also with the social preconditions for individual and family effectiveness generally.

Consistent with this characterization, new objectives and strategies are being associated with resident participation in the antipoverty projects. Three interrelated objectives can be identified:

(1) Fostering the participation of low-income people in a variety of local associations;

(2) Enhancing the effective influence of low-income people on the policies and practices of institutions which serve the low-income community;

(3) Establishing the conditions for effective individual and family life by altering the social context of individual behavior.

These objectives for resident participation reflect the concern of the poverty programs with political problems pertaining to democratic participation and influence, as well as with the social-welfare problems to which the programs are principally addressed. The conception we have attributed to urban-renewal programs, in contrast, emphasizes another kind of political problem—that of integrating local groups to the support of a larger public policy. It should be noted, however, that the poverty programs are only less immediately charged with the problem of reconciling divergent group interests. To the extent that the programs do pursue objectives oriented specifically to the interests of the poor, they will, as they develop, require changes and accommodations from larger institutions. Problems of political conflict and integration will inevitably arise and rebound on the objectives of local resident participation and influence.[4]

The CAP Problem

The Population

While the poor are obviously composed of diverse groups, certain attributes can be identified which are pertinent to any efforts to encourage resident participation among the poor, in terms of the objectives outlined above.[5]

Several aspects of low-income urban life contribute to disorganization and political ineffectiveness. Low-income people are overwhelmed by concrete daily needs. Their lives are often crisis-ridden, deflecting any concern with community issues. Low-income people often do not believe in their ability to affect the world in which they live, and so they are not easily induced to try to affect it. Low-income people frequently lack the necessary resources of knowledge and information to scrutinize social policies. Leadership capabilities are also scarcer among the poor. Moreover, when leaders do emerge, the poor have few incentives to offer them, and scarce means of controlling them. Potential leaders therefore tend to take advantage of opportunities for their own advancement which move them quickly away from low-income concerns. Finally, the institutions whose services might offer incentives for low-income interest and activity are

[4] We already have evidence of such problems in the controversy over the Mobilization for Youth project. Recent testimony from local leaders before a Congressional committee suggests, moreover, that such problems may smolder without becoming so publicly evident.

[5] The discussion which follows is addressed specifically to the urban poor. The problems and potentialities in involving the rural poor would appear to be quite different, and to require examination in their own right.

often effectively insulated from the low-income community by their structure, practices, and cultural style.

These several aspects of low-income life are interrelated and cumulative in their effects. Thus, lower-class interpretations of the world stress the inability of most men to affect the conditions under which they live. These beliefs take form in a sense of political inefficacy, which discourages political participation and thus further reinforces conditions of actual powerlessness. Low-income people have little to offer in the way of material resources as political inducements, and they are separated by their social location from the exercise of personal influence on decision-makers. Thus they are not easily able to secure the benefits of political influence which might serve as inducements for political participation, and as inducements to overcome the disadvantages in education and skill which inhibit participation.

The organizational life of the low-income community both reflects these individual attributes and serves to maintain the conditions which produce them. Participation and influence do not consist only in the relations between disparate individuals and official decision-makers. The influence of individuals is mediated by organizations. It is through organizations that diverse individual resources are coordinated into coherent patterns of effective influence. But lower-class people have few of the requirements out of which stable organizations are generated: they have less organizational skill, less professional expertise, less money, and fewer personal relations with officials. In any case, they do not have the resources lent by a stable livelihood which are required merely for regular participation in organizations. The instability of lower-class life and the character of lower-class beliefs further discourage the poor from organizational participation. It is, in turn, partly because of the meagerness of organizational life that the poor community is so little able to retain or control its potential leaders.

This characterization of low-income urban life may be modified or even overcome when, for example, a community is bound by a strong ethnic culture. It is a characterization which tends to apply to vast numbers of our urban poor today, however, and a characterization which marks those groups who share least in organizational and political life. The meager success of traditional approaches to involving the poor, which rely upon exhorting them to participate or upon civic education, can be understood in terms of the interlocking and reinforcing relationships between actual powerlessness, apathetic beliefs, and scarce skills and resources. These circumstances, in turn, both produce and are maintained by the paucity of organizational life in the low-income community.

The antipoverty projects can address these problems in resident participation in two different contexts. They can attempt to facilitate resident participation in a variety of areas of community life and with regard to a variety of institutions. This is typically the approach of community-organization efforts. The antipoverty project is, however, itself a public-policy arena. The focus may therefore be specifically on resident participation in the policy and program of the local project.

Program Strategies

Various strategies for facilitating resident participation in community life generally are being employed by projects already under way. These can be identified and reviewed in terms of early experiences.

1. Concrete services are provided, such as help in processing housing complaints or in consumer problems. These services are located in places easily accessible to local people and are expected to attract low-income people as recipients. The goal, however, is to induce recipients to take on more active roles through associations formed around the provision of service. Thus, for example, tenant associations may be organized in housing clinics, in the hope that tenants will become interested in sponsoring and operating the clinic and eventually, as a group, will become more articulate and aggressive concerning the issues in housing policy which their daily problems reflect.

2. Existing low-income organizations in the project area are helped with staff and facilities. It is expected that adding to the capability of these groups will enable them to attract more participants and also will encourage them to take more alert and forceful positions on social issues of concern to the membership.

3. (a) A short-run approach to the problem of scarce leadership resources in the community is the engagement of professional staff in community-organization activity. Whether the engagement of professionals in this role is indeed merely an in-

terim solution depends on the success of attempts to develop
local leadership.

(b) Potential leaders are sought among local people. Efforts are made to interest persons who seem to show leadership
qualities in organizing activity and to educate these persons
about issues considered critical to low-income people. These
individuals may be paid as a kind of "community worker" or
they may be coached and encouraged to perform actively as
volunteers.

4. The social contiguity provided by ethnic, religious, occupational, or residential groups is a natural basis for affiliation
and therefore is a reference in organizing group activity.

5. Participation in social-protest action is sometimes encouraged by staff assigned to local organizations. Facilities required to pursue such actions may also be provided to these
organizations, or even to formally unaffiliated individuals who
seem to play a leader role. These protest actions may range from
participation in nationwide events to demonstrations to city
agencies over particular complaints involving perhaps only a
few residents.

Some early experience with these program strategies reveals
persisting problems in overcoming barriers to low-income participation and influence in community affairs.

When concrete services are the incentive for initial participation they tend to remain the focus of activity. The extent of
need for such service among the poor seems to overwhelm any
less urgent activities, and the provision of services consumes the
energies of staff and recipients alike.

Existing low-income organizations are weak and seem often
to be mere emblems of power for leaders whose personal ambition is tied, not to a low-income following, which has little to
offer them, but, rather, to the service organization.

The role of professionals in community organization remains
problematical. Local people tend to regard them as strangers and
with uneasiness. The professionals themselves must accommodate
a strain between the style and actions indicated by their role in
low-income organizations, the dictates of their professional
training, and the organizational requirements of the antipoverty
project itself.

Other problems seem to reside in the strategies for selecting
and cultivating indigenous leadership. When these individuals

are paid, in an effort to compensate for the absence of incentives for leadership in the low-income community, they tend to orient themselves predominately to the organization which is the source of funds. Volunteers, when they can be cultivated, come to expect similar compensation.

Social-protest actions, because they offer simple and dramatic definitions of problems, may penetrate apathy and override the puzzled disengagement bred of lack of information. These actions also require less personal and economic stability than sustained organizational participation. It should be noted that urban-renewal programs elicited protest action from local groups, in response to the threats posed by renewal. Social protest is likely, however, to incur hostile and repressive reactions from other groups in the community and from public authorities. Low-income groups may in consequence be even further cut off from channels to influence, and also from the services which can serve as a basis for more stable organization. We already have experience with antipoverty programs which testifies dramatically to this risk.

Organizational Participation in the CAP

The antipoverty project itself is a potential arena for resident participation. This has lately become something of a public issue, and several different organizational forms for participation are being recommended:

1. Residents should participate on policy-making structures—ordinarily the Board—either on the city-wide or local level. These residents are regarded as representatives of the resident population.

2. Residents should participate as staff. These programs are generally referred to as the employment of indigenous, or nonprofessional, workers.

3. Residents should be formed into active constituent groups. These groups are sometimes recommended as a program resource for professional staff, providing feedback for program evaluation, or they may be regarded as pressure groups which properly influence the project in its activities.

These proposals can be reviewed for problems and potentialities in the light of the foregoing characterization of low-income urban life.

1. Persons from the resident community who are selected to participate in policy-making structures will, if they are to be effective, ordinarily be distinguished by superior abilities or resources. To this extent their representative character is qualified. Moreover, what has been said about the scarce resources for control of leaders in the low-income community applies to the control of these representatives as well. The community has little in the way of an alert and able citizenry or organizational resources to review, control, and direct what its ostensible spokesmen do. The antipoverty program, on the other hand, and the organizations with which it is affiliated, constitute an active source of pressure and inducement to the presumed representatives.

2. To some extent these problems also pertain when residents are employed as staff. Their sense of themselves as employees, however, facilitated by unionization, may create something of a bulwark enhancing resident identity. The tendency of supervising professionals to become overly protective and directing with resident staff, usually in the name of professional guidance and training, may also strain against the goals of participation and influence. This may be mitigated if the resident staff are organized in cadres enhancing their resident identity and providing group support.

3. When constituent groups are restricted to "feedback" participation there may be little incentive for their continuing viability. Feedback in the form of more active pressure and influence by these groups, in the course of which the project could deliver incentives for continued engagement, might be more successful. This requires organizational arrangements which try to ensure the project's responsiveness to constituent groups. For example, local public hearings can be held on various program practices provided that these practices are deemed appropriate for review and change in response to constituent groups.

Whatever patterns for resident participation are developed in the antipoverty projects will reflect answers to two sets of questions:

1. Who should participate? In what actions should they participate? Where should this participation be located in the organizational structure? What conditions should govern this action?

2. How can participation by the specified groups, and in the prescribed forms, be elicited and maintained; i.e., what are the effectuating mechanisms for the forms of participation prescribed by the answers to the first set of questions above?

The answers to these questions must reflect some of the fundamental ambiguities of our political values and must take account of the fluidity of social and political arrangements. Moreover, they require knowledge of processes of social and political change which we do not yet have. For these reasons, the questions will not be answered entirely explicitly or comprehensively. Nevertheless, decisions made in antipoverty programs will establish patterns of participation, and the questions must be confronted. Decisions pertaining to program activities designed to foster resident participation in community life generally will imply answers which properly vary with the kinds of participation considered and the institutional contexts of participation. The full scope of such decisions will reflect the political philosophy of the antipoverty program, as well as a range of assumptions regarding the conditions of social action. Insofar as these decisions pertain to participation in the projects themselves, they will imply answers which describe the antipoverty program as a political subsystem, and the place of residents of the local community in this political subsystem.

Part Four

THE LOW-INCOME
NONPROFESSIONAL

CHAPTER TEN

The Low-Income Nonprofessional*

by GEORGE A. BRAGER

As a result of chronic staff shortages for social-welfare tasks, increasing attention is being given to the use of nonprofessional personnel in social work. There is wide agreement that auxiliary personnel ought to be used as assistants to relieve the heavy work load of the harassed social worker. There is also considerable, although less widespread, sentiment for the development of a "social work associate" position, requiring independent functioning.[1] Under the latter scheme, work loads are differentiated: the social worker handles the more "vulnerable" client in circumstances that require a relatively high degree of worker autonomy, and the associate deals with less vulnerable persons in situations that permit greater bureaucratic control.[2] Both "solutions" presuppose well-educated technicians who, although less trained and experienced than the professional, function essentially in his image. By definition they must be middle class.

The employment of low-income persons in social services has certain advantages as well. It serves, of course, to increase vocational opportunities for the undereducated slum-dweller. Since automation is eliminating more and more unskilled and semi-

* Presented at the National Conference on Social Welfare, Los Angeles, California, May 1964, and published as "The Indigenous Worker: A New Approach to the Social Work Technician," in *Social Work*, April 1965, pp. 33-40. Reproduced with permission of the National Association of Social Workers.

[1] Bertram M. Beck, "Wanted Now: Social Work Associates," paper delivered at the National Conference on Social Welfare, Cleveland, Ohio, May 1963, mimeo.

[2] Willard C. Richan has developed this formulation. See "A Theoretical Scheme for Determining Roles of Professional and Nonprofessional Personnel," *Social Work*, Oct. 1961, pp. 22-28. See also "Utilization of Personnel in Social Work: Those with Full Professional Education and Those Without," a report of the Subcommittee on Utilization of Personnel, Commission on Practice (New York: National Association of Social Workers, 1962), mimeo.

skilled positions, there is great need to accelerate the development of service occupations appropriate for untrained persons. Furthermore, helpers often gain more from the helping process than the person who ostensibly is being helped.[3] Programs such as Alcoholics Anonymous and Synanon may be viewed in part as substituting for the addiction to alcohol and narcotics the addiction to helping. Engaging in a helping occupation enhances the self-image of low-income persons; it provides them with psychological support, and they themselves report considerable satisfaction in the job.[4] Thus, from a broad social perspective, providing new roles for low-income persons is a highly salutary objective.

Programmatic Goals

Other objectives in using nonprofessionals have barely been considered, and until recently there was virtual silence on the possibility that low-income persons might perform program tasks.[5] This paper explores the use of the indigenous worker to achieve these more programmatic goals. These goals must be specified in detail, for they determine the characteristics sought in the nonprofessional, the tasks to which he is assigned, his means of performing those tasks, and the organizational arrangements that guide his work.

One important programmatic goal in hiring nonprofessionals is to increase the meaningful participation of other urban-slum residents in social-welfare and community programs. Belief that the employment of nonprofessionals can contribute to this end stems from a number of assumptions and takes into account social-class variables often neglected in social-welfare considerations. One assumption is that low-income persons can establish contact with other slum residents more easily and maintain communication with them more effectively than can professionals. The "likeness" of the indigenous worker to clients may facilitate rapport with them and encourage them to use the agency's program, whether it provides individual services or community

[3] See Frank Riessman, "The 'Helper' Therapy Principle," below, pp. 217-26.

[4] See Gertrude Goldberg, "Nonprofessional Helpers: The Visiting Homemakers," below, pp. 175-207.

[5] See Arthur Pearl and Frank Riessman (eds.), New Careers for the Poor (New York: Free Press, 1965).

action. The social climate of the service may be affected significantly by drawing persons from and of the community, representative of the style, values, needs, and wants of the community's low-income residents. The indigenous worker may also serve as a "bridge," interpreting the residents to the agency and its personnel and vice versa.

This social-class-mediating function is one of the major objectives in the employment of low-income persons in the three programs on which this article is based. These programs, all part of Mobilization for Youth, are a visiting homemaker service, a parent-education aide unit, and a community-development program. Approximately fifty low-income inner-city residents are employed in these three activities.

The visiting homemaker service works with individuals and families to increase their competence in home management. In addition, homemakers teach the use of community resources (e.g., help clients to establish eligibility for public assistance and public housing), offer companionship and psychological support, and provide escort and mother's-helper services. Group teaching and community activity are minor components of the service.

At the other end of the service spectrum is the community-development program, whose goal is to encourage community residents to engage in autonomous and collective protest designed to improve social conditions. Services to individuals and groups, such as finding jobs, filing housing complaints, and organizing social events, are a necessary but peripheral feature of the community-organization program.

The parent-education aide unit has engaged in individual problem-solving, group teaching, and community action, as the situation required. Parent aides try to help residents make home conditions such as to facilitate school achievement. They also try to increase the responsiveness of school personnel to the low-income family. "Generalists," they welcome in-migrants, facilitate parent-teacher interaction, suggest appropriate referrals, organize informal discussion groups and building committees, and assist in mass efforts to protest school conditions.

In addition to attracting low-income residents to these programs and making their participation meaningful, the indigenous worker serves as an effective role model for other residents. Such a worker has a special expertise in coping with the life problems of the inner city. Persons who themselves have negotiated slum conditions and welfare resources can be of great assistance to others. Homemakers, for example, know how to stretch leftovers, use surplus foods, recognize bargains, plan children's schedules, as well as deal with merchants and even with public and private agencies. Their abilities and attainments, while considerable, may yet be within the grasp of other, more impoverished, residents.

Characteristics Sought

In employing indigenous workers to affect social climate broadly, it is neither possible nor desirable to draw a "representative" sample from the low-income community. The specific goals of the program will be a major determinant of the characteristics sought. If, for example, an important objective of the service is to enable working-class persons to strive for and reach middle-class status, it might be desirable to employ low-income people who are oriented to middle-class life. One consequence of such a decision, of course, is that, if other factors are equal, less striving persons will then be likely to avoid participation. To cite another example: if the agency's intention in hiring nonprofessionals is to give the appearance of minority-group or low-income representativeness without impinging on the middle-class value base or organizational prerequisite of the agency, it will choose low-income persons who are willing to accommodate to these requirements.

These are, of course, gross characteristics and cannot at this stage of our knowledge be refined further. In the three MFY programs mentioned, however, the following rough criteria provided the framework for recruitment decisions:

(1) Persons with some expertise in the program's area were sought—i.e., reasonably good home managers, though not compulsive cleaners, were hired as homemakers, parent aides were required to have had children in school, and community-development workers were expected to have some experience in leading formal or informal groups.

(2) Persons who seemed to be identified with other working- and lower-class people and especially with their own culture group, but who did not reject their less striving neighbors, were preferred.

(3) Especially within the community-development program, and to a lesser extent in the others, action-oriented residents

were sought—those who believed in group solutions to the problems of impoverishment and minority status and who were militantly oriented to changing social conditions.

Beyond these criteria, the intent was to recruit a cross-section of the stable working-class community as regards such demographic characteristics as ethnicity and to select those with some personal experience in dealing with social problems. Many workers were, in fact, drawn from the department of welfare rolls. Others had close relatives who exhibited some significant social problem, such as school maladjustment, delinquency, or addiction. The workers reflected the minority-group composition of the low-income community. Subsequent review indicated that the parents of the nonprofessionals employed by MFY were educationally equivalent to current community residents, so that educationally, at least, the nonprofessionals were one generational rung up the ladder.

A random survey of the attitudes and perceptions of community residents was conducted prior to the action phase of the MFY project.[6] Similar questions were subsequently asked of the agency's professional and nonprofessional staff. Analysis of these responses indicates that the attitudes and perceptions of the nonprofessional, as expected, conform more closely to those of the community than do the professional's. Asked to rate the Lower East Side as a place in which to live, for example, 70.5 per cent of the professionals answered poor or very poor. Only 37.5 per cent of the indigenous staff agreed with this designation, while the community response was a close 34.4 per cent.[7]

"Style" of the Indigenous Worker

The following report by an observer of a tenants' meeting led by a community-development worker (Lila) illustrates some differences between the ways in which nonprofessionals typi-

[6] *A Proposal for the Prevention and Control of Delinquency by Expanding Opportunities*, New York: Mobilization for Youth, Dec. 1961, Appendix I.

[7] Charles F. Grosser, "Perceptions of Professionals, Indigenous Workers, and Lower-Class Clients," unpublished doctoral dissertation, Columbia University School of Social Work, 1965. See also Grosser, "Middle-Class Professionals and Lower-Class Clients," above, pp. 64-71, and "Class Orientation of the Indigenous Staff," below, pp. 208-16.

cally approach their task and the more traditional methods of the social worker.

> Two persons whose building had been cleaned as a result of Lila's efforts came to the meeting to enlist the aid of the group in alleviating other building violations. One of them explained that he could not convince his neighbors to take part. Lila detailed the necessity of their signing a building complaint and kept saying that if people did not want to help themselves, she could not do anything for them. However, as she said this she let them know what the results could be if they were to unite. At her suggestion the meeting adjourned and all the members went down the street to the building to convince the tenants to sign the complaint form. It was an extremely impressive and moving scene, in which old women, children, and other adults were strung along the dark stairways of the apartment building while Lila knocked on the doors to urge tenants to sign.

The action of the community worker was immediately responsive to the needs of the two tenants. It was spontaneous and partisan. The worker was in the center of activity, exhorting her "clients," training by demonstration, and providing direction. Another illustration of the central role of the nonprofessional is furnished by a parent aide's record, which notes that "a chairman and secretary were elected to assist me in planning for the group." Cursory analysis of records further supports the conclusion that the nonprofessionals tend to provide active direction, for the reports reveal that they "decided," "announced," and "insisted." This differs sharply from professional recording, in which workers are more likely to "suggest" and "enable."

The nonprofessionals are considerably less formal. They hug clients, accept (and repay) their hospitality, and share first-name designations. The tenants' association meeting described was attended by children with balloons and bubble gum, as well as by adults of all ages. Although they were wrestling with problems resulting from serious housing violations, there were laughter and gaiety; although much business was conducted, this was no formal meeting.

Mutuality of interest between the nonprofessional and the program participant and shared group loyalties are sharply evident. Thus, record material refers to "we Puerto Ricans," "us Negroes." There is considerable reciprocity and sharing of favors. A group of residents will picket a building because of discrimination by a landlord against a parent aide. A client will give surplus food to a homemaker.

Professionals in all three programs report that much information is shared with the nonprofessional that the professionals working with the same client receive later or not at all. Enhanced communication is undoubtedly a consequence of the mutuality of interest of nonprofessional and community resident. The nonprofessional has no need to validate his presence in the community, which gives him a considerable advantage over the professional from the outset. Communication can be short-cut and friction eliminated because much is taken for granted as a result of the common background. The nonprofessional has a sense of life's meaning to the client out of their shared experience. The peer status of the nonprofessional and community resident further facilitates communication.[8]

Nonprofessionals are unencumbered by "professional role," a concept that low-income clients rarely understand. Although these clients tend to define impersonality in the professional as unfriendliness, a homemaker supervisor notes that the hostility and apparent prejudice some of the indigenous workers displayed apparently did not impair their relationship with clients.[9] This may be due, in part, to the reality in the relationship, to the fact that it reflects a more "natural" interaction of persons than is prescribed in a professional relationship. In addition, the subtle intimidation of the middle-class professional's authority is eliminated as a factor. Clients do, nevertheless, view the nonprofessional as a representative of the organization, and in spite of initial congeniality testing does occur.

The nonprofessional tends to give stronger weight to external life circumstances than to internal factors. In instances when caseworkers have defined a client's behavior as "neglectful," nonprofessional staff have been more likely to see it as a response to depressed conditions. A homemaker touchingly ascribed the impulsive credit buying of a woman to the fact that "being young, she wants everything in life." When the same

[8] Organization theorists have demonstrated amply that interaction between equals is greater than between persons with status differential. See, for example, Peter M. Blau and W. Richard Scott, *Formal Organizations* (San Francisco: Chandler Publishing Co., 1962).

Gertrude Goldberg, "Report on Visiting Homemakers" (New York: Mobilization for Youth, July 1963), p. 70, mimeo.

young woman reported a conversation with her dead husband, the homemaker acknowledged the woman's mental illness and recommended referral to a mental-hygiene clinic, although her further comment suggests that such diagnosis and referral may be the result of supervisory influence: "My *honest* opinion is that she needs to remarry."

The nonprofessional accepts information at face value and acts directly on it. A woman with low self-esteem is invited by a parent aide to her house for dinner, told she is worth something, and urged to go out and buy something for herself. A surface definition is, of course, of limited value, since it may lead to an obvious but erroneous action. It can, however, serve as a corrective to overreliance on intrapsychic interpretation. The indigenous worker's diagnosis also provides an important clue to the low-income client's perception of the problem.

Since they themselves have had extensive dealings with public services, indigenous workers tend to look askance at bureaucratic authority. In their service function as well, they quickly see the barriers to the resolution of individual and community-wide problems stemming from organizational rigidity or disinterest. They are, furthermore, less interested in or sensitive to the maintenance requirements of the agency that employs them. There is suspicion, not wholly unfounded, that agency policy reflects the views of conventional and powerful interests rather than of their people. Since their predilection is to respond immediately and directly, they are led to confrontation with other agency systems.

Some Structural Considerations

It is, of course, essentially inaccurate to ascribe the method of practice of the nonprofessional group wholly to the characteristics of certain types of low-income persons. One must also take into account the immediate environment that conditions their functioning, in this case the social agency. Who trains the nonprofessional, for what purpose, and, most important, how that relationship is structured are crucial factors in a review of his performance. Nonprofessionals are quite likely to convey the wishes of their employers, subtly but effectively. It has been asserted, for example, that some parents are hired by schools to aid the system by deflecting parental criticism. Community militancy may be reduced by hiring local leaders to "cool off" others.

Indigenous workers were employed in the programs described in this paper in order to attract other impoverished persons who ordinarily avoid social services, to encourage the development of services meaningful to these persons, and to bring about their active involvement in individual and collective community problem-solving. The milieu of the program was intended to reflect low-income style and method. The characteristics sought in the workers and their performance on the job stem from these purposes. Structural considerations are a further aspect of this formulation.

Indigenous workers were assigned a wide range of tasks and given great freedom in carrying them out. They gave advice, processed complaints, made referrals, offered support, and guided the development of community-action strategies, in addition to performing other, more concrete and specific functions. Because of this holistic, nonsegmented role, much of their activity had to take place outside the purview of professional observation. Since written material is not a viable supervisory tool with undereducated workers, professional control inevitably was limited.

Logically, tasks requiring discretion are allocated within organizations in accordance with staff training and experience. Inexperienced and undereducated persons usually perform functions that do not require or permit significant decision-making. The Chicago Area Project, long an advocate of the use of indigenous workers, notes that "one of the most distinctive features of project procedure was the employment of local residents, in appropriate categories and under the tutelage of staff sociologists."[10] While visiting homemakers, parent aides, and community-development workers were supervised by professionals, they had vast discretionary powers. If their functions had been delimited, however, or their tasks too closely defined, the differences in style noted between the nonprofessional and the professional would not have emerged so clearly. Dilution of the nonprofessional's impact on program climate might be the consequence.

[10] Solomon Kobrin, "The Chicago Area Project—A 25-Year Assessment," *Annals of the American Academy of Political and Social Science*, XXXII (March 1959), p. 24.

The nonprofessional will make frequent practice mistakes. These are ordinarily neither serious nor irreparable, nor do they resemble in effect the condescension, indifference, misunderstanding, and even cruelty that impoverished persons encounter all too often in dealing with conventional institutions. The holistic role of nonprofessionals poses other problems. Their assignment to some traditional social-work tasks implicitly derogates the enabling role of the professional. When, in addition, high value is placed on the low-income worker's difference from the professional, there is the further implication that nonprofessionals can do what professionals cannot. On the other hand, the nonprofessional is encouraged to vie with his trained and higher-status colleague when functions are shared. Status anxiety and hostility between the two groups are the consequence.

Strains can be minimized or exaggerated by structural arrangements. The visiting homemakers both provide auxiliary service to clients of agency caseworkers and offer assistance independently; the parent-education aides are part of a separate program with its own clientele. Not unexpectedly, tensions are greater in the former program. If the 15 homemakers were dispersed throughout the project and supervised by individual caseworkers rather than by the two unit supervisors to whom they are currently responsible, strain would be reduced and greater integration of individual services would be achieved. Once again, however, an attenuation of the distinctive "flavor" of the indigenous staff might be the result. The choice of structural arrangement will depend on the clarity with which an agency views the interrelationship of structure and goal, as well as its choice among the conflicting values that underlie different objectives. In the present example, a milieu congenial to lower-class persons was favored over tension reduction and more effective integration.

Indigenous workers are all too easy to "professionalize." In the early stages of the community-development program, it was recognized that the assignment of nonprofessionals to individual community organizers in varying subunits of that program encouraged them to imitate their supervisors. In becoming less-skilled professionals, they were undermining a basic purpose of their employment. This problem can best be met by providing the nonprofessionals with the safety of numbers. Their tendency to withhold information and opinion in one-to-one contacts with middle-class professionals is significantly less evident in group sessions. Within the alien confines of a social agency, they need one another's support. When they are together, on the other hand, it is the supervisor who may need help! If it is not possible, for programmatic reasons, to assign the nonprofessionals as a collective unit, one solution might be a group training program.

Assessment of Effectiveness

An assessment of the effectiveness of using indigenous workers in the three programs is implicit in many of the preceding comments. It is a documented fact that the programs serve vast numbers of low-income persons heretofore unreached by private agency services.[11] Although this probably has more to do with the nature of the service than with the use of nonprofessionals, it is safe to assume that they are a contributory element. A vivid example of their ability to engage participation is provided by the project's voter-registration drive. Both professionals and nonprofessionals did extensive door-to-door canvassing, with dramatic differences in achievement; the extensive success of the nonprofessionals was matched by the extensive failure of the professionals.

For good and ill, the nonprofessionals have placed their stamp on agency programs. They have been a source of pressure on the agency to move in an activist direction. The lack of felt social distance between nonprofessional and client has facilitated rapport and enhanced communication.

Whether the nonprofessional has contributed to the particularistic objectives of the specific programs is impossible to determine. Homemaker supervisors indicate a considerable upgrading of home-management skills, with other benefits as well. Reports on the other programs are similarly positive. Like most social-work evaluation, however, they reflect the educated but essentially subjective judgments of interested professionals and therefore have limitations as evidence.

One major failure has been the inability of the nonprofessional to facilitate communication between the low-income resident and conventional persons and institutions. Within the agency,

[11] The Records Development Unit of the Mobilization for Youth Research Department has reported to this effect.

nonprofessional staff tend to be unheeded, except in their own particular programs. Their efforts with outside institutions have been even more disappointing. As persons of minority-group status, without material or educational attainment, they are frequently dismissed by the personnel of the large service systems, barely accorded legitimacy in their official contacts with them. Language difficulty, lack of "polish," and working-class status create a gulf. Their advocacy of their people and their cause widen it.

The use of indigenous persons in program roles tends to be challenged by responsible persons and institutions. Internal and external pressures are brought to bear to dilute their impact. Resistance to these pressures may well result, however, in an organization more accountable to and "in tune" with the lower-income population of the community it serves.

CHAPTER ELEVEN

Nonprofessional Helpers: The Visiting Homemakers*

by GERTRUDE GOLDBERG

Having spent its professional infancy severing ties with Lady Bountiful, social work may find itself enlisting the aid of another kind of untrained person, the neighborhood or indigenous worker. For increasingly, we note that the middle-class professional worker has difficulty both in developing rapport with lower-class clients and in offering them practical help with the everyday problems of slum life. The professional lacks skilled experience in budgeting or shopping on a low income, in caring for a large family, in housekeeping under substandard conditions, and in using the public-welfare agencies as a client.

In an attempt to meet this problem, Mobilization for Youth employed 15 neighborhood women as "visiting homemakers." Their job was primarily to teach low-income families greater competence in home management.[1] Assigned to a home for several full or half days a week, homemakers helped families to improve their skills in such tasks as shopping, cleaning, sewing, budgeting of time and money, child care, and cooking. In addition to this home teaching, homemakers offered some services traditionally performed by case aides, such as escorting persons to clinics and helping them to establish eligibility for public assistance or public housing (which were often efforts to teach

---

* This article is a revised and expanded version of "The Use of Untrained Neighborhood Workers in a Homemaker Program," New York: Mobilization for Youth, 1963. Parts of it appeared in Arthur Pearl and Frank Riessman (eds.), *New Careers for the Poor* (New York: Free Press, 1965).

[1] The homemaker service and a number of the observations and conclusions of this article owe a great deal to the imagination and skill of my colleague, Dorothy Yates. For help in preparing the text, I am also indebted to Florence Galkin and Phyllis Melnick.

the use of community resources). Like case aides, they also provided companionship or psychological support as part of a casework plan. Homemakers maintained a baby-sitting center where
mothers could leave their youngsters while they did errands or
kept appointments. Finally, they performed the mother-substitute or mother's helper type of assignment when it became
necessary to complement existing city-wide homemaker services.

The visiting homemakers were able to be helpful to a large
proportion of the families served, many of whom would probably not have been receptive to casework or counseling. During
the first six months of service, homemakers were assigned to
approximately 48 cases in which there were teaching components. Of these, only six families failed to improve in some
area of home management or to learn how to use community
resources more efficiently.[2] Even among the cases regarded as
failures in both respects, the homemaker generally developed a
good relationship with the client. In cases requiring escort,
mother-substitute, or companionship functions, homemakers
were often very helpful, although it is somewhat more difficult
to estimate the results of service.[3] The apparent ability of the
visiting homemakers to decrease the self-defeating behavior of
low-income clients makes it important for us to try to understand their contribution to a social-welfare program.

Recruitment and Selection

Manner of Recruiting

Candidates for the position of visiting homemaker were referred by various community agencies, by personal acquaint-
ances of the supervisors who lived in the neighborhood, and by
other applicants. Individual recruiters and staff members of
settlements, churches, day-care centers, schools, the housing

[2] These figures do not pertain to changes in interpersonal relationships,
nor is there any claim that a family was "cured." Rather, each of the
families with whom we had some success learned to cope better with some
aspect of home management.

[3] To measure the effectiveness of the homemaker service, a much more
scientific evaluation covering a longer period is, of course, necessary. The
impressionistic evidence given herein is all that is currently available and
is cited only as a general indication of the value of neighborhood workers.

authority, and the like simply described the job to neighborhood women who they felt might be interested. Within a month there were many more qualified applicants than openings.

Characteristics Sought

In recruiting homemakers, the agency sought persons whose social distance from the target population (the most deprived group in the community, consisting mainly of low-income Puerto Ricans and Negroes) was much less than that of the professional staff but who appeared to have the warmth, friendliness, and understanding which are usually sought in candidates for social work and related professions. Persons with skill in various areas of home management or with wide knowledge of community resources were favored. At least some of the homemakers, it was hoped, would belong to the same ethnic groups as the majority of the client population.

Rejectees

In choosing among the sixty-odd candidates, we tried to avoid both upwardly mobile slum dwellers who tended to shun their less-striving neighbors and persons too deprived to be helpful to others.

We felt that by setting no formal educational requirements except ability to read, write, and fill out simple forms and reports we would be likely to attract a lower-class group. However, we did turn down persons who seemed to lack basic intelligence or who were unable to grasp the point of the service or to understand how the position differed from domestic employment.

We excluded persons who showed no special interest in the work and could not see how it would offer more satisfaction than a factory job, for example. On the other hand, we were wary of those who emphasized the missionary aspects of the work to the exclusion of pecuniary rewards. If a candidate seemed to derive little satisfaction from managing her own home, we felt she would be unsuited to teach others.

Candidates who exhibited blatant prejudice against minority groups, welfare recipients, or delinquents were considered unsuitable. Similarly, if they regarded themselves as utterly apart from deviant or severely deprived persons, they were excluded. For this reason, we were favorably impressed when a candidate conceded that she could have used a homemaker at one time or that she had "gone through some bad times."

Selection Process

Applicants who were at all promising were seen twice, once by each supervisor. At an initial office interview, we discussed the position, had the candidate fill out a simple application, and formed a general impression of her interest, availability, and ability.

Applicants were asked to give three references other than former employers. They usually tended to give friends' names, but we urged them to list at least one "official"—i.e., such leaders as school principals, ministers, and social workers, whose opinions we might better evaluate. (It was probably a mistake to insist on these recommendations since we were not necessarily seeking persons with community connections. Actually, three persons who became quite satisfactory workers had no community leaders to recommend them.)

We scheduled a home visit to those candidates who seemed to be good prospects. This second interview helped us to assess the applicant's attitudes toward her home, homemaking, and family life and gave us a better opportunity to determine her proximity to the client population. (Several candidates who had seemed to be in good circumstances because they were well dressed at the first interview actually lived in substandard tenements and appeared to have meager possessions.)[4] More important, several of the candidates responded more spontaneously when they were interviewed at home. In the absence of trustworthy references, the home interview was particularly important.

Characteristics of the Homemakers

It was our goal to hire persons who, unlike many middle-class professionals, had natural rapport with the target population or the lower class. In describing the homemakers, it seems important, therefore, to determine both how close they were to the clients and how different they were from the professional staff.

---

[4] It has been observed that today's poor are misleadingly well clad but nonetheless ill housed and ill fed. See Michael Harrington, *The Other America: Poverty in the United States* (New York: Macmillan, 1962), pp. 4-7.

The fact that the 15 homemakers were able to help a large number of very deprived persons suggests either that they were close enough to form good relationships with members of the target group or, if they seem to be quite different from the clients, that the social-distance variable may be less important than we postulated.

Social Pathology

Although we sought persons who were not so overburdened as to be unable to help others, the homemakers were by no means problem-free. To a much greater extent than professional staff (who are more frequently troubled by interpersonal problems), they revealed, either at the onset or in the course of employment, a wide gamut of social problems. At least five had close relatives, either sons or brothers, who exhibited serious social pathology, such as drug addiction, desertion, delinquency, or school maladjustment.[5]

Income

The income of most homemakers was relatively low. Three of them were receiving public assistance at the time they were hired. For all of them, their $4,000 salary as homemakers, perhaps supplemented by sporadic contributions of spouses or small Social Security benefits, represented an economic step up. One of these women commented that the salary for visiting homemakers was about as good as she could expect in view of her limited skill and education. At least one of those who were not receiving public assistance at the time of hiring had an income low enough to qualify for the surplus foods distributed by the department of welfare. Nine homemakers resided in low-income

[5] Because of the social problems of neighborhood staff, it was necessary to spend considerable supervisory time offering casework help (mainly referral) to those who requested it. We referred a daughter to a vocational-guidance service, obtained casework service for a brother, discussed a marital upheaval, saw a homemaker's mother who was concerned about a delinquent son, etc. In addition to the obvious justification of this use of time—that of extending help to persons who asked for professional assistance—we felt that it was an important supervisory role. The homemakers would never have believed we cared about people and therefore would not have respected our judgment if they felt we could respond only to clients' problems.

public-housing projects. Four of those who lived in tenements were in very old buildings in problem-ridden areas. One homemaker lived in a middle-income, partially subsidized cooperative. Only three had a family car. Most of their husbands (12 were married) were steadily employed but in lower-status occupations, such as railroad laborer and elevator operator. The two most affluent women were married, respectively, to a bass player in a well-known Spanish band and to a school custodian. Thus the homemakers were neither the "down and out," although some have been at one time or another, nor the stable working class, with skills and homes and cars. They were, as a group, somewhere between lower class and stable working class as measured by objective factors such as income, occupation, and education.

Attitudes Toward Work

It is sometimes maintained that working-class and lower-class persons regard work differently from middle-class people. For the former, it is said, work is just a means of making money and a necessary evil. Often lower-status employment involves considerable physical activity, little cerebral effort, and highly routinized behavior. Although the financial aspect of middle-class work is very important too, the middle-class employee usually has a more responsible job requiring greater intellectual ability than that of the lower-class worker. The middle-class person is sometimes a member of a profession, which is associated with a way of life and a means of intrinsic as well as monetary satisfaction. The middle-class white-collar worker is thought to be more reliable and conscientious than the lower-class employee because he cares more about his job. The lower-status person is reputed to work only as hard as he has to.[6]

[6] In a study of a group of working men, it was found that about 80 per cent of the workers would want to keep working even if they inherited enough money to stop. The only group which deviated from this over-all pattern was composed of unskilled workers. Only slightly more than 50 per cent of them would want to continue working. The authors also found that middle-class people see work as a chance to accomplish something or to make a contribution, whereas working-class people see it as synonymous with activity; the alternative to working would be "to lie around." (Nancy Morse and R. S. Weiss, "The Function and Meaning of Work and the Job," *American Sociological Review*, XX [March 1955], pp. 191-205.)

On the other hand, some commentators have emphasized that there is very

Our experience with the visiting homemakers leads us to three possible conclusions: (1) they are not typical working- or lower-class women, (2) the assumptions regarding differential class attitudes toward work should be questioned, (3) this particular position or social opportunity evoked a conscientious response regardless of the employee's class orientation. The homemakers responded very seriously to a demanding job. At times they seemed to resent being compelled to work so hard and complained of fatigue. The truth is, though, that they drove themselves hard. With the exception of such vestiges of jobs with little responsibility as taking a two-week "vacation" with one day's notice or failing to be circumspect in leaving messages when they called to report an illness, they were very reliable. They were frequently more prompt than members of the professional staff and quite apologetic when they had to miss work. One voluntarily cut her vacation short to be available for shopping when a client's welfare check arrived. To miss a day's work was regarded as to fail one's personal obligation to the client rather than to the job.

Their enthusiasm and spirit were infectious. As a result, the supervisors were overburdened with work. Homemakers called on weekends and in the evening to report successes and to discuss "emergencies" that could not possibly keep until Monday or the next morning. Curiously, these women, who had walked close to misery all their lives, treated every problem as an emergency once they were in the helping role.

The enthusiasm of the homemakers impressed even the usually impassive institutional personnel. Teachers in neighborhood schools frequently lauded "these dedicated women who are doing such a wonderful job," at the same time faintly concealing their disdain for the "cold" professional social worker. The administrator of the local welfare center declared to a group of new social investigators that "these women are the best thing that ever happened to the neighborhood."

Regardless of where we assign the homemakers in the class hierarchy or in relation to clients or professional staff, the nature

little work available today that is creative and satisfying, regardless of one's social class. (See Paul Goodman, "Youth in the Organized Society," *Commentary*, Vol. 26 [Feb. 1960], pp. 95-107; and C. Wright Mills, "Work Milieu and Social Structure," *People at Work: A Symposium* [San Francisco: Mental Health Society of Northern California, 1954], pp. 20-36.)

of the job and the type of employment opportunity it provided had important effects on their response to the work. The specific characteristics of the position of visiting homemaker, its social purpose and involvement with persons in need of their help, account partly for their dedication. In addition, the scarcity of purposeful work and of jobs with such attributes of steady employment as vacations, increments, and sick leave may have led persons with scant formal education to strive hard to succeed or to use a rare opportunity well.

A program to orient the homemakers to the agency attempted to convey to them our feelings that they would perform an important service. They were welcomed at a tea attended by the executive director and other administrative staff. They toured every division and were given an introduction to the various services by supervisory personnel. In the middle of the first week, one of the more noncommittal homemakers remarked, "I took this job as if it were any other job, but now I see it's different: we really have a chance to do something for our people and our neighborhood." Her statement indicated that a sense of self-help rather than "pure" altruism had been generated. Homemakers began to feel both that the work was important and that they would derive satisfaction and status from it.

The very low turnover rates among nonprofessional staff are probably an indication of the lack of comparable jobs for this group as much as of their reaction to this particular job. Similarly, the zeal of the homemakers may stem from their desire to hold onto a job that provides them with satisfaction and status rather than from a wish to keep a job that involves helping others. Similarly, the homemakers' attitudes toward the impermanence of the job (as part of a temporary demonstration program, it was scheduled to last only a few years) reflect a fear of losing the employment opportunity rather than of losing the chance to perform a social service.

The experience of the Youth Worker Training Program, an effort to recruit and train persons for nonprofessional and subprofessional jobs in youth work, tends to support these conjectures concerning the effect of the employment opportunity on homemakers. The trainees, all school dropouts and offenders, were selected from residential treatment centers of the New York State Division for Youth. When given a Kuder Preference Test, they scored higher on the social-service scale than college graduates planning to enter youth work or a related field. The higher scores of the socially disadvantaged group were interpreted as "more a function of the paucity of career opportunities for such youth than of enthusiasm for the youth-work field."[7]

Attitudes Toward Child Care

The responses of most homemakers to caring for children in our center differed from a middle-class approach. Most of them persisted in offering custodial care only (i.e., gave only the necessary physical attention to the children) despite our having stressed the importance of playing with the children and supervising their activities. They felt it essential only to feed the youngsters, take them to the bathroom, and give them an occasional affectionate hug or pat. In fact, were it not for the constant prodding of the supervisors, they would have left the children in the playroom, returning only to respond to a cry or to arbitrate a quarrel.

Manner of Relating

The informality of the homemakers was striking as compared with the more inhibited behavior of the professional staff. One homemaker sucked lemons throughout a conference with the assistant director of the agency. At the staff Christmas party, the homemakers distinguished themselves by "twisting" with abandon. Disgusted with the men who stood around talking "like faggots" instead of dancing, they were forced to choose female partners (generally one another) and displayed much less self-consciousness about dancing with members of the same sex than middle-class women would have shown. They were well aware and rather proud of being less constrained than the professionals. They asked their supervisors if they were acting inappropriately or indecorously but at the same time complained that many of the social workers were stiff and unfriendly.

Some of them had a saucy manner that is not particularly lady-like but very charming. They exchanged wisecracks with anyone visiting the center who responded to their informality. One of

[7] Edmund W. Gordon and Gertrude S. Goldberg, *Two-Year Report of the Youth Worker Training Program* (New York: Ferkauf Graduate School of Education, Yeshiva University and New York State Division for Youth, 1965).

them, for example, was describing Puerto Rican foods to a group of school teachers when a rather pedantic gentleman asked, "Is there any medical reason why you don't eat *platanos* (plantains) raw?" She retorted, "Any medical reason why you don't eat potatoes raw?"

Social Attitudes

It was believed that their proximity to slum life would free neighborhood staff from some of the negative attitudes toward clients which should be handled by the professional training of middle-class persons. However, this assumption was not necessarily valid, for we found that even these persons, who had themselves lived in poverty, had many of the prevailing middle-class attitudes toward the poor (e.g., that persons are responsible for their social circumstances, that those who do not pay for a service are getting a "favor" and have relinquished the right to make demands on the dispensers of that service). These attitudes stem partly from negative self-images and internalization of the majority viewpoint; they are also the familiar reaction of persons who have bettered themselves, even if slightly, toward the group from which they have risen.

It is important to recognize that pejorative attitudes toward the deprived are shared not only by the middle classes and the more striving members of the lower classes but by the better-functioning low-income persons as well. Indeed, their need to distinguish themselves from their neighbors may increase in proportion to their proximity to poverty. After all, one's need to shun the delinquent is greater when one lives on the same street or in the same housing project. We were, in effect, asking our indigenous staff to walk through those very doors which they had managed to slide past most of their lives.

In considering the apparently middle-class attitudes of some of the homemakers toward the poor, we must distinguish between what they really thought or said among themselves and what they believed others wanted to hear and, in effect, demanded of them. In some layer of their personalities, unlike persons who have not experienced economic and social deprivation, they both felt and knew that social opportunities are important and that middle-class norms and values do not necessarily apply to their way of life.

A comparison of sentiments expressed by homemakers early in the program and later, when they were more capable of candor, illustrates the difference between real and assumed attitudes. Early in her employment, we gave a homemaker some material on teenage behavior prepared by one of the large insurance companies. She accepted the interpretation without qualification on the ground that it was "just what the teachers say." Somewhat later, she took issue (quite rightly) with a school principal's extreme concern over a pornographic note written by the homemaker's 11-year-old daughter.

The disparity between middle-class compliance and genuine attitudes was also illustrated when, during a training session, a Negro homemaker vigorously denied that color affected one's opportunities. "If you don't get a job, it's your own fault," she maintained. Later we learned that she was one of the staff who most keenly felt the sting of inequality. Her attempt at blatant denial of her opinions suggests that she was not accustomed and probably feared to express her feelings in a mixed group, particularly in the presence of a middle-class person who was also her supervisor.

Evidently, the homemakers, despite greater conservatism than professionals, were more critical of slum conditions than were typical lower-class community residents. The results of a survey administered to a random sample of the Lower East Side community and to the Mobilization staff indicate that in this and many other respects the attitudes of indigenous staff members resembled those of the middle-class professionals more than those of the low-income residents with whom they shared class, ethnic, cultural, and residential ties.[8] One conclusion suggested by this finding is that, despite our efforts to eschew upwardly mobile slum dwellers, our indigenous staff were middle-class-oriented.[9] When asked to estimate the responses of lower-class community residents to the same questions, the neighborhood staff, however, were significantly more accurate in their per-

[8] Charles Grosser, "Class Orientation of the Indigenous Staff," below, pp. 208-16.

[9] Some of the items on the questionnaire were part of national samples and have been proved to be sensitive indicators of class-linked attitudes; thus the indigenous group is thought to have responded in a way characteristic of the middle class in general rather specifically like the professional sample.

ceptions of the community than their professional colleagues, probably as a result of their proximity, if not similarity, to other lower-class residents.

Representativeness of Nonprofessional Staff

Impressionistic evidence and objective data seem to offer somewhat conflicting conclusions regarding the representativeness of indigenous staff. On the one hand, they were, before they obtained stable employment at Mobilization, either working-class or lower-class by such indices as occupation, income, and education. Their behavior also seemed markedly different from that of middle-class staff. One simply could not visit the homemaking center without tasting their salt, whether one enjoyed the flavor or preferred something more bland. They, in turn, felt different from other staff and thought they had a distinctive contribution to make. On the other hand, although they were more knowledgeable about the community than professionals, their attitudes, as measured by the questionnaire reported above, were closer to those of middle-class persons than of community residents.

As Mobilization staff members, neighborhood workers acted differently from slum residents traditionally employed as helpers in such middle-class organizations as schools and settlements. Yet the difference may be more the result of the manner in which they were used by the agency than of a difference in class orientation. Thus, a role which gave them status and *bona fide* employment as a result of their knowledge of and rapport with the lower class may have led them to be more accepting of themselves and of the class to which they belonged and, in turn, less inclined to emulate the middle class. Ironically, the modes of behavior typical of his class of origin become for the indigenous worker, as for the politician with roots and bailiwick in the slums, a means of upward mobility. Regardless of their social attitudes and aspirations, such persons have at their disposal the style of behavior characteristic of their original class. Indeed, such traits as the manner of forming relationships and of speaking often persist long after one has assumed the attitudes of or achieved the desired class. Further investigation is necessary to determine how the performance of nonprofessional workers is affected by such variables as style of behavior, social attitudes, agency function, lack of professional training, and proximity to client group and professional staff.[10]

In the next section we shall provide more detailed observations concerning two of these factors, their style of relationship with clients and their role in the agency.

The Homemaking Relationship and Role

As supervisors of the visiting homemakers, we felt that they were helpful to clients for two principal reasons. First, regardless of their middle-class attitudes, they could form relationships with low-income persons with a facility that surpassed that of many competent professional workers. Secondly, they were able to offer clients a service which they genuinely needed. Thus success hinged on their relative proximity to the client group and on the type of helping role the position of visiting homemaker permitted them to perform. Although these two facets of the homemakers' success will be discussed separately for purposes of analysis, they are interrelated in practice. We shall also attempt to answer some questions about problems of motivation and dependency which, because of the homemakers' closeness to the client group and the nature of the helping role, appear to be less crucial considerations in a service of this type than is customary in social work.

Relationship

The capacity of homemakers to develop rapport with their clients is evident from a cursory reading of cases, even some in which failure is noted. Above all, one is impressed by the unusual evidence of warmth between worker and client.

The relationship resembled that of friends rather than that of

[10] This discussion has omitted ethnic differences among the homemakers. (There were six American Negroes, six white Puerto Ricans, one American of Cuban descent, a second-generation Italian-American, and a first-generation German-American.) Although significant differences in behavior and attitudes could be noted, especially between the two major groups, the social-class variable seems most pertinent to a consideration of assistance to low-income clients. One observes, furthermore, that professional workers who are Negro or Puerto Rican experience many of the difficulties and disadvantages of other middle-class workers in developing relationships with lower-class Negro or Puerto Rican clients. Obviously, further study of the ethnic variables is necessary, as well as of those related to social class and agency function.

worker and client. Like friends, they were usually on a first-name basis. Significantly, some homemakers felt snubbed when a client failed to offer them coffee or a snack. (The supervisor sometimes felt that such hurt reactions were inappropriate to the helping role, partly because she failed to recognize the wish to be friendly that they implied.) Clients invited homemakers to parties and other social events; they would come to the center to chat or visit when there was no pressing problem or official business. It is not surprising that clients revealed themselves quickly to homemakers and that a homemaker could obtain information in a few visits that would have taken her supervisor a number of interviews to elicit. One homemaker was asked to be the godmother of a client's child. Another was invited to be matron of honor at a client's wedding.

Although the homemakers were better off or better able to manage than most of their clients, there was a lack of *felt* social distance. There was, of course, less actual disparity in life circumstances between indigenous staff and clients than between clients and professional workers. Although the neighborhood workers had some "status," they were within the pale of the clients' set, visible enough to respect and aspire toward. Thus a homemaker, speaking of a client who was a very poor housekeeper, remarked, "I wouldn't see her socially." Although the worker was snobbishly rejecting the possibility of social contact with the client, at least it had occurred to her, whereas it probably would not have entered the mind of the professional worker.

The difference between the professional's ability to form relationships and that of the homemakers was apparent when a supervisor introduced a neighborhood worker to a family. The supervisor sometimes felt like an inhibiting influence. When she left, worker and client could speak freely in their own vernacular. They had something to talk about instead of problems—the neighborhood, a mutual friend, a place on the island if they were both Puerto Rican, or other common experiences.

One indication of the lack of condescension is the reciprocity between client and worker. For example, one family gave a homemaker some surplus butter that they did not intend to use. When another homemaker lost a family member, two clients who had heard the news paid her a condolence call. Another family surprised a worker by bringing her gifts on Mother's

Day. A housewife stopped by the center to tell a homemaker about some bargains because the worker had given her so many good tips previously. The homemakers were not perceived as belonging to the "giving class." And, in turn, clients did not see themselves as the "receiving class." Homemakers were neighbors, perhaps a little better off, but nonetheless persons with whom one exchanged help, favors, and information.

It would be inaccurate to stress the warm feeling between homemakers and their clients without also pointing out that homemakers in some respects were less accepting than trained middle-class staff. As was noted previously, they sometimes looked down on deprived people, partly because they themselves had poor self-images. More important, they were contemptuous of persons who managed less well than they did in what seemed to be comparable circumstances. Some homemakers were particularly offended by slovenly housekeepers. Those who had budgeted thriftily when they were penurious or who had adjusted to a husband's desertion were often intolerant of persons who handled similar troubles with less pluck. Then, too, like any untrained staff, they were less disciplined in their responses to clients than professional workers. For example, they would fail to recognize that berating a deprived client for inappropriate behavior often compounded her deprivation. Similarly, they would show favoritism to one child in a family, scold a deviant youngster by saying "If you were my child . . . ," or become offended if a client was not "grateful" enough.

Ironically, these "mistakes" and rather punitive attitudes impaired relationships between workers and clients less than might be expected. For example, a homemaker with genuine contempt for a wretched housekeeper nonetheless helped her to improve her housekeeping. Rather than reacting negatively to the worker's judgmental attitude, the family responded warmly to her. One is led to conclude that the professional worker may also harbor prejudices toward low-income clients which are apparent to them despite the fact that he tends to express them in subtle ways. Then, too, the disciplined response of the professional worker may seem colder or more rejecting to the client than the homemaker's direct, candid reaction, even when it is harsh. Furthermore, such outward behavior as forms of greeting, use of physical gestures in speaking, and overt displays of emotion may be more important in developing worker-client rapport than such intrinsic factors as motivations, attitudes, and ideological commitments, which are often viewed as crucial. Another reason for this seeming paradox may be one that we shall discuss below; namely, the difference in the type of helping roles performed by professional and indigenous workers.

Although homemakers were in some respects less accepting than professional workers, they were more tolerant in others. They did not perceive people as problems, or at least they disagreed with professionals about what constitutes a problem. They reacted more strongly to bad housing, illness, and lack of money, perhaps because they had experienced these deprivations. They could understand that a client's refusal to discuss interpersonal problems when her welfare check had not arrived was a manifestation, not of "resistance," but of preoccupation with physical survival. A client whom the homemaker regarded as well-meaning, easily misunderstood, and temperamental ("She falls out with everyone but me") appeared to the caseworker to be "paranoid, rejecting, and abusive to her children." The homemakers were clearly judgmental in their approach to clients. In many respects, professional workers are equally judgmental, but they cloak their censure in psychiatric terms which are not merely diagnostic or descriptive but moralistic. Thus the terms "sick" or "problematic" behavior are sometimes euphemisms for "bad" or immoral actions.

The homemakers, on the other hand, thought professionals made too much over "little things." "That child didn't try to commit suicide; he ran up on the roof to hide." The point is not that homemakers could not diagnose psychological causation but that they were less likely to assume it, partly because they were untrained, and partly because they were not trained to emphasize psychological problems. More important, deviance did not suggest to them that a situation was hopeless or that people were beyond help. Indeed, homemakers sometimes brought about changes in persons who had seemed too self-destructive to be aided.

Type of Helping Role

The homemakers were untrained, but they were not unskilled. As we have suggested, they had considerable ability to cope with their environment and therefore much to offer clients who were less resourceful than they. They knew how to live on a low income, how to stretch leftovers, how to use surplus foods (including powdered skim milk and canned meat, which must have the preservative removed before it is edible), where to buy inexpensive material and how to sew an attractive garment with it, how to recognize a bargain. They knew which detergents would best clean an icebox or a stove and which made sense on a low income. They knew their neighborhood, which stores were good, and where bargains could be found. They also had learned how to deal with the local merchants. They were familiar with the neighborhood clinics, the welfare center, the child health stations, and the schools, and they could show a client how to fend with these institutions—not in the manner of a professional, who relies partly on the agency's power and partly on his polish, but the way a lower-class person does it for himself. Most of them had taken care of a large family and had planned their schedules well enough to have some time for themselves. They were both skilled and experienced in caring for young children.

A homemaker's know-how makes it possible to get by on a little, to negotiate life in a slum. She exploits every opportunity—the barber school for free haircuts, the thrift shop, the remnant heap, free recreation, public clinics, surplus foods (if she qualifies or if her neighbors do and don't use their supply). She is not under any illusion that it is easy to get ahead (and she did not get far), but she creates some regularity and routine, some security, and some freshness amidst the uncertainty, squalor, and chaos that surround her. Her children are well fed and healthy. They have the energy and strength to study and perhaps to achieve more than their parents.[11]

[11] The homemaker service was part of a program that was attempting to help clients to forego self-defeating patterns of behavior so that they might efficiently exploit new and existing opportunities. Like other MFY programs, the homemaker service was not based on a static concept of opportunities; it was very clearly recognized that it is much more difficult to manage a home under adverse conditions than with an adequate income and modern conveniences. There is, however, abundant evidence that some lower-class persons, largely because of the effects of social barriers, do not make maximal use of the advantages that are available. Far from lulling persons to accept their lot, a program of this sort helps them to assert their rights and to have the confidence and competence to work for their own social betterment. The homemakers themselves were examples of lower-income persons who made the most of their opportunities but were hardly content with their situations. Some of them were active in efforts to improve conditions in the neighborhood, and few would allow themselves to be taken advantage of.

The position of visiting homemaker permitted the neighbor-hood worker to impart her skill and know-how to clients. By imagining a client's description of the homemaking service, we can perhaps illustrate how the workers combined aid and in-struction:

> The homemaker didn't talk about how to shop or bargain or sew. She showed me how, helped out, lent a hand. She went along when I might have been afraid to go alone. When we went to the project office to ask them to fix the broken window, nobody hit her when she spoke up for me. She didn't do all the talking for me. I said enough to have the courage to do it alone next time. If we'd just talked about how to ask them to make a repair it wouldn't have helped.

> When she came, we got things done together . . . she ironed while I cleaned, or sewed while I cooked. When we budgeted and shopped I found it was possible to have a full icebox even when you live on welfare. I also began to believe that a cleaner house and a better way of running the house would really make a difference to the kids and me.

> It was nice to have her around. She was someone to talk to. I don't have much of a chance to get out and see grown folks. It seemed like the only people I knew were the kids. The time went fast when she worked along with me. I hardly knew we were working. Meantime she got me into the swing of things. Sometimes she made it a little easier for me to do things, like she stayed with some of the kids while I took the others to the clinic or came along to help watch a few during the long wait. Sometimes when I had to go somewhere she would come early to help me feed the kids and get them dressed. Once she even made dinner when I came back from welfare feeling too tired to do anything.

The important component in this admittedly idealized descrip-tion of the service is not so much the homemaker's personality or her ability to form a relationship with the client but what she could teach and do for the client. If a child was sick, they went to the clinic, the homemaker serving as interpreter, guide, and supportive companion. When this type of active and immediate service was offered, the client did not have to wonder whether the homemaker meant what she said or liked her. The service itself demonstrated the worker's concern.

The role of visiting homemaker led to a friendly peer relationship. Someone who shops, sews, or cleans with a client is perceived differently from someone who offers help from behind a desk. In addition, a worker who spent considerable time in a client's home was likely to develop an informal relationship with her. In those circumstances, they sometimes got on each other's nerves, but the homemaker did not seem distant or aloof.

Motivation and Dependency

Two traditional concerns of social work, and particularly of social casework, have thus far been missing from this discussion. The reason is that limited motivation and hostility resulting from dependence on the helping person were less important obstacles to effective use of the visiting homemaker service than some behavioral theories would lead us to expect.

Homemakers were able to help some persons who lacked what might be called superficial motivation—for example, a client who could verbalize neither her problem nor her need for homemaking help. They were able to be helpful to some clients who had barely tolerated their presence during intake as well as to others who were more friendly but who had been referred without discussion of their problems or how homemaking service might benefit them. They could work not only with some persons who were unclear about how the homemaker was aiding them but also with others whose motivation was artificial. Among the latter were tenants of the housing authority whose initial reason for being served was that the authority had defined them as poor housekeepers and threatened to evict them if they did not improve. Often such a client did not accept the housing manager's opinion of her but would respond to the idea of improving so that she would no longer be plagued by the fear of losing her apartment.[12]

[12] We did not necessarily accept the judgment of the housing authority that a tenant was a bad housekeeper. In those cases where we differed, we reported our dissenting opinion to the management. Whether or not we agreed with the individual decision of a manager, the authority's action against someone considered a poor housekeeper was a problem for that person. In all instances, we pointed out that we were a voluntary agency, separate from the housing authority. The client was free to accept or reject our offer of service. She was also told that we were not involved in determining whether her housekeeping standards were "acceptable," either at the time of referral or after homemaking service had been provided.

The crucial determinant of whether the homemaker could enable a client to change her patterns of home management was not her superficial motivation but the homemaker's ability to demonstrate quickly that the service was valuable. Once the homemaker had shown the client that it was possible for her to live better, then underlying motivation became important. If a client did not know whether she really preferred a clean to a dirty apartment or a full to an empty icebox, once such goals appeared attainable, then we were unable to help her. Many clients who lacked surface motivation, however, were able to forego self-defeating patterns of behavior when the homemaker showed them how to do so. We found that it was not important to demand initial motivation for a teaching service. We were, however, unable to develop any means of diagnosing underlying motivation or to predict who would profit from the service. Underlying motivation was revealed only in the client's response to homemaking assistance.

A homemaking service in which the worker actually did some of the client's work might be expected to conjure up severe feelings of dependency. It was our observation, however, that while some clients did rely too heavily on the homemaker, hostile feelings engendered by excessive dependency usually did not keep them from being helped by the service, nor did such feelings need to be handled in depth through casework intervention. Frequently the client became more restive as she became more efficient. We felt that this was an appropriate response and that the service should be gradually reduced, if not terminated quickly, in these cases. Sometimes a client would resent demands made on her by a homemaker (e.g., if she had to work much harder than usual in order to move to a new apartment) and would discharge her. If we were convinced that the client could use additional help and that she would be unable to accomplish an important task without it, we attempted to persuade her to keep the homemaker until the task was completed. One client whom we influenced in this way was able to sustain substantial homemaking gains when the homemaker left two weeks after a flare-up. If the service had been terminated when the client requested, she would probably have regressed to her previous very disorganized manner of homemaking. Other clients either became too dependent on the homemaker or tried to use her as a maid. In the case of a woman who learned from a homemaker but began to lean too heavily on her help, we slowly tapered the service. If the client was using the homemaker as a domestic, we instructed the worker to do household chores only when the client did; if the client could not respond to this setting of limits by working along with the homemaker, we probably could not help her and would have to withdraw completely. (In this technique of handling excessive dependency we were using a time-honored method of social work: doing *with*, not *for*, the client.)

Several additional factors account for our failure to be stymied by the roadblocks of motivation and dependency. We were offering a concrete, goal-oriented rather than relationship- or process-oriented service. As long as we could help clients to solve substantial bread-and-butter problems, we did not have to worry about their desire for aid or their feelings of anger toward us for assisting them. (When a service seems to offer little, it may be the service and not the client's motivation that is lacking. Insufficient help or help that is not really geared to the needs of the person served is resented more than genuine assistance.)

The client may feel less dependence if he is convinced that while receiving help he is becoming progressively better equipped to fend for himself. The analogy of a patient's response to a physician may be appropriate here. The patient is clearly dependent on the doctor's help and frequently has little understanding of what the doctor is doing for him. Yet he is usually not too upset by his reliance on medical treatment unless he does not seem to be getting well. He becomes hostile to the doctor when treatment fails to bring improvement or to make him less dependent on medical service or care. As long as the patient can see that he is getting better, the temporary dependence on the doctor is usually not unduly hard to bear, or, at least, does not prevent him from continuing to use the service until he no longer needs it.

The nature of an indigenous staff is another factor which may mitigate problems of dependency in a service for low-income clients. We have noted that there seemed to be less condescension between homemaker and client than between professional worker and client. The relatively small social distance between homemaker and client may have made it easier for the client to accept help. The homemakers seemed like older, better-established women who traditionally help less capable or experienced neighbors. They also conveyed to clients that they had themselves faced similar problems. What they were doing for clients benefited the neighborhood as well as the particular individuals being helped, and therefore benefited the homemakers themselves. Homemakers may have communicated this feeling to clients, thus relieving their need to feel grateful.

Training, Supervision, and Administration

The chief hazard in supervising, training, and administering an indigenous staff and program is that workers might be molded in the professional image, which would dissipate their ability to help the client group. Because of their tendency to comply with middle-class expectations, particularly in an employment situation, the homemakers had to be helped to feel that they had much to teach clients. Because they could easily be induced to act like middle-class persons, we had to encourage them to be themselves rather than to behave as they felt was expected of them. A number of important aspects of training, supervision, and administration might be described. However, because our penchant to professionalize neighborhood workers is most crucial, we shall focus here on several ways in which we tried to maintain the indigenous flavor of our staff.

Training

The training period was really a two-week orientation in which we tried to set the tone of our service and to introduce homemakers to the agency. Although we did not want to give them the false impression that treatment decisions or interpretations of client behavior were theirs to make, we did wish to make it clear that when it came to homemaking under the conditions faced by low-income clients, they were the experts. There were a number of specialists—a psychiatrist, a day-care center director, a nutritionist, a home economist, and a nurse—who served as resource persons during the training sessions. However, these persons were there, not to teach homemaking or offer formulas for understanding or reacting to clients' behavior, but to evoke the homemakers' comments and stimulate their discussion. Skills sessions were provided to refresh them, for time had elapsed since some of them had taken care of babies, for example, or to fill in gaps in their ability, since they had talents in different areas of home management.

We employed several methods to make the sessions lively and informal. Rather than a didactic format, we used the case method in nearly all sessions. That is, we described a family with budgeting, health, nutritional, or other homemaking problems. Trainees were asked to interpret the behavior described and to say how they would handle the problems if they were assigned to the case. There was much discussion and argument over interpretations. We continually prodded them to state what they really thought; when a response seemed pat or an attempt to tell us what they thought social workers wanted to hear, we would express skepticism until the discussion became more candid.

Role-playing was an excellent technique for achieving spontaneity. We often asked one trainee to play the homemaker and another the client in order to give them practice in certain aspects of the work. In the dramatic situation of role-play, it was very hard for them to maintain middle-class compliance.

The theme of our orientation sessions was a constant question, "Is this how it's really done?" Never mind what the "experts" say—how *does* one budget on a very low income, keep house in an overcrowded, substandard apartment? One worker who had monopolized several early discussions by bragging about her role as a community leader became the expert when we discussed a rat-infested apartment: "I'll be honest; I've lived in some pretty rotten tenements, and this is how I plug a rat hole." Evidently she had become convinced that status is derived from acknowledging and then imparting one's skill in coping with slum life.

Supervision

We found that individual conferences were necessary for assigning a homemaker to a family and for emergencies or special problems faced by a client, but that the group was generally a more suitable medium for supervision. We initially chose group supervision to save time but discovered that it encouraged greater informality and freer participation than the one-to-one situation.

The most important reason that group supervision was effective was that it helped to mitigate authority and status problems.

It was probably asking too much of the indigenous worker to expect her to be relaxed in a one-to-one supervisory situation with a trained person, no matter how much self-confidence she had. In a group with five homemakers and two supervisors there was more equality. In such a group supervisors were able to argue more forcefully without the fear of overpowering the homemakers. There was also the likelihood that some of the "desired conclusions," particularly regarding social attitudes, would come from a member of the group, so that the supervisors could support that viewpoint rather than dictate it. If role-playing was one of the activities of the group, the supervisor had to demonstrate her ability to help a client by assuming a role. She thus became a member of the group.

Administration

If the indigenous character of a service is to be retained, it must be administered less formally and bureaucratically than many social-work programs. Not that we failed to develop forms and procedures consistent with good practice. As much as possible, however, we let the homemakers set the pace and determine the atmosphere of the center. The supervisors seldom sat behind desks or closed doors and were accessible to homemakers for spot conferences, success stories, and "emergencies." Neighborhood persons, both workers and clients, chatted and gossiped in the office. It was the professional staff rather than indigenous people who felt like outsiders.

The physical plan of the center—an apartment in a housing project rather than an office—owed much to the homemaker's tastes. After giving the homemakers the assignment of furnishing it as a model apartment on a low-income budget, we suggested that they visit an apartment which had been done by the housing authority's interior designer. They felt this apartment was nice but not in their taste or that of the clients. They pointed out for example, that the area rugs used by the professional decorator might be stylish, but that to a poor person a small rug indicates that one cannot afford a large one. To a certain extent, the problem in furnishing the apartment was to find a solution between big and small rugs—to expose clients to economical and sound home decorating and at the same time to offer something they would like, something not too remote from their life-styles.

Problems Posed by the Employment of Neighborhood Workers

Because of the inevitable tendency, in describing a promising innovation, to stress its positive aspects, it seems particularly important to discuss the problems the employment of neighborhood workers poses for a social agency.

To the extent that we succeed in hiring persons who have rapport with lower-class clientele and in avoiding the tendency to professionalize them, we face difficulties in working with them. The visiting homemakers were more difficult to get along with than their nonprofessional predecessor, Lady Bountiful. Most of the problems inherent in successful recruitment and appropriate utilization of nonprofessional staff are related to strains between the professional and nonprofessional workers. The difficulties stem from two sets of mutually enforcing status factors. These include the class differences (and sometimes racial and ethnic differences) between middle-class and indigenous workers and the different agency status and function of the two sets of workers. Another important source of conflict is the professional culture itself, which tends to reinforce disparities between the two classes of staff.

Even if members of the neighborhood staff were more like middle-class persons than the client group, they had experienced economic hardship and in many cases racial and ethnic discrimination. Such experiences heightened their empathy with lower-class clients but frequently threatened or undermined their relationships with the professional staff. The latter were either from middle-class families or had themselves achieved middle-class status. They were therefore members of a group which some lower-status workers perceived as responsible for discrimination. As social workers, the professionals also had certain group handicaps, for many neighborhood workers had received prejudicial treatment or inadequate help from teachers, social investigators, and social workers. It would have been possible to hire neighborhood staff who were less inclined to be suspicious of the several reference groups of trained workers. But such persons, because of unequivocal middle-class leanings, might tend to denigrate their former peers.

Among the variables that contributed to social-class and professional barriers between the two staff groups was the expected

wariness of lower-class Negroes and Puerto Ricans toward middle-class, particularly white, persons. One homemaker remarked
to the author: "You impress me as some rich girl down here trying to make it with us." When I walked in one Monday morning,
another homemaker announced sarcastically to her colleagues:
"She always looks so rested and we're so worn out." This kind of
suspiciousness exists regardless of the manner in which professionals act toward indigenous staff. In fact, some lower-status
persons have become so accustomed to being treated unfairly
that they find it difficult to deal with different behavior. Like
Herzog, they are unable to handle kind or considerate treatment.

The homemakers' testiness was based not only on past experiences, but on the behavior of some social workers which
reinforced their perceptions of middle-class and professional
persons. This behavior included blatant and subtle manifestations of prejudice by the professional staff as well as characteristics of the professional culture that were misunderstood by the
untrained workers. Professionals are often uncomfortable in a
close working relationship with lower-class staff. The homemakers were very quick to perceive this, and no amount of fair
treatment, respect for their work, and consideration for their
personal and agency problems could erase their resentment of
a half-hearted hello.

Certain characteristics of the professional culture also were
galling to the homemakers. For example, the professional pro-
clivity for labeling social phenomena was misconstrued. The
neighborhood workers felt that the term "lower-income" was
being used not merely in a descriptive but in a pejorative sense.
The author's writing a report about the service was viewed as a
betrayal of confidence and, to some extent, a denigration of those
aspects of their behavior that were described as different from
that of professional workers. They refused to view the report as
an attempt to analyze their service and to extend the professional
dialogue.

We may respond to this type of reaction by trying to interpret
the professional culture to these workers, but we would not wish
to alter the professional traits that call it forth. On the other
hand, some aspects of professional behavior which workers resented should be modified. In addition to the prejudices expressed toward them by professionals, the professional style and
mannerisms were a source of conflict. Social-work training tends

to encourage controlled if not controlling behavior and to discourage what is termed overidentification with clients. Significantly, on her first day, a homemaker did a role-play imitation of a caseworker who had learned her professional lines and recited them without feeling or conviction. What we must recognize is that spontaneous action and unrelenting efforts to find a resource or a way to help are necessary behaviors in poverty programs, if not in all types of social-work programs.

We might have utilized neighborhood staff in such ways as to minimize the expression of status barriers. We have noted that it is not difficult to evoke middle-class compliance from persons in the position of the homemakers; however, if we had not encouraged their candor, feelings of resentment and malaise would simply have remained underground, and we would have lost the opportunity to develop working relationships based on honesty and trust. In this sense, initial expressions of hostility or skepticism rather than feigned amiability are desirable preludes to sound working relationships. If we had not encouraged and rewarded self-assertion among lower-status staff, they would have been less likely to provide models of more aggressive behavior to their clients. In addition, when members of a neighborhood staff are enabled to regard their circumstances as socially rather than personally induced, they are more accepting of themselves and have greater empathy with clients. Finally, if we wish indigenous staff to help us to adopt behavior that is more compatible to the clientele, then we must stimulate them to speak frankly and be willing to respond to what may often be their criticism of our social and professional class.

We might, on the other hand, have encouraged neighborhood workers to respect us or at least defer to us by using them in a clearly subordinate role rather than as workers with their own area of competence. If they are employed as aides, their skill will always be regarded as less than that of a trained worker, and they will depend entirely on the superior judgment and skill of the professional staff. However, if they are led to view themselves as experts in certain areas of service, then they will be more assertive in their relationships with professionals. For example, after we had urged them to describe actual as opposed to theoretical homemaking, they responded to the budgeting suggestions of a professional home economist as "too middle-class" or impractical for persons with low income.

A final source of interstaff conflict, the differences in service roles, would probably exist in the more traditional homemaking services as well as in a visiting homemaker service. Homemakers were continually expressing their disdain for caseworkers who were not able to react to the problems of clients they jointly served with sufficient rapidity and energy. The indigenous workers did not realize that while they had two or three clients with whom they spent several half or full days a week, caseworkers were assigned to many families. The social workers had neither the extent of personal involvement that results from such intensive contact nor the time to be wholly available and responsive in the way that the structure of the homemaking service permitted. Conversely, caseworkers seemed to resent the homemakers' involvement with clients and were upset when other workers, particularly nonprofessionals, knew more about a client than they did. Just as the homemakers failed to understand the implications of the caseworkers' roles, so the caseworkers did not anticipate that a person who spent several days in a client's home would be closer to the family than one with a more restricted role.

Although Mobilization for Youth took important steps toward recognizing the worth and contribution of indigenous staff, it failed to provide career mobility for them, perhaps because it was a demonstration program rather than a permanent institution. It taught the neighborhood staff to regard their role as important and unique, but the indigenous workers still had lower status in the agency than professionals and were not afforded an opportunity for significant advancement. The reward for able performance was an increment, but there was no position of greater responsibility or higher status to which they could be promoted as a result of competence. The California Department of Corrections has probably done more than most agencies to advance nonprofessionals.[13] There, probation officers without high-school diplomas have been enabled, as a result of in-service training and changes in agency structure, to compete for jobs formerly reserved for professionals. However, the probation officers must in effect become professionals in order to be promoted. So long as we are unable to create a system of advance-

[13] J. Douglas Grant, "A Strategy for New Careers Development," in Arthur Pearl and Frank Reissman (eds.), *New Careers for the Poor* (New York: Free Press, 1965), pp. 215-17.

ment within nonprofessional ranks, we shall be encouraging ambivalence, dual striving, and anomie among nonprofessionals. On the one hand, we urge them not to feign middle-class values. On the other hand, they recognize that prestige and social advancement lie along professional routes and imitation of professional and middle-class behavior. Ultimately we probably need to provide them with educational opportunities comparable in principle to those offered to college graduates and professionals in some social agencies. Instead of graduate training, these would include tutoring for high-school equivalency examinations, two-year college programs geared to social welfare, and the like. At the same time, we need to explore ways of providing greater responsibility and rewards within the nonprofessional ranks or of extending the concept of what constitutes a professional welfare service.

Tasks Suited to an Indigenous Homemaking Staff

In our experience with a neighborhood staff, we found that they could perform a number of service tasks well. There are undoubtedly other roles that indigenous staff can perform, such as that of neighborhood organizer in a community-organization program. However, this discussion will be confined to those assignments which we have observed the homemakers doing or which fall into the general area of home management.

Teaching the newcomer, the young housewife, or the inadequate homemaker how to manage her home and exploit community resources was the most significant task done by homemakers. Here they were imparting the methods they themselves had acquired in coping with slum life. Unlike the case aide who is an untrained social worker, they were the experts in this special area of competence. When the homemaker went with the client to the clinic she was not a substitute for the caseworker who can intervene in behalf of the client or influence bureaucratic personnel. Rather, the homemaker showed the client how to use the clinic. It would be a mistake, therefore, to have homemakers do the leg work for caseworkers, for they move quite differently from middle-class staff.

Homemakers did group teaching or community education as well as individual assignments. That is, they offered sessions to groups of clients on such homemaking subjects as budgeting, shopping, cooking with surplus food, and sewing.[14] Again, one should not expect a class similar to that taught by a professional home economist. Instruction will be informal. There will be no basic orientation or scientific approach to cooking or meal planning. Lower-class clients will be more responsive to this type of teaching because they can identify more readily with the leader and because the presentation will not be academic.

Education of professional personnel was another important task of the indigenous staff. For example, homemakers introduced school teachers in the neighborhood to Puerto Rican cuisine by cooking a meal for them and talking to them informally about the various *productos tropicales.* The workers' enthusiasm and pride helped teachers to gain more respect for Puerto Rican culture. Homemakers also explained to professionals how it feels to be a newcomer, to try to talk to a teacher when you do not speak well, to live in public housing, to receive public assistance.

During the session with the psychiatrist, for example, a homemaker offered an interesting interpretation of a client's behavior that would not be likely to occur to someone who had not had experience similar to the client's. A tenant in a public-housing project, the client was described as having few friends. The implication was that she did not form relationships well. The homemaker remarked that public-housing policies sometimes encourage a tenant to report his neighbors' income, employment, or family composition to management, and that it was therefore unwise to be too friendly with anyone in the project. She concluded, "It's a lonely thing to live in a project." It was possible, then, that the client was more circumspect than alienated.

In addition to developing the professional's understanding of the culture of poverty and of various ethnic groups and under-privileged minorities, the indigenous worker can help the professional know how he is perceived and how certain of his methods and techniques are viewed by lower-class clients.

The homemakers easily developed rapport with clients and were good companions. Because so many low-income mothers are isolated from their neighbors, the friendship function is

[14] Within a year's time the only class offered on an ongoing basis was a sewing class. There were a few scattered cooking sessions, too. We had little doubt, however, that classes in other areas of homemaking are feasible and could have been developed had time permitted.

quite useful. However, this help was less artificial when it was either a by-product or a part of a teaching service in which the client and homemaker did certain tasks together. For example, a homemaker had been assigned to a depressed mother of four, chiefly to help her furnish and develop some enthusiasm for her home and for homemaking. We learned that this person stayed indoors all the time and knew no one in the neighborhood. While she and the homemaker were doing the shopping and the sewing assignments, the worker took her to the park and encouraged her to meet some of her neighbors. The goal was for the client to develop some ability to make friends so that she would be less alone when she could no longer rely on the homemaker's companionship. Although a homemaker can relieve some of a client's isolation and offer sound advice about homemaking, it is important to recognize that, unlike a case aide, she is not an assistant caseworker. She can speak with the client as a friend but not as a caseworker.

There is a specific community-organization task which homemakers can perform. If community resources such as a public clinic are underutilized because of poor transportation, then failure to obtain medical service is not simply a matter of self-defeating patterns of behavior. In such a situation, indigenous workers can involve residents in a campaign to procure adequate transportation. Similarly, shopping and budgeting may be difficult because neighborhood stores sell overpriced items (as do many shops in slum areas) or do not stock special products used by members of certain ethnic groups. Homemakers could organize a boycott, complain directly to a merchant, or publicize exploitative practices in the newspapers in order to alter actual conditions which prevent sound home management.[15]

The mother-substitute service performed by our homemakers is not new to social work but can be offered more effectively as a neighborhood program. The proximity of a neighborhood-based service to clients makes it possible to assign workers more

---

[15] Other social problems, notably substandard housing and restrictive policies of the housing authority and department of welfare, bear directly on home management. However, social action required in these areas is too extensive for a homemaking staff to mount without dissipating their function in regard to self-defeating behavior. Such activities are also beyond their range of competence. However, homemaking staff should certainly lend appropriate support to community action to improve these conditions.

rapidly. A smaller neighborhood program is also likely to involve less red tape. Further, the service can be shaped to the particular problems and needs of the neighborhood. Finally, the home-makers are thoroughly familiar with the homemaking resources if they are assigned on a neighborhood, rather than city-wide, basis.

Child care out of the home or a group baby-sitting service is appropriately staffed by neighborhood workers. The home-makers were ill-suited to develop a formal program or to cater to what might be called the nonessential needs of children. They were, however, perfectly able to give adequate physical care while parents did errands or kept appointments. They might also be used to help organize cooperative baby-sitting groups among low-income residents, staffing them initially to encourage par-ticipation and to demonstrate the usefulness of such a facility but eventually turning the task over to participating parents.

Conclusions

An indigenous staff can be an invaluable part of a social agency's efforts to help low-income clients, provided that the agency appreciates and knows how to realize their potentiality. Untrained neighborhood workers are sometimes regarded as poor substitutes for professionals, hired because of a shortage of funds or trained staff. Consequently, the goal of supervision, training, and administration may be to make them as "profes-sional" as possible. The aim is sometimes to teach them without learning from them. (Of course, they must be oriented to agency and social-work goals as well as freed, if possible, of social atti-tudes and actions which are clearly hostile and damaging to clients.) Because we would sometimes prefer to hire profes-sionals if given the choice, we tend to seek out upwardly mobile slum dwellers or middle-class persons who lack social-work edu-cation. We find such persons, who usually serve as case aides, easier to get along with than lower-class persons because they are more likely to share our values. Unfortunately, these middle-class and middle-class-oriented workers also share our difficulties in developing rapport with clients. They have neither the know-how of the lower-class worker nor the skill of the trained worker.

To a certain extent, a lack of respect for the work of lower-class neighborhood staff stems from a clinical approach to the problems of the poor. We have acknowledged that our neighborhood workers were indeed unskilled when it came to psychosocial diagnosis and to psychotherapy. However, if we regard social deprivations as critical barriers for many lower-class clients, then providing them with skills for coping with difficult management problems (as well as expanding social opportunities) is an important goal of social-work practice. In this type of social treatment, indigenous staff can make a substantial contribution. Even where there are severe psychological problems, bread-and-butter difficulties often need to be alleviated before the client can concentrate on intrapsychic problems. In several cases, the homemakers' help with environmental problems was an important prelude to psychological treatment by the casework staff.

A truly professional service is one in which diagnosis is based on social as well as psychological problems. Based on this comprehensive understanding, help is then offered by the staff best qualified to assist the "client-in-situation." In seeking the most suitable staff, it is important to acknowledge the limitations of trained workers, who cannot be expected to know how to manage a low-income household or to cope with slum life. It is, however, possible to find neighborhood workers who have this competence and who can thus make it possible to offer a professional service.

CHAPTER TWELVE

Class Orientation of the Indigenous Staff*

by CHARLES F. GROSSER

In an attempt to bridge the anticipated gap between its professional staff and its lower-class clientele, Mobilization for Youth employed some fifty local residents in such program capacities as community organizer, homemaker, school–parent liaison, and work-crew chief. The perceptions and perceptiveness of this group in regard to the community were measured and compared with those of the professional staff and a sampling of the community residents.[1] One purpose of this study was to discover whether these indigenous workers, chosen in part for their similarity to their lower-class neighbors, did in fact perform the bridge role.

The bridge role, it has been pointed out, is made possible by the fact that the indigenous worker

> . . . is poor, is from the neighborhood, is often a member of a minority group. He is a peer of the client and shares a common background, language, ethnic origin, style and group of interests . . . he "belongs," he is a "significant other," he is "one of us." . . . The style of the non-professional is significantly related to his effectiveness, because it matches the client's.[2]

The indigenous staff group at MFY mirrored the community sample in ethnicity, social class, welfare status, residence, contact with public agencies, and similar demographic measures. In addition, residents were recruited who had successfully mastered the intricacies of urban slum life and who were therefore able

---

* Abstracted from Grosser, "Perceptions of Professionals, Indigenous Workers, and Lower-Class Clients," unpublished doctoral dissertation, Columbia University School of Social Work, 1965.

[1] For a description of this study, see Grosser, "Middle-Class Professionals and Lower-Class Clients," above, pp. 64-71.

[2] R. Reiff and F. Reissman, *The Indigenous Non-Professional* (New York: National Institute of Labor Education, 1964), pp. 8-10.

to live as productively as one can in the backwash of the city. At the time they were hired, these workers were lower class by all the customary indicators (education, occupation, income, and residence). Subsequent to their employment, they fell within the general parameters of the middle-class staff sample, since their positions and salaries with MFY significantly raised their occupational and income levels. For all practical purposes, however, we can continue to consider this group lower class.

As has previously been reported,[3] it was found that the views of the community held by indigenous staff before their employment generally fell between the views of the professional staff and those of the community but more closely approximated the former on almost two-thirds of the items.

Staff respondents were also asked to estimate the perceptions of community residents, and a prediction index was developed based on the accuracy of these estimates. A comparison of the prediction ratings of indigenous and professional staff indicates, as might be anticipated, statistically significant difference: 52 per cent of the indigenous group and only 26 per cent of the professional group scored in the top third.

We have sufficient knowledge about prediction to say that the relatively greater accuracy with which the indigenous group gauged the community's attitudes is related to social class. Our study indicates that lower-class staff predict lower-class residents' views more accurately than do middle-class staff. We may hypothesize that in a middle-class community, middle-class staff would predict more accurately than lower-class staff. To generalize even further, we might expect that staff similarity with the client in ethnicity, class, cultural background, or religion will result in greater perceptual accuracy regarding the client and his community.

Our finding that the nonprofessionals in our sample were significantly more accurate in assessing the community's views than were their professional colleagues suggests, also, that the professional education of the respondents who had received training was not such as to overcome a distorted view of the urban poor. (Since professional and social-class status are inevitably linked, we may assume that such attitudes were brought to, rather than produced by, a professional career.) The implica-

[3] Grosser, *op. cit.*

tion of this finding for professional and in-service training is that the ingredients necessary to correct these inaccurate perceptions must be sought outside our present repertory of knowledge, techniques, and strategy for intervention on behalf of people in need, or that new kinds of staff members—i.e., indigenous persons—must be sought in whom these requisite qualities will be found.

The study did not attempt to document the extent to which groups endemic to deprived urban communities, such as those on public assistance, minority-group members, and new immigrants, are kept from professional services by the lack of understanding implied by the low prediction ratings of professionally trained workers. We can at least hypothesize, however, that the alienation of some slum residents stems in part from the inaccuracy with which service professionals anticipate their attitudes. Similarly, although neither the literature nor the evidence at hand offers conclusive support, we presume that agency service will also be affected adversely by distortion in the staff's view of the community. It is true, of course, that when such realities as size of school classes and number of juvenile delinquents are misperceived by community residents, staff's failure to recognize this distortion may result in more appropriate actions and thus may facilitate service. Where prediction ratings are developed on items which cannot be validated easily or at all (i.e., most people can't be trusted, nothing can be done to cut graft in government, nobody cares about voting), one may very well argue that accuracy in estimating community perceptions is irrelevant to service. There is certainly a danger that acting on irrelevancies either may be overtly dysfunctional to clients or may inadvertently shatter their protective illusions without providing material resources or programs to take their place.

It is our belief that good client-related service is positively correlated with a high degree of accuracy in estimating community perceptions. We cannot, of course, measure this hypothesis in statistical terms, but it is attested by the extraordinary success of a group of professionals who rated very high on the prediction index and who were regarded by local residents in charismatic terms. These professional staff members functioned as if they were locally selected leaders. Their reputations have spread quite beyond the borders of the project. They have been recognized as spokesmen for neighborhood residents, both by the poor themselves and by the community at large. A retest of this group would unquestionably show an over-all increase in prediction scores. We suggest that the acquisition of expertise by this staff group in welfare law and regulations, code-enforcement procedures, and public-housing rules is itself a positive indicator of client-related service.

The data do not enable us to link accuracy in prediction and high performance as rated by agency supervisors within either the indigenous or the professional group. As a group, indigenous staff were found to be higher perceivers and better performers than the professionals, but within this indigenous group 89 per cent of the low and medium perceivers and only 79 per cent of the high perceivers were rated as good or excellent performers. Professional staff showed the opposite tendency: a discernible, although not statistically significant, trend toward a positive correlation between high performance and accurate prediction.

If we assume that our measures are valid, what does a lack of correlation between accurate community prediction and good performance mean? It may indicate that behavior does not necessarily conform to belief or attitude. It may mean that client-related behavior (i.e., the performance of accurate predictors) is not regarded as excellence by professional evaluators.

We do not find the lack of correlation between performance and prediction anomalous. From the fact that professionals who, as a result of factors not related to their professional training, happen to be accurate predictors are rated better performers than professionals whose predictions are less accurate, we might conclude that certain qualities of professionalization help to convert accurate insights into effective actions. Although professional training cannot increase the practitioner's ability to predict, it may contribute to his ability to apply these predictions so as to improve performance.

This contention would lead us to expect a neutral relationship between performance and prediction in untrained persons. Such relationship as we find, however, is negative. It may be that in untrained persons relatively great perceptiveness and ability to predict are inhibiting factors which affect performance adversely. Sensitivity to one's surroundings plays a considerable role in the system of defenses by which individuals achieve and maintain social and personal equilibrium. It is possible to conclude that heightened acuity regarding the community, coupled with the dual status of being both indigenous and an agency staff member, produces a set of circumstances which decreases performance effectiveness.

Further, since local residents frequently hold inaccurate views of their environment, staff with low prediction ratings may actually be accurate objective perceivers of the community. Conversely, high prediction scores might accompany inaccurate objective views of the community and thus be positively correlated with poor performance.

Professional attributes related to objectivity probably contribute heavily to the ability to produce good performance from accurate appraisal of community, for one can readily see the pitfall of over-identification coupled with high accuracy. The learned objectivity of the professional plus the heightened perceptivity of the indigenous worker would appear to be the ideal combination of qualities for producing excellent performance.

It has also been found that the participation of indigenous people heightens the awareness of the staff as a whole to the problems of the local community. It thus contributes to the social climate of the agency, resulting in organizational decision-making which more accurately reflects low-income needs and interests. A simple and obvious example of this is Mobilization's production of materials in Spanish as well as English and its inclusion of Spanish-speaking persons in all programs. Although this decision is unrelated to the performance of indigenous staff, one would strongly postulate its relevance to professional-staff performance.

The attempt to improve service by recruiting and hiring local nonprofessionals to undertake program assignments has not been limited to social-work practice; it has also been undertaken or proposed in such diverse settings as education, medicine, mental health, and recreation.[4] Most of these innovations are still to be evaluated. The present study offers some empirical data in general support of the intuitive–deductive processes from which these new helping roles have been developed. It also poses certain questions relative to the employment of indigenous workers. The findings of the study suggest that persons indigenous to a given community may have the most accurate perceptions of

[4] Reiff and Reissman, op. cit., pp. 44-48.

that community but do not necessarily demonstrate high performance as a result; they may, in fact, perform less well than others with poorer perception. If the quality we seek in the indigenous worker is the ability to predict the views of lower-class persons, we must investigate means of capitalizing on this quality so that it will significantly affect performance, as it does not do now. If it is accurate perception that we seek, we ought to bear in mind that the findings of this study are relative; indigenous staff are better perceivers than their professional counterparts, but they are themselves quite inaccurate in judging community attitudes. They err in the same ways as professional staff, but to a lesser degree.[5] How do we maximize accuracy? In which particular indigenous persons will we find it to be most pronounced?

It has often been suggested, as we pointed out earlier, that what we seek in the local resident worker is a bridge between the lower-class client and the middle-class professional. Some of the findings of this study are particularly relevant to this goal. We have found, as we might expect, that the attitudes of indigenous staff themselves were closer to the community's attitudes than the professionals' were on 77 per cent of the survey items. However, on 63 per cent of the items, the indigenous staff's responses were closer to the professional group's than to the community's. In other words, although the indigenous group falls between the professionals and the community on 77 per cent of the items, their position is not closer to that of the lower-class respondents with whom they share class, ethnic, cultural, and residential ties; nor is it midway between the position of these respondents and that of the middle-class professionals. It is, instead, closer to the position of the professional staff almost two thirds of the time. This suggests that the beliefs of the indigenous group are more like those of professionals than like those of locals. Since certain of the items used in our question-

---

[5] Using as a standard the community's responses to the 40 questions in the survey instrument, 62 per cent of the professionals' responses and 42 per cent of the indigenous workers' answers were "incorrect." Even on responses that were "correct," indigenous staff tended to diverge from the community in degree of response, but less so than the professionals. For example, 73 per cent of the community indicated disagreement with the statement that Protestants have a better chance to rise in the world. This response was ascribed to residents by 62 per cent of the indigenous respondents and 48 per cent of the professionals.

naire had proved on national polls to be sensitive indicators of class-linked attitudes,[6] we may conclude that our indigenous group was responding in a way characteristic of the middle class in general rather than specifically like our professional sample.

Essentially, these findings present the apparent anomaly of indigenous staff responding more like middle-class staff than like lower-class clients. One might conclude from this response that, despite its efforts to the contrary, MFY did not recruit "truly" endemic folk. By objective criteria such as income, residence, education, and ethnicity, the indigenous group was lower-class, but the responses noted suggest that by such subjective criteria as style, attitude, and aspirations, they had strong middle-class tendencies. A significant problem for further research is whether the outgroup attitudes of indigenous workers are induced as part of the socialization process accompanying the new job role. We suspect that recruitment, socialization, and indoctrination strengthen the tendency toward middle-class values in indigenous staff. Newly acquired staff are apt to be assigned to conventional organizational roles and inducted through training programs which are likely to induce emulation and conformity to the host disciplines. Our data, of course, were gathered shortly after personnel arrived on the job and can be interpreted only as reflecting on the way in which indigenous staff were recruited from the Lower East Side community.

Reference-group literature strongly suggests that persons who are upwardly mobile tend to overidentify with new acculturation patterns as they vigorously reject the old. Merton points out that while anticipatory socialization is functional in aiding persons to rise to the group they aspire to, it is dysfunctional to the solidarity of the group being abandoned. To the degree that a person identifies with another group, he alienates himself from his own. This is recognized in the "value-laden connotations of those terms (renegade, traitor, deserter) used to describe identification with groups other than one's own."[7] Our findings at least

[6] H. H. Hyman, "The Value Systems of Different Classes: A Social-Psychological Contribution to the Analysis of Stratification," in R. Bendix and S. M. Lipset (eds.), *Class Status and Power* (Glencoe, Ill.: Free Press, 1963), p. 434.

[7] R. K. Merton, *Social Theory and Social Structure* (Glencoe, Ill.: Free Press, 1957), p. 269. See also pp. 262-71.

suggest the possibility that a major function of indigenous-staff status is the facilitation of the worker's adjustment to a new reference group and his consequent alienation from the very group to which a bridge was being sought.

Referring to the effects of insecurity and acculturation on discriminatory tendencies, social status, and family relationships, Blau states,

> . . . the upwardly mobile differ widely in these respects from members of their class of origin and seem to overconform with the practices prevalent among their new social class.[8]

Having eschewed the style of the lower class, upwardly mobile persons embrace the style of the middle class. Over a period of time, for example, Mobilization's indigenous homemakers developed an aversion to their titular designation, requesting that they be referred to as "case aides," showed increasing resistance to such responsibilities as baby sitting to free mothers to meet other obligations, began to refuse to go into certain "terrible" buildings in the neighborhood, and requested such symbols of professional status as office space, desks, and individual supervisory conferences. Our indigenous group is probably high in community perception because of its familiarity with, proximity to, and participation in lower-class community life. However, their outgroup orientation affects their attitudes and their own perceptions in a way that skews them toward the middle class.

The lack of correlation between performance and perception suggested by our data can also be understood as an indication that the indigenous high performer aspires toward and emulates the middle class. We would postulate, then, that these middle-class values act as intervening variables, producing the performance results we have found.

This line of inquiry is of great significance to the professions, particularly now that many thousands of subprofessional employment opportunities are being proposed as part of the effort to defeat poverty. Our limited experience indicates a tendency to use these new strategies merely to create an illusion of service

[8] P. M. Blau, "Social Mobility and Interpersonal Relations," in H. D. Stein and R. A. Cloward (eds.), *Social Perspectives on Behavior* (Glencoe, Ill.: Free Press, 1958), p. 473.

while the needs of the vast majority of the poor continue to remain unmet. Further study is needed to ascertain how indigenous persons can successfully fulfill the functions being sought for them, and how to avoid the pitfall of simply providing channels for upwardly mobile lower-class persons so as to help fill existing professional and institutional needs. Although there is function and purpose in solving operational problems, one would hope that the professions would utilize the resource and promise of indigenous staff toward the much grander purpose of significant engagement in the social issues of the day.

CHAPTER THIRTEEN

The "Helper" Therapy Principle*

by FRANK REISSMAN

An age-old therapeutic approach is the use of people with a problem to help other people who have the same problem in more severe form (e.g., Alcoholics Anonymous). But in the current use of this approach, it may be that emphasis is being placed on the wrong person. Although attention is generally centered on the individual receiving help, it is frequently the person who is providing the assistance who improves.

It may not always be certain that people receiving help are being benefited, but it seems likely that the people giving help usually profit from their role. This appears to be the case in a wide variety of self-help "therapies," including Synanon (for drug addicts), Recovery Incorporated (for psychologically disturbed people), and Alcoholics Anonymous. Mowrer notes that there are more than 265 groups of this kind.[1] The official publication of the American Conference of Therapeutic Self-Help Clubs, entitled *Action*, describes some of the functions of these groups.

Although there is still a need for firm research evidence, various reports on these programs (many of them admittedly impressionistic) point to improvement in the givers of help rather than in the recipients. There are, however, numerous contaminating factors that may be contributing to their success, such as the leadership of the therapist, the selection of subjects, and the novelty of the program.

Although much of the evidence for the helper principle is observational and uncontrolled, there is one experimental investigation that provides at least indirect verification. In a study by

* Adapted from *Social Work*, Vol. 10, No. 2, April 1965. Reproduced by permission of the National Association of Social Workers.

[1] O. Hobart Mowrer, *The New Group Therapy* (Princeton, N.J.: Van Nostrand, 1964), p. iv.

King and Janis in which role-playing was used, it was found that subjects who were asked to improvise a speech supporting a given point of view tended to change their opinions in the direction of this view more than subjects who merely read a prepared speech for an equivalent amount of time.[2] They describe this effect as "self-persuasion through persuading others."

Volkman and Cressey identify helper therapy as one of five social–psychological principles for the rehabilitation of criminals:

> The most effective mechanism for exerting group pressure on members will be found in groups so organized that criminals are induced to join with noncriminals for the purpose of changing other criminals. A group in which criminal "A" joins with some noncriminals to change criminal "B" is probably most effective in changing criminal "A," not "B." . . .[3]

Perhaps, then, social work's strategy ought to be to devise ways of creating more helpers or, to be more exact, to find ways of transforming recipients of help into dispensers of help, thus reversing their roles, and to structure the situation so that recipients of help will be placed in roles requiring them to give assistance.

In most of the programs mentioned thus far the helpers and the helped have had essentially the same problem or symptom. The approach is carried one step further in Recovery Incorporated, in which emotionally disturbed people help each other even though their symptoms may differ.

A somewhat more indirect application of the principle is found in the sociotherapeutic approach reported by Wittenberg some years ago.[4] Wittenberg found that participation in a neighborhood block committee formed to help other people in the neighborhood led to marked personality development and growth in a woman who had had considerable personality difficulty.

[2] B. T. King and I. L. Janis, "Comparison of the Effectiveness of Improvised Versus Non-Improvised Role Playing in Producing Opinion Changes," *Human Relations*, I (1956), pp. 177-86.

[3] Rita Volkman and Donald R. Cressey, "Differential Association and the Rehabilitation of Drug Addicts," *American Journal of Sociology*, LXIX, 2 (Feb. 1963), p. 139.

[4] Rudolph M. Wittenberg, "Personality Adjustment Through Social Action," *American Journal of Orthopsychiatry*, XVIII, 2 (March 1958), pp. 207-21.

The Work of Nonprofessionals

Another variant of this principle is found in the work of indigenous nonprofessionals employed by social-service agencies as homemakers, community organizers, youth workers, recreation aides, and the like. Some of these people have had serious problems in the recent past. Some are former delinquents. It has been observed, however, that in the course of their work their own problems diminished greatly.[5] One of the important premises of the HARYOU program is that "indigenous personnel will solve their own problems while attempting to help others."[6]

The helper-therapy principle has at least two important implications for the employment of the nonprofessional of lower socioeconomic background: (1) Since many of the nonprofessionals to be recruited are former delinquents, addicts, AFDC mothers, and the like, it seems quite likely that placing them in a helping role can be rehabilitative for them. (2) As the nonprofessionals benefit from their new helping roles, they may actually become more effective workers and may therefore provide more help to others at a new level. Thus, a positive upward spiral may result. The helping role may be highly beneficial to the helper, who in turn becomes more efficient and better motivated and reaches a new stage in helping skill.

Therapy for the Poor

The helper principle probably has universal therapeutic application, but it may be especially useful in low-income treatment projects, for these two reasons:

1. It may circumvent the special interclass role-distance difficulties that arise from the fact that the middle-class-oriented therapy (and therapist) is often at odds with the low-income client's expectations and style. The alienation that many low-income clients feel in regard to professional treatment agents and the concomitant rapport difficulties may be greatly

[5] See Gertrude Goldberg, "The Use of Untrained Neighborhood Workers in a Homemaker Program," an unpublished report of Mobilization for Youth, 1963; and "Nonprofessional Helpers," above, pp. 175-207.

[6] *Youth in the Ghetto* (New York: Harlem Youth Opportunities Unlimited, 1964), p. 609.

reduced by utilizing the low-income person himself as the helper-therapist.

For the same reason, much wider employment of neighborhood-based nonprofessionals in hospitals and social agencies as aides or social-service technicians is recommended. Like the helper-therapist, such workers are likely to have considerably less role distance from the low-income client than does the professional.

2. The helper principle may be especially attuned to the cooperative trends in lower socioeconomic groups and cultures. In this sense it may be beneficial to both the helper (the model) and the helped.

Students as Helpers

In Flint, Michigan, a group of fourth-grade pupils with reading problems was assigned to the tutelage of sixth-grade pupils who were also experiencing reading difficulties. It is interesting to note that while the fourth-graders made significant progress, the sixth-graders also learned from the experience.[7] Mobilization for Youth has used homework helpers with a fair amount of success, in that the recipients of the help showed some measurable academic improvement.[8] Even more significant changes took place in the high-school youngsters who were used as tutors. Not only did their school performance improve but, as a result of their new role, many of these youngsters began to perceive the possibility of embarking on a teaching career.

Schneider reports on a small study in which youngsters with varying levels of reading ability were asked to read an "easy" book as practice for reading to younger children. She observes:

> For the child who could read well, this was a good experience. For the child who could not read well it was an even better experience. He was reading material on a level within his competence and he could read it with pleasure. Ordinary books on his level of interest were too difficult for him to read easily and so

[7] Frank B. W. Hawkinshire, "Training Needs for Offenders Working in Community Treatment Programs," *Experiment in Culture Expansion* (Sacramento, Calif.: State of California Department of Corrections, 1963), pp. 27-36.

[8] "Progress Report" (New York: Mobilization for Youth, July 1964).

he did not read books for pleasure. Reading for him was hard, hard work; often it left him feeling stupid and helpless. This time it was different . . . he would be a giver; he would share his gift with little children just as a parent or teacher does.[9]

In a sense these children were role-playing the helper role in this experience, reading aloud to adults in anticipation of later reading to small children.

The classroom situation illustrates an interesting offshoot of the helper principle. When children are removed from a class in which they are below average and placed in a new group in which they are in the upper half of the class, some of them manifest many new qualities and are in turn responded to more positively by the teacher. This can occur regardless of whether or not they play a helper role. But some of the same underlying mechanisms are operative as in the direct helper situations: the pupil in the new group is responded to more, he stands out more, more is expected of him, and generally he responds in turn and demands more of himself. Even though he may not be in the helper role as such, similar forces are at work in both cases, stimulating more active responses. (Unfortunately, this principle may be counteracted if the teacher treats the entire class as a "lower" or poorer group and this image is absorbed in an undifferentiated manner by all the members.)

A related issue worthy of mention is that in the new situations in the schools, where (it is hoped) integration will be taking place, youngsters coming from segregated backgrounds will need help in order to catch up in terms of reading skills and the like. It is generally argued that the white middle-class children who do not need this extra assistance will suffer. Their parents want these youngsters to be in a class with advanced pupils and not to be "held back" by youngsters who are behind.

However, in terms of the helper principle, it may very well be that the more advanced youngsters can benefit in new ways from playing a teaching role. Not all fast, bright youngsters like to be in a class with similar children. We have been led to believe that if a child is fast and bright he will want to be with others who are fast and bright, and this will act as a stimulus to his growth.

[9] Gussie Albert Schneider, "Reading of the Children, By the Children, For the Children," unpublished manuscript, 1964. (Mimeo.)

It does for some people, but for others it most certainly does not. Some people do better in a group in which there is a great range of ability, in which they can stand out more, and, finally—and this is the point of the helper principle—in situations in which they can help others. It may be that some children develop intellectually, not by being challenged by someone ahead of them, but by helping somebody behind them, by being put into the tutor-helper role.

As any teacher can report, there is nothing like learning through teaching. When one must explain something to someone else one's attention is focused more sharply. This premise seems to have tremendous potentiality that social workers have failed to exploit.

Leadership Development

Carried one step further, the helper principle allows for the development of leadership in community organizations and the like. In tenant groups, for example, it has been found that an individual might be relatively inactive at meetings in his own building and yet display quite different characteristics when helping to organize another building. In the new situation, in which he is forced to play the helper role, leadership begins to emerge. The character of the new group, in which the individual is in a more advanced position vis-à-vis the remainder of the group, contributes toward the emergence of new leadership behavior. This is simply another way of saying that leadership develops through the act of leading. The art of leadership training may lie in providing just the right roles to stimulate the emergence of more and more leadership.

While some individuals fall more naturally into the helper or leader role (in certain groups), this role can be distributed more widely by careful planning with regard to the sociometry and composition of the group. When the group is fluid, the introduction of new members often encourages older members who were formerly in the follower role to assume a more active helping role.

Following the lead of King and Janis, role-playing can be utilized by having a person who formerly was the recipient of help in the group now play a helper role, thus aiding him to persuade himself through persuading others. Many similar group-dynamics approaches can be used in order to fully exploit the potentialities of the helper principle. Seating arrangements can be altered, individuals can be placed in key positions—for example, chairing small committees—and temporary classroom groupings can be formed in which pupils who were previously submerged by more advanced classmates are now allowed to become helpers or models for less advanced youngsters. The idea behind this is to restructure the groups so that different members play the helper role at different times.

Helper-Therapy Mechanisms

It may be of value to speculate briefly regarding the various possible mechanisms whereby the helper benefits from his helping role.

Brager comments on the improved self-image that may result from helping someone in need.[10] As we have noted, King and Janis suggest that one becomes committed to a position through advocating it. Pearl finds that many helpers (such as the homework helpers) are "given a stake or concern in a system," and this contributes to their becoming committed to the task in a way that brings about especially meaningful development of their own abilities."[11]

There are undoubtedly many other mechanisms that will be clarified by further research. Probably also the mechanisms vary depending on the setting and task of the helper. Thus helpers functioning in a therapeutic context, whether as professional therapeutic agents or as nonprofessional "peer therapists," may benefit from the importance and status associated with this role. They also receive support from the implicit thesis "I must be well if I help others." People who themselves have problems (e.g., alcoholics, drug addicts, unwed mothers) should derive benefit from this formulation. Moreover, their new helper roles as such may function as a major (distracting) source of involvement, thus diverting them from their problem and general self-concern. There is no question also that individual differences are important: some people derive much greater satisfaction than

[10] George Brager, "The Low-Income Nonprofessional," above. pp. 163-74.
[11] Arthur Pearl, "Youth in Lower Class Settings," paper presented at the fifth Symposium on Social Pathology, Norman, Okla., 1964, p. 6.

others from "giving," "helping," "leading," "controlling," "persuading," and "mothering."

Helpers operating in a teaching context, again both as professionals and nonprofessionals, may profit from the cognitive mechanisms associated with learning through teaching. They need to learn the material better in order to teach it. More generalized academic sets may emerge from the teacher role. Finally, the status and prestige attached to the teacher role may bring unforeseen benefits to them.

The helper in the leader role may benefit from some of the same factors related to the teacher and therapist roles as well as from "self-persuasion through persuading others" and the "stake in the system" mechanism. In essence, then, it would seem that the gains are related to the actual demands of the specific helper role (whether it is teacher, leader, or therapist), plus the new feelings associated with the meaning and prestige of the role and the way the helper is treated because of the new role.

Cautions and Conditions

In a sense, the helper principle seems to run counter to the widely accepted psychological dictum that warns against therapist projection. The well-known danger, called to our attention by all of psychoanalytic theory and practice, indicates that a therapist with a specific problem may, unless he understands and has control of it, project it onto the person he is treating, who actually does not suffer from the same malady. When rehabilitated nonprofessional workers are hired to work with people who either have no specific problem or do not have the problems of the helper, the possibility of projection as well as of psychological contagion has to be considered.

Two controlling devices are suggested to guard against the potential risk: (1) the helper should not be involved in any intensive treatment function unless he has considerable awareness of his problem and the projection issue, and (2) professional supervision is absolutely necessary. Perhaps one of the difficulties of the amateur therapeutic self-help programs is the antiprofessionalism that frequently characterizes them.

There is another potential danger residing in the helper-therapy principle, especially if it is to be applied on a large scale. Much of the intrinsic value of the technique may depend on its operating in a relatively subconscious fashion. Once people know that they are being placed in certain helping roles in order to be helped themselves, some of the power of the principle deriving from feelings of self-importance and the like may be reduced. That this is not entirely true is evident from role-playing situations in which the subjects know the object of the game but still are affected. Nevertheless, the question of large-scale manipulation of the principle, with the increased likelihood of mechanical and arbitrary application, does hold some danger that only careful observation and research can accurately evaluate.

Implications

The helper principle may have wide application in hospital groups (both in- and outpatient), prisons, correctional institutions, and the like. Scheidlinger suggests that the principle may have powerful implications for social work's understanding of the therapeutic process in all group therapy. Not only are individual group members aided through helping other members in the group, but the group as a whole may be greatly strengthened in manifold ways as it continually offers assistance to individual group members.[12]

Levine suggests that in a variety of types of habit change, such as efforts to curtail cigarette smoking, the helper principle may have considerable validity. Smokers who are cast in the role of persuading other smokers to stop smoking have themselves been found to benefit from their commitment to the new antismoking prescription.[13]

The helper principle does not imply that only the helper profits or even that he benefits more than the person receiving help. In the Flint, Michigan, study, for example, the fourth-graders receiving tutoring benefited at least as much as the sixth-grade givers of help.[14] The helper principle only calls attention to the aid the helper receives from being in the helper role.

[12] Conversation with Saul Scheidlinger, Community Service Society, New York, N. Y., January 18, 1964.
[13] Conversation with Sol Levine, Harvard University School of Public Health, Cambridge, Mass., January 12, 1964.
[14] Hawkinshire, *op. cit.*

The helper principle has been utilized with varying degrees of awareness in many group situations. What we are calling for is more explicit use of this principle in an organized manner. Conscious planning directed toward the structuring of groups for the widest possible distribution of the helper role may be a decisive therapeutic intervention, a significant leadership-training principle, and an important teaching device. It is often said that one of the best ways to learn is to teach. Perhaps also psychiatrists, social workers, and others in the helping professions are helping themselves more than is generally recognized.

Part Five

NEW ROLES FOR THE SOCIAL WORKER

Selecting Methods and Points of Intervention in Dealing with Social Problems: The House on Sixth Street*

by Francis P. Purcell and Harry Specht

The extent to which social work as a profession can affect the course of social problems[1] has not received the full consideration it deserves. For some time the social-work profession has taken account of social problems only as they have become manifest in behavioral pathology. Yet it is becoming increasingly apparent that, even allowing for this limitation, it is often necessary for the same agency or worker to intervene by various methods at various points.

In this article the case history of a tenement house in New York City, taken from the files of Mobilization for Youth,[2] is used to illustrate some of the factors that we believe must be considered in selecting methods and points of intervention in a social problem. Like all first attempts, the approach described

* Reproduced from *Social Work*, October 1965, with permission of the National Association of Social Workers.

[1] Many social-work practitioners use the term "social problem" as synonymous with "environmental problem." The sense in which it is used here corresponds to the definition developed by the social sciences. That is, a social problem is a disturbance, deviation, or breakdown in social behavior which (1) involves a considerable number of people and (2) is of serious concern to many in the society. It is social in origin and social in effect, and it is a social responsibility. It represents a discrepancy between social standards and social reality. Additionally, such socially perceived variations must be viewed as corrigible. See Robert K. Merton and Robert A. Nisbet (eds.), *Contemporary Social Problems* (New York: Harcourt, Brace and World, 1961), pp. 6, 701.

[2] All case material used in this article is based on recordings and notes prepared by Ezra Birnbaum of MFY. We are indebted to Mr. Birnbaum for the care and thoroughness with which he conducted his work. We are also indebted to Dr. Frances Piven and Valerie Jorrin of MFY, and to Michael Coffey of the Citizens Housing and Planning Council, for their helpful comments and suggestions.

here can be found wanting in conceptual clarity and systematization. Yet the vital quality of the effort, and its implication for
social-work education and practice, seem clear.

The Problem

"The House on Sixth Street" became a case when "Mrs. Smith"
came to a MFY Neighborhood Service Center to complain that
there had been no gas, electricity, heat, or hot water in her
apartment house for over four weeks. She asked if the agency
could help her. Mrs. Smith was 23 years old, Negro, and the
mother of four children. Three of her four children had been
born out of wedlock, and at the time she was unmarried and
receiving assistance from public welfare. Mrs. Smith came to the
Center in desperation because without utilities she was unable
to run her household. Her financial resources were exhausted,
but not her courage. The Neighborhood Service Center worker
decided that in this case it appeared to be the building—all the
tenants, the landlord, and the circumstances affecting their relationships—that was of central concern.

A professional social worker then visited the Sixth Street
building with Mrs. Smith and a nonprofessional member of the
community-organization staff. Because some of the tenants were
Puerto Rican, a Spanish-speaking community worker, himself a
resident of the area, was chosen. His easy manner and knowledge of the neighborhood enabled him and the social worker to
become involved quickly with all the tenants.

Their first visits confirmed Mrs. Smith's charge that the entire house had been without utilities for over four weeks. Several
months earlier, the City Rent and Rehabilitation Administration
had reduced the rent for the 28 apartments in the building to
one dollar a month each because the landlord was not providing
services, but this agency was slow in taking further action. Elev-
en families were still living in the building. The landlord was
several thousand dollars in arrears to the Consolidated Edison
Company, which had consequently removed the meters from the
house. Because most of the tenants were welfare clients, the department of welfare had "reimbursed" the landlord directly for
most of the unpaid electric bill and refused to pay more money
to the electric company. Without services in the building, food

had spoiled, and the department of welfare was slow in meeting the emergency needs of tenants. Most of the 48 children in the building had not been to school for a month because they had colds or lacked proper clothing.

The mothers were terribly tired and demoralized. Dirt and disorganization were increasing daily. The tenants were afraid to go to sleep at night because the building was infested with rats. There was danger of fire from the candles tenants were using. The 17 abandoned apartments were being used by homeless men and drug addicts. Petty thievery is common in such situations, but the mothers did not dare to seek protection from the police for fear that they would chase away all men who were not part of the families in the building, including the men living with some of the unmarried mothers. (One of the few means of protection from physical dangers available to such a woman is to have a male live with her. However, mothers on public assistance are threatened with loss of income if they are not legally married.) The anxiety created by these living conditions was intense and disabling.

The workers noted that the mothers were not only anxious but fighting mad—not only seeking some immediate relief to their physical dangers and discomforts but eager to express their fury toward the landlord and toward the public agencies, which they felt had let them down.

The circumstances we have described are by no means uncommon, at least not in New York City. Twenty per cent of all housing in the city is still unfit, in spite of all the public and private residential building that has been done since World War II. At least 277,500 dwellings in New York City need major repairs if they are to become safe and adequate shelters. In terms of human misery this means that approximately 500,000 people in New York City live in below-standard dwelling units, and as many as 825,000 people live in buildings which are considered unsafe.[3] In 1962 the New York City Bureau of Sanitary Inspections reported that 530 children were bitten by rats in their homes and that 198 children were poisoned (nine of them fatally) by nibbling at peeling, exposed lead paint, even though

[3] U. S. Census 1960, as reported in *Facts About Low-Income Housing* (New York: Emergency Committee for More Low-Income Housing, 1963).

the use of lead paint has been illegal in the city for over ten years. Given the difficulties involved in lodging formal complaints with city agencies, it is safe to assume that unreported rat bites and poisonings far exceed these figures.

The effects of such actual hardships on the well-being of children are obviously of great humanitarian significance. Of even greater significance is the sense of powerlessness which is generated when families go into these struggles barehanded. It is this sense of powerlessness in the face of adversity that induces pathological anxiety, intergenerational alienation, and social retreatism. Actual physical impoverishment alone is not nearly so debilitating as poverty attended by a sense of powerlessness which becomes generalized and internalized. It is this sense of powerlessness that causes the poor to regard much social learning as irrelevant, since they do not believe that it can effect environmental change.[4]

Selecting Methods of Intervention

Selecting a point of intervention in dealing with this problem would have been simpler if the target of change were Mrs. Smith alone, or Mrs. Smith and her co-tenants, the clients in whose behalf intervention was planned. However, Mrs. Smith and the other tenants had a multitude of problems emanating from many sources, any of which would warrant attention of a social agency. The circumstantial fact that a prospective client walks into a setting which offers services to individuals and families should not be a major determinant of the method of intervention. Identification of the client merely helps the agency to define goals; other variables are involved in the selection of methods. As Burns and Glasser have suggested:

... it may be helpful to consider the primary target of change as distinct from the persons who may be the primary clients. . . . The primary target of change then becomes the human or physical environment toward which professional efforts via direct intervention are aimed in order to facilitate change.[5]

[4] F. P. Purcell, *The Brief Contact* (New York: Mobilization for Youth, 1963).

[5] Mary E. Burns and Paul H. Glasser, "Similarities and Differences in Casework and Group Work Practice," *Social Service Review*, 4 (Dec. 1963), p. 423.

The three major factors that determined the manner by which MFY attempted to combat the social problem presented by Mrs. Smith were as follows:

1. Knowledge of the various social systems within which the social problem was located (i.e., social-systems assessment);
2. Knowledge of the various methods (including non-social work methods) appropriate for intervention in these different social systems; and
3. The resources available to the agency.[6]

The difficulties of the families in the building were intricately related to other elements of the social system within which the housing problem was located. For example, seven different public agencies were involved in the questions of the maintenance of building services, and another group of agencies was involved in the questions which arose later regarding the relocation of the tenants. There is no centralized agency in New York City which handles housing problems, and tenants have little hope of getting help on their own initiative. In order to redress a grievance relating to the water supply (which was only one of the many problem areas in this building), one must know precisely which problems belong in which city departments:

No water	Health Dept.
Not enough water	Dept. of Water Supply
No hot water	Buildings Dept.
Water leaks	Buildings Dept.
Large water leaks	Dept. of Water Supply
Water overflowing from apartment above	Police Dept.
Water sewerage in the cellar	Sanitation Dept.

And this is only a partial listing.

As if the task of determining which agencies are responsible for code enforcement in various areas were not difficult enough, one must also know that the benefits and services available for tenants and for the community vary depending on the course of action chosen. For example, if the building were taken over by

[6] Harry Specht and Frank Riessman, *Some Notes on a Model for an Integrated Social Work Approach to Social Problems* (New York: Mobilization for Youth, June 1963).

the Rent and Rehabilitation Administration under the receiver-ship law, it would be several weeks before services would be re-established, and the tenants would have to remain in the building during its rehabilitation. There are, however, some compensations: tenants in this case would not have to leave the neighborhood, and their youngsters would not have to change schools. If, on the other hand, the house were condemned by the Buildings Department, the tenants would have to move, but they would be moved quickly and would receive top relocation priorities and maximum relocation benefits. But once the tenants had been relocated, at city expense, chances are that the land-lord would sell the building, which would then be renovated for middle-income housing. In the Sixth Street house, we suspected that forcing his tenants to move had been the landlord's motive to begin with. If the building were condemned and renovated, 28 low-income housing units would be lost to the neighborhood.

Scores of tenements in the neighborhood of the Sixth Street house were experiencing similar problems because the area is one in which new middle-income housing is being built. Some landlords withhold basic services or use other harassing tactics to force tenants to leave so that they can renovate their build-ings for middle-income tenants. Others allow their buildings to deteriorate in the expectation that urban-renewal agencies will soon be purchasing them.

Even if we were to limit our analysis to the social systems which are related to one tenement, the Sixth Street house, the problem is obviously enormous. Although the tenants were the clients in this case, Mrs. Smith, the tenant group, and other com-munity groups were all served at one point or another. It is even conceivable that the landlord might have been selected as the most appropriate recipient of service. Rehabilitation of slum tenements is in many cases at present a near-impossible task. Some landlords do regard such property purely as an investment and quite ruthlessly attempt to squeeze out the maximum profit. But under present conditions it would be financially impossible for many landlords to correct all the violations in their buildings even if they wanted to. If the social worker chose to intervene at this level of the problem, he might apply to the Municipal Loan Fund, make arrangements with unions for the use of non-union labor in limited rehabilitation projects, or provide expert consultants on reconstruction. These tasks are part of a non-social-work method, akin to that used by city planners. Even if the problems of landlords were not selected as a major point of intervention, they would have to be considered at some time since they are an integral part of the social system within which this problem exists.

We are not concerned here with the correctness of our definition of the interacting social systems in this case or with that of the social worker's choice of methods and points of intervention. What we wish to emphasize is what this case so clearly demonstrates: that although the needs of the client system enable the agency to define its goals, the points and methods of intervention cannot be selected properly without an awareness of, and substantial knowledge about, the social systems within which the problem is rooted.

Dealing with the Problem

Work with the problems of the tenants in the building on Sixth Street involved many staff members. Since it is not possible to describe the entire process here, only some of the salient features will be presented.

The social worker remained with the building throughout a four-month period. In order to deal effectively with the problem, he had to make use of all the social-work methods, as well as the special talents of a community worker, a lawyer, a city planner, and various civil-rights organizations. The social worker and the community worker functioned as generalists with both individuals and families, calling upon caseworkers as needed for specialized services or at particularly trying times, such as during the first week and when the families were relocated. Because of the division of labor in the agency, much of the social work with individuals was done with the help of a caseworker. The group work, administration, and community organization were handled by the social worker, who had been trained in community organization. However, in many instances he dealt with the mothers as individuals, as they encountered one stressful situation after another. Agency caseworkers also were used to provide immediate and concrete assistance to individual families, such as small financial grants, medical care, homemaking services, baby-sitting services, and transportation, and thereby to relieve the intensity of the pressures on these families. The caseworkers were especially helpful in following through on some of the very knotty and highly technical problems connected with the public agencies.

With a caseworker and a lawyer experienced in handling tenement cases, the social worker began to help the families organize their demands for the needed service and utilities to which they were legally entitled but which the public agencies had consistently failed to provide.

The ability of the mothers to take concerted group action was evident from the very beginning, and Mrs. Smith proved to be a natural and very competent leader. With support, encouragement, and assistance from the staff, the mothers became quite articulate and effective in their negotiations with the various agencies involved. The interest and concern of the agencies increased remarkably when the mothers began visiting the agencies, making frequent telephone calls, and sending letters and telegrams to agencies and politicians demanding action.

With the lawyer and a city planner (an agency consultant called in by the worker), the mothers and staff members explored various possible solutions to the housing problem. For example, the Department of Welfare had offered to move the families to shelters or hotels. Neither alternative was acceptable to the mothers. They refused shelters because they would not consider splitting up their families, and they refused the hotels because they had discovered from previous experience that many of the hotels selected were flophouses or brothels.

The following excerpt is taken from the social worker's record during the first week:

Met with the remaining tenants, several Negro men from the block, and [the city planner]. . . . Three of the mothers said that they would sooner sleep out on the street than go to the Welfare shelter. If nothing else, they felt that this would be a way of protesting their plight. . . . One of the mothers said that they couldn't very well do this with most of the children having colds. Mrs. Brown thought that they might do better to ask Reverend Jones if they could move into the cellar of his church temporarily. . . . The other mothers got quite excited about this idea because they thought that the church basement would make excellent living quarters.

After a long discussion about whether the mothers would benefit from embarrassing the public agencies by dramatically exposing their inadequacies, the mothers decided to move into the nearby church and instructed the worker to attempt to have the Sixth Street building condemned. At another meeting, attended by tenants from neighboring buildings and representatives of other local groups, it was concluded that what had happened to the Sixth Street building was a result of discrimination against the tenants as Puerto Ricans and Negroes. The group, which was now becoming an organization, sent the following telegram to city, state, and federal officials:

> We are voters and Puerto Rican and Negro mothers asking for equal rights, for decent housing and enough room. Building has broken windows, no gas or electricity for four weeks, no heat or hot water, holes in floors, loose wiring. Twelve of 48 children in building sick. Welfare doctors refuse to walk up dark stairs. Are we human or what? Should innocent children suffer for landlords' brutality and city and state neglect? We are tired of being told to wait with children ill and unable to attend school. Negro and Puerto Rican tenants are forced out while buildings next door are renovated at high rents. We are not being treated as human beings.

For the most part, the lawyer and city planner stayed in the wings and were used by the worker only on a consultative basis. But as the tenants and worker became more involved with the courts and as other organizations entered the fight, the activity of the lawyer and city planner became much more direct and visible.

During this helping process, tenants in other buildings on the block became increasingly militant concerning similar problems in their buildings. With the help of the community-development staff and the housing consultant, local groups and organizations, such as tenants' councils and the local chapter of CORE, were enlisted to support and work with the mothers.

Some of the city agencies believed that the social worker had engineered the entire scheme to embarrass them, steadfastly disregarding the fact that the building had been in unlivable condition for many months. Needless to say, the public agencies are overloaded and have inadequate resources to help. Many workers at such agencies see it as their function to squelch criticism of the inadequacies of services. In the case of the house on Sixth Street, the social worker believed that the tenants —and other people in their plight—should make their needs known to the agencies and to the public at large. The worker

knew that when these expressions of need are backed by power
—either in numbers or in political savvy—they are far more likely
to have effect.

Other movements which were taking place in the city at this
time gave encouragement and direction to the people in the
community. The March on Washington and the Harlem Rent
Strike became confluent with the activities of the tenants and
the local groups and organizations.

By the time the families had been relocated in different
housing, several things had been accomplished. Some of the
public agencies had been sufficiently moved by the actions of
the families and the local organizations to provide better services for them. When the families refused to be moved to a
shelter and instead moved into a neighborhood church until they
could be given better housing, one of the television networks
picked up their story. Officials in the housing agencies came
down to see what was wrong, and several local politicians lent
their support to the tenants. Most important, several weeks after
the tenants moved into the church a bill was passed by the City
Council designed to prevent some of the abuses which the landlord of the Sixth Street house had practiced with impunity. The
councilman who sponsored the new law referred to the house
on Sixth Street to support his argument.

Nevertheless, the accomplishments in this case were far out-
weighed by the problems that remain. A disappointing epilogue
to the story is that in court, two months later, the tenants' case
against the landlord was dismissed on a rather flimsy techni-
cality. The judge ruled that because Consolidated Edison had
removed the meters from the building it was impossible for the
landlord to provide services.

Some of the tenants were relocated out of the neighborhood,
and some were relocated in housing almost as bad as that which
they had left. The organization that began to develop in the
neighborhood has continued to grow, but it is a painstaking job.

Implications for Social-Work Practice and Education

Social-work helping methods as they are currently classified
are so inextricably interwoven in practice that it no longer seems
valid to think of a generic practice as consisting of the application of casework or group-work or community-organization skills,

as the nature of the problem demands. Nor does it seem feasible to adapt group methods for traditional casework problems, or to use group-work skills in community organization or community-organization methods in social casework.

In the case reported here it was the manifestation of a social problem—housing—around which social services were organized. The social worker's major intellectual task was to select the points at which the agency could intervene in the problem and the appropriate methods to use. In order to perform such a task, it seems clear that the worker must understand, not only individual patterns of response, but the social conditions which form the context in which behavior takes place.

As "The House on Sixth Street" makes abundantly evident, the "poverty system" is enduring and persistent, and its parts intermesh with clocklike precision and disturbing complementarity. Intentionally or not, a function is thereby maintained, producing severe social and economic deprivation. Certain groups profit enormously from the maintenance of this system, but other groups suffer. The social-welfare enterprise, and social work in particular, must examine the part it plays in either maintaining or undermining this socially pernicious poverty system.

Whether the failure of traditional welfare organizations can be attributed to accident or to design, its consequence for the poor is devastating. The oft-cited rationalization that these organizations are manned—or, even worse, *under*manned—by "untrained" workers gives rise to the question whether the consequences would be different if the organizations were "fully" manned by workers "fully" trained in our present educational institutions.

In the case of "The House on Sixth Street," much depended on the way in which the situation was defined by Mobilization for Youth. Had it been defined in traditional terms, the caseload of one worker would have become filled, and, although comfort and help would have been provided, discouragement soon would have overwhelmed the most valiant worker as the cases mounted in geometric order. But how effectively can an organization carry out a plan based on a novel definition of a situation when the staff are trained only to perform tasks growing from other, traditional definitions?

Although the sheer quantity of the work to be done in the case reported required the services of specialists as well, the worker with major responsibility was engaged in "generalist" activities, using methods evolved in all three areas of full-fledged specialization. What appears to have guided him consistently, whether he was dealing with an individual mother, an expressive group of mothers, or their organization, was a general set of beliefs, attitudes, norms, assumptions about people, perspectives about slum housing and poverty, ethical principles attesting to man's dignity and rights, a relationship to his agency, and other sets which are commonly shared by social workers. Rather than shift self-consciously from method to method, the worker pursued the problem from system to system, applying various social-work skills to various facets of the social problem. This kind of process needs agency backing and conceptual understanding and clarity. Certainly it should be closely studied, for it may reveal a single helping process which is operant.

If the concept of social problem has any basis in reality, then the line of action would quite naturally lead from an individual manifestation of this condition to a group or groups and eventually to several interconnected organizations which are key elements in the problem. "The House on Sixth Street" is an example of social-work practice that starts with a typical case situation—a mother in need—and leads ultimately to formation of a group with social action as its goal—first a group of mothers who were experiencing acute housing problems, and then an organization of several groups which played some part in social action at the local level.

Despite the lesson to be learned from such cases, the movement away from specialization and narrow technicism in social-work education has been disappointingly slow. The kind of practice that requires intervention by the use of more than one method is not being taught; nor are schools particularly responsive to agencies which are pointing their efforts in these directions. If social-work education is to produce professionals who are able to address social problems in the manner we have described, the opportunity agencies provide for broader experience should be exploited, and those agencies which deliberately intervene in the various systems in which social problems are located should be fully utilized.

The idea which MFY has advanced is that the social worker can best fulfill his professional function and agency responsibility by addressing social problems directly, in an attempt to bring about institutional change, rather than by focusing on individual problems in social functioning. This is not to say that individual expressions of a given social problem should be unattended. To the contrary, this approach is predicated on the belief that individual problems in social functioning are, to varying degrees, both cause and effect. It rejects the notion that individuals are afflicted with social pathologies, holding, rather, that the same social environment which generates conformity also encourages certain forms of deviance. As Nisbet points out, ". . . socially prized arrangements and values in society can produce socially condemned results."[7] This should direct our attention to institutional arrangements and their consequences. The approach suggested does not lose sight of the individual or group, since the social system is composed of various statuses, roles, and classes. It takes cognizance of the systematic relationship of the various parts of the social system, which includes the client. It recognizes that efforts to deal with one social problem frequently generate others, with debilitating consequences.

Thus it is that such institutional arrangements as public assistance, state prisons, state mental hospitals, and slum schools are regarded by many as social problems in their own right. The social problems which these arrangements were designed to solve or relieve—poverty, criminality, mental illness, failure to learn—still remain, and the proposed solutions pose almost equally egregious problems.

In order to prepare students for a frontal attack on social problems, the social-work curriculum must focus on the development of the analytical and synthesizing skills necessary to make accurate appraisals of problem situations. In the methods sequence the present emphasis on fields-of-practice content should be abandoned in favor of social-work skills in work with individuals, groups, and communities. Such social problems as mental illness, juvenile delinquency, and slum housing could provide a framework for the currently fragmented methods sequence. In course work, the student would be expected to explore the cause, nature, and scope of these problems and the means by which social agencies, their agents, and the profession's developing methodology can help to prevent or ameliorate them. Even if a narrow case focus were maintained, the student should

[7] Merton and Nisbet, *op. cit.*

be taught how certain strategies and tactics can affect the various systems in which social functioning through groups takes place, how others can lead to social action, and still others to social-policy development.

This paper has described an innovation of social-work practice. The knowledge, values, attitudes, and skills were derived from a generalist approach to the social-work profession. Agencies which attack social problems by attempting to effect institutional change will need professional workers whose skills cut across the broad spectrum of social-work knowledge.

If the academic preparation we propose were adopted, undoubtedly a transitional period would be required while field-instruction placements were developed. But certainly the schools can do no less than broaden the base of social-work education so that agencies which require and are developing new methods have a source for recruitment. And certainly specific agencies with a need for specific methods should not be favored in the curriculum, as so often seems to be the case today.

CHAPTER FIFTEEN

Neighborhood Community-Development Programs Serving the Urban Poor*

by CHARLES F. GROSSER

Neighborhood community development, as we use the term here, refers to community-organization efforts taking place with lower-class, minority-group, urban-slum residents. The goal of such efforts is to engage the poor in the decision-making process of the community. The poor man's involvement is seen as a way of overcoming his own apathy and estrangement and as a means of realigning the power resources of the community by creating channels through which the consumers of social-welfare services can define their problems and goals and negotiate on their own behalf.

For some time, a discrepancy has existed between this theory or expressed goal of community organization and the methodology employed by the field. Kahn, among other writers, points out:

> Until recently, community-organization method was conceptualized entirely in relation to the enabling role. . . . The enabling took the form of facilitating leadership development of consensus about direction to be taken or winning local assent to leadership-sanctioned direction and plans—not of shaping planning out of true community-wide involvement in goal setting.[1]

Today, however, the field is paying increased attention to the client group with which it is engaged. Community-organization specialists are beginning to work directly with the recipients, rather than exclusively with the providers, of social-welfare service. It is the purpose of this article to explore some of the consequences emerging from community organization's growing involvement with the poor man.

* Presented at the Alumni Conference, Columbia University School of Social Work, April 24, 1965, and published in *Social Work*, July 1965. Reproduced with permission of the National Association of Social Workers.

[1] A. J. Kahn, "Trends and Problems in Community Organization," *Social Work Practice, 1964* (New York: Columbia University Press, 1964), pp. 9, 19.

Substantive Areas and Issues

The poor, more than any other group in our society, expend a major portion of their efforts to achieve the "good life" in interaction with agencies of city government. It is with the local branches of the department of welfare, the police, the housing authority, the board of education, and similar agencies that the poor man negotiates for his share of the community's resources. Striving toward the equitable distribution of these resources is the programmatic strategy which must accompany any bona fide effort to encourage the residents of the inner-city slum to help themselves. Neighborhood development which denies or ignores this fact is, in the eyes of the local residents, at best sham and window-dressing and at worst deceit. Lower-class, minority-group persons cannot be expected to feel that they have a part in the determination of their own destinies in the face of such grievances as the denial of welfare to nonresidents; the categorization of a tenant as "undesirable" with no right to face his accusers and no recourse, brutal arrest and interrogation procedures, and an inferior and segregated school system. To attempt to facilitate the client's adjustment to such a social system is to betray his interests.

If local community-development programs are to be successful, they must, therefore, be prepared for the fact that local efforts at self-expression will be directed to the agents of government in an attempt to bring about solutions to such injustices as those listed above.

Further, in order to arouse people who have been systematically socialized into apathy and inaction, some over several generations, it may be necessary to teach them that solutions to their problems lie in the hands of certain governmental agencies, and that these agencies are sensitive to well-publicized mass efforts, particularly in election years. Lower-class, alienated, nonparticipating people will not be induced to organize by appeals to their civic duty, patriotism, or morality, or by any other exhortation to exercise their obligations of citizenship. Such persons will organize only when they perceive organization as a means to an immediate end. Although we wish to eschew the means–ends, process–content colloquium, we feel impelled to point out that the programs we are discussing require a great deal more attention to material objectives than we have been

wont to give. After all, community development in slum neighborhoods is essentially a process for the redress of grievances
which are the cumulative result of the differential distribution of
community resources. To avoid partisanship in the name of objectivity and service to the "total community" is in effect to take
a position justifying the pittance which has been allotted from
the economic, educational, and social-welfare coffers to the
residents of the inner-city slum.

An example of the application of the foregoing remarks is the
voter-registration campaign conducted by Mobilization for Youth
in the summer and fall of 1964. The campaign, geared to the
registration of eligible minority-group nonvoters, was not run on
the model of the League of Women Voters. It was focused on
Proposition 1 on the ballot that year, which provided for additional low-income housing, and on the recently enacted "stop
and frisk" and "no knock" laws. Both issues have great saliency
in the Lower East Side slum community and hence were used to
encourage voter registration. Campaigners were careful to avoid
creating unrealistic expectations of immediate success regarding
these two issues; rather, they argued that Proposition 1 was sure
to be defeated unless the people of New York City carried it by
a large enough plurality to overcome the upstate opposition, and
that the "stop and frisk" and "no knock" laws, which violate the
rights and dignity of the suspect, were a reflection of lack of
political accountability in general and of the abstinence from
voting of the poor man, who is the most often arrested and in-
terrogated.[2]

The Role of the Worker

The traditional stance of the community organizer as enabler
is based on two assumptions: one valid, the other invalid. The
valid assumption is that actions which are self-imposed, which
grow out of a community's assessment of its own needs, have a
value and permanence which do not inhere in actions imposed
by some outside force. The invalid assumption is that the enabling role is the only one by which this desirable end may be
brought about. In this section we shall suggest some alternatives
which we believe to be viable.

It should be noted, first, that the role of enabler, geared to

[2] Betty Jo Bailey and S. Pinsky, *1964 Voter Registration Drive* (New
York: Mobilization for Youth, 1965), unpublished report.

process, may itself be limited as a strategy for the facilitation of the community self-help process. For example, one of the texts on community-organization method draws on the experience of a special governor's committee set up to deal with serious and pervasive problems in the state's mental institutions, as illustrative of proper work by a community organizer. The committee had recommended certain corrective legislation, which "did not get very far in the ensuing session of the State Assembly." The text points out:

> . . . a more substantial program might have resulted if the committee, or even a considerable bloc within the committee, had been willing to manipulate or use undemocratic methods. It was *rightly* felt, however, that this might jeopardize future working relationships—in short, that process or means was as important as the immediate goal.[3]

Although this kind of judgment may be defensible in dealings with a state-wide interdisciplinary committee, direct contact with those immediately affected by such decisions in a neighborhood community-development program precludes such cavalier disposal of the client's fate.

The role of broker, familiar in such contexts as real estate and stocks and bonds, was instituted in the Mobilization for Youth program in 1962. To our knowledge, it was first suggested for social-work practice by Wilensky and Lebeaux in 1958. These writers postulated a need for "guides, so to speak, through a new kind of civilized jungle," and identified social work as "an example par excellence of the liaison function, a large part of its total activity being devoted to putting people in touch with community resources they need but can hardly name, let alone locate."[4]

In its "pure" form, however, the liaison or broker role has its limitations, as the following report, by a Mobilization for Youth community organizer, illustrates:

> Residents of the Lower East Side have brought their welfare problems . . . such as late checks, insufficient funds to pay large utility bills, no winter clothing, dispossess notices, and a host of

---

[3] C. Murphy, *Community Organization Practice* (New York: Houghton, Mifflin, 1954), p. 22. Emphasis added.

[4] H. Wilensky and C. N. Lebeaux, *Industrial Society and Social Welfare* (New York: Russell Sage Foundation, 1958), p. 286.

others. . . . These problems were handled by the case workers. . . . All too often, no real change seemed to result, either in the lives of the clients or in the procedures of Welfare. The same clients tended to come over and over again, from emergency to emergency.[5]

The community organizer brings the component of collective action to the broker role, and this adds a potent factor to the process. Through collective brokerage activity we introduce the notion of collective solutions: that is, administrative and policy changes which will affect whole classes of persons rather than a single individual.

As a result of experiences like the one described above, two community-organization efforts were launched in the welfare area: a welfare information center, and an organization of welfare clients holding court-support orders. The latter group sought a collective resolution to the problems created when budgets are determined on the basis of income that is directed by a court order but rarely received by the family.

It has been the experience of neighborhood community-development workers that the brokerage role is frequently insufficiently directive. We have therefore co-opted the role of advocate from the field of law. Often the institutions with which our local residents must deal are not even neutral, much less positively motivated, toward handling the issues brought by community groups. They are frequently, in fact, overtly negative and hostile; they often conceal or distort information regarding rules, procedures, and office hours. Thus, by their own partisanship on behalf of instrumental organizational goals, they create an atmosphere which demands advocacy on behalf of the poor man. If the community worker is to facilitate productive interaction between residents and institutions, it is necessary for him to provide leadership and resources directed toward eliciting information, arguing the correctness of a position, and challenging the stance taken by the institutions.

In short, the worker's posture, both to the community residents and to the institutional representatives with whom he is engaged, is that of advocate of the client group's point of view. Although the worker uses all available techniques, the impar-

[5] D. Kronenfeld, *Community Organization and Welfare* (New York: Mobilization for Youth, 1965), unpublished report.

tiality of the enabler and the functionalism of the broker are absent. Nor is the worker expert, consultant, guide, or social therapist.[6] He is, in fact, a partisan in a social conflict. His expertise is available exclusively to serve client interests, since other actors in this social conflict may be using their expertise and resources against the client. Thus, the community organizer may find himself arguing the appropriateness of the issuance of a permit and the police its inappropriateness, or the worker may contend that building violations exist which warrant the tenant's withholding of rent and the landlord may argue that they do not. There may be differences between social workers; for example, a community organizer may claim certain welfare benefits for a group of clients over the opposition of a social investigator. A community organizer and a housing-authority worker may take opposite sides in a dispute regarding the criteria by which the housing authority causes tenants to be evicted as undesirable.

In jurisdictional disputes or when organizational prerogatives are at issue, it is not uncommon to find social workers arrayed on opposite sides. With regard to issues of professional ideology or politics, vigorous advocacy is the rule rather than the exception, as a casual glance through the professional journals will show. Why is it not possible for the poor to recruit such advocates from the ranks of social workers? This we believe is one of the orders of today's business.

Once outside the courthouse, attorneys for defendants and plaintiffs often mingle in an atmosphere of congeniality and good fellowship. The field of social work does not enjoy this style of professional relationship. It is likely that the partisan advocacy we have postulated will call forth virulence from the public agency directed against the worker. Thus school principals attacked MFY staff in response to actions of a local group of parents who were part of the MFY community-organization program:

> We find that a group in its staff is fomenting suspicion and enmity toward the schools . . . this group is largely in the C.O. program.
> Mobilization workers have been engaged in a war on the schools. . . .

[6] Cf. M. G. Ross, *Community Organization* (New York: Harper and Row, 1955), pp. 220-28.

Parents and children are encouraged to make such complaints. This means that MFY is accumulating a secret dossier on the teachers in the area. . . .

The social worker from MFY began to assume the mantle of "guardian." . . .

It should be noted how . . . a controversy between MFY and the principals is transformed into a conflict between the community and the school.[7]

Such response is not surprising, for advocacy, if effective, will require the public agencies to spend more money, will create more work for already harassed staff, and will focus community attention on their shortcomings.

Once we recognize the fact that community-development efforts on behalf of the poor will produce partisan situations, we must concede further that the community organizer—or, for that matter, any other service worker in the urban slum—must choose which side he is on. The same logic that legitimates the roles of broker and advocate leads inevitably to a further role, that of activist.

Morris and Rein have pointed out:

Political knowledge and skill to achieve one's ends have often been considered by social workers to be unprofessional. We have somehow believed that strong advocacy of a particular point of view and the development of techniques to achieve those ends violate our professional commitment to the democratic process. The question for us is whether our commitment to professional neutrality and non-involvement is to continue to sustain our professional practice.[8]

The traditional neutrality of our profession has much to recommend it, but we feel that it has been exercised to the detriment of certain client groups. Morris and Rein suggest that if this policy of noninvolvement persists, the function of community-organization practice will be limited to coordination. If community organization is to find a role in community development, it cannot be exclusively neutral; it must embrace the role of activist.

Except for the heroes of the American Revolution, this nation

[7] Report of 26 Principals of Districts 1-4, 1964.

[8] R. Morris and M. Rein, "Emerging Patterns in Community Planning," *Social Work Practice, 1963* (New York: Columbia University Press, 1963), p. 174.

has had a cultural alienation from the political and social activist. Despite their ultimate vindication, the abolitionist, suffragette, and the labor organizer are still viewed as historical mutants by the community at large. Activists are characterized as "outsiders" and "agitators" to this very day, whether they play their roles in Selma, Alabama, or between Houston and Delancey Streets.

We believe that the activist role is, and has been, a legitimate stance for the social worker, especially the community organizer. It must be available as a strategy, to be chosen from among others when community needs require it. The passivity and objectivity of the service professions are, after all, something of a myth. We do urge people to action of all sorts—to visit a dentist, to sit up straight, to curb their dogs, to contribute to the Red Cross, and even, in some communities, to register and vote and to support the PTA. In neighborhood community development, we urge students to stay in school, tenants to keep off project lawns, dropouts to join the Job Corps, and mothers to use the well-baby clinics. Why may we not also urge tenants who are without heat to withhold rent, parents with grievances to boycott the schools, or citizens without franchise to take to the streets in legal public demonstration to redress grievances?

The answer to this point has been a matter of contingency, not reason. Some have expressed concern that recourse to roles other than that of enabler, and particularly to that of activist, entails manipulation of the client group or community. We are convinced that the choice of role bears no relevance whatsoever to the issue of manipulation. Manipulation, which is an attempt to achieve goals determined by the worker rather than the clients, can be accomplished by many techniques. Activists and advocates, no less than enablers and brokers, must make judgments on the basis of their professional appraisal of client needs, without regard to political expedience, personal ideology, or agency vested interests.

Where, and by whom, is significant neighborhood community development with the impoverished being done today? We suggest that it is being done in the Negro ghettos of the North and South by nonprofessional activists in such organizations as the Congress of Racial Equality, the Council of Federated Organizations, the Student Nonviolent Coordinating Committee, and the Southern Christian Leadership Conference. With very few exceptions, neighborhood community development is taking place outside the field of social work. This state of affairs reflects, not a paucity of professional resources, but a narrowness of concept. Law students have already undertaken systematic participation in the organizing drives of such organizations as SNCC and CORE. For a number of years, community-organization practice and the training of C.O. students has existed within such groups as the NAACP and the Urban League. I suggest, therefore, that it would be appropriate for social work to place students in more activist areas within the civil-rights movement.

A body of literature is beginning to evolve based on the philosophy and tactics of nonviolent direct action. In *A Manual for Direct Action*,[9] for example, Oppenheimer and Lakey describe such techniques as "haunting" (silently following a person about), renouncing honors, hartal (demonstration by absence, a form of boycott), boycott, demonstrations, leafleting, picketing, vigils, and role-playing. They also suggest forms for record-keeping and typical budgets for voter-registration projects, provide notes on security in the Deep South, and offer advice on how to conduct oneself if arrested, including such specific suggestions as wearing two sets of underwear to absorb the shock of being dragged and sticking one's head in a bucket of water to remove traces of tear gas. Let us not be intimidated by the notion of incorporating some of these suggestions into our method: their strangeness stems largely from their unfamiliarity. It might be noted that the many civil-rights workers who sought counsel and technique from social workers frequently found our methods somewhat strange also, and wondered how they might be incorporated into the methodology of nonviolence.

The Organizational Forms of Neighborhood Development

Those in community organization who have wrestled with the problems of neighborhood development in urban slums have found it difficult to decide on the organizational forms which their efforts should take. When we examine the forms characteristic of voluntary associations in the middle-class community, we find a proliferation of styles, purposes, and patterns of participation, as varied as the personalities and social circumstances of those who participate in them. We would not have the temerity

[9] M. Oppenheimer and G. Lakey, *A Manual for Direct Action* (Chicago, Ill.: Quadrangle Books, 1965).

to suggest that there is a single optimal form for middle-class voluntarism. The assumption that such a form exists for collective action in the slum community is equally untenable.

Rather than a debate on the relative merits of various alternatives, what is needed is a determination of the strategies that will be most effective.

> Forms of organization, their structure, and their affiliations if any will depend on the job decided on and the personnel available. The worker may want to join an existing group in order to influence it; he may want to set up an ad hoc or temporary group composed either of individuals or of representatives of other groups; or he may want to create a new group.[10]

Neighborhood work has been conducted in groups based on common cultural patterns (home-town clubs), common social problems (welfare or housing organizations), physical proximity (building or block organizations), social movements (civil-rights groups), specific task orientation (voter-registration campaigns), and the operation of a resource center (storefronts). The success or failure of these groups has little to do with their form.

We would note, in conclusion, that if they have not yet created the technology or method of neighborhood community-development work, social-work efforts at community organization in urban slums have at least established the legitimacy of such efforts.

Commenting editorially on this issue as reflected in the Mobilization for Youth experience, the *New York Times* stated:

> . . . If Mobilization for Youth is to do more than merely ameliorate the lot of the poorest elements of the community, it must teach them to help themselves by concerted efforts. . . . Any form of social protest is bound to generate controversy, and some forms clearly raise serious questions of propriety for an agency that draws so much of its support from government funds. . . . But the poor must be encouraged to believe that there are ways to express their views on the need for social betterment. . . . The right to fight City Hall is as much a prerogative of the poor as of any other group of citizens; it is only when those who dwell in the slums and have too little to keep themselves and their families in dignity surrender to a supine sense of total futility and helplessness that the community has real cause to worry.[11]

[10] *Ibid.*, p. 43.
[11] *New York Times*, Editorial, Nov. 11, 1964.

CHAPTER SIXTEEN

The Storefront on Stanton Street: Advocacy in the Ghetto*

by RICHARD A. CLOWARD and RICHARD M. ELMAN

The Welfare State on Stanton Street

Stanton Street is one block south of Houston Street on New York's Lower East Side, the city's oldest slum. At the westernmost end of Stanton Street is a playground; to the east are the Gompers Houses—a project which rents primarily to low-income people with jobs. Lying between these two points are the usual blocks of deteriorating old-law tenements, built before the turn of the century, but there are also some middle-income, high-rise apartment buildings which went up just before the second World War.

On the ground floors of apartment buildings as well as of tenements are dusty-looking storefronts, some vacant, others housing Spanish travel agencies, CPA's, insurance brokers, tin fitters, and wholesale jobbers. Most are occupied by grocery stores. The fact that there are twelve busy grocers within many fewer blocks along Stanton Street testifies to the adequacy of food supplies, but it also tells us something about the short supplies of cash in the neighborhood. In most of these stores, the ringing of the cash register is heard less frequently than the customers' insistent pleas for credit. Typically, about 14 per cent of the residents are on public assistance, including some large families whose marginal incomes have to be supplemented by the Department of Welfare even though they have a regular breadwinner. If we also take into account the many social-

---

* This article records the experience of Mobilization for Youth's storefronts to the end of 1965. Since then, changes have taken place in the storefront program and in some of the laws, policies, and practices of the Department of Welfare. A condensed version of this article appeared in *Trans-Action*, December 1966, pp. 27-35.

security pensioners living in the area, it must be said that one
of the street's chief commercial activities is the cashing of government checks.

Mail for Stanton Street residents—including government checks
—usually arrives a day later than in the more prosperous areas
of the city. This can cause problems, for many of the residents
are dependent upon these checks to redeem their credit with
local merchants. Mail or no mail, they are expected to pay their
semimonthly rentals on time. Thus, as early as the third or 18th
of the month, the dispossess notices begin to appear in hallway
mailboxes and under the rat-catchers of Stanton Street doorways.
To avoid a default judgment, tenants must appear in Landlord-
Tenants' Court on Center Street, many blocks away. Other tardy
mail deliveries for some might bring dunning letters from Consolidated Edison after gas and electricity have already been cut
off; summonses to appear in Family Court on the day before
yesterday; "reminders" to come to the Mental Hygiene Clinic;
or truancy notices from the Bureau of Attendance. There will
also be summonses to appear in Civil Court to explain why the
purchaser was reluctant to pay nearly three times the real value
in credit or service charges on a sewing machine or TV set of
dubious mechanical function. If, in general, Stanton Street residents are not litigious, they are confronted throughout their
daily lives by individuals and institutions which are.

The Lower Manhattan Welfare Center

A major point of encounter between Stanton Street residents
and the social-welfare state is the Lower Manhattan Welfare
Center on Fifth Street. At this center more than 6,000 individual
cases a month—including those of 500 new applicants—are processed by a staff of 119 caseworkers and field investigators, 20
assistant supervisors, five case supervisors, and an approximately
equal number of clericals. Many residents of the Stanton Street
vicinity are also cared for by a newer center on East 28th Street.
If a welfare recipient has moved to Stanton Street from the area
to the north of Houston Street, he must continue to deal with a
center in the Yorkville neighborhood, more than 60 blocks away.
If an applicant for public assistance is a recent arrival to the
state of New York, he must deal with a center for "non-residents"

on West 31st Street. The staff at all these centers are part of the
DW bureaucracy of nearly 14,000 employees.

An applicant for public assistance enters the Lower Manhattan
Welfare Center past a uniformed guard. Almost immediately,
he confronts a clerk seated at a small desk, where he is given his
first brief interview. This initial orientation, or "softening-up"
interview, as one investigator described it, serves the specific
purpose of making certain that the person has come to the right
office for the right type of assistance, but it also fits into the
general purpose of interviewing procedures at DW: to cast immediate suspicion on the applicant, to make him come forth with
proof that he does not have an income. Although it is usually
conducted by an untrained clerical, the interview customarily
inquires into motives as well as matters of fact. Because it is a
major premise of all DW interviewing procedures that "mere
unsubstantiated assertions of need" are never sufficient to establish eligibility, even the clericals may endeavor to shake the
applicant's credibility. Not knowing what may lie ahead of them,
applicants often rattle off lengthy tales of adversity at this very
desk, only to be peremptorily informed to "save it for the
investigator."

Single men applying for relief usually get no further than this
desk. Here they will be issued a voucher for a meal and a night's
lodging at the Municipal Shelter, where efforts may be made to
find them work or otherwise to "rehabilitate" them. These men
are automatically assumed to be bums. The initial interviewer
has the liberty to speak as harshly to them as he deems necessary.

The interviewer is charged with keeping a numerical roster of
all applicants and with arranging contacts between long-term
clients and their investigators. It is only after the applicant has
been assigned a number that he is allowed to pass around the
clerk's desk into a bull pen, in dimensions about twenty by thirty
yards, which is surrounded on all sides by the glass-walled
cubicles of the "intake" investigators.

The area in which welfare petitioners are required to wait
their turns is similar to the waiting rooms of many of our public
hospitals and unemployment offices: rows of folding chairs are
packed into dense squares with narrow aisles between them; the
light is dim, yet harsh, changing the institutional shade of the
walls to dingy grey; and wherever the eye wanders during the

many hours of waiting, there are posters in doggedly cheerful colors exhorting the applicants to

> Eat well!
> Be ready for breakfast!
> Eat a square lunch!

Distributed by the federal Department of Health, Education and Welfare, these posters may show designs for healthful and nutritious meals with tables of calories, columns of mock-up fruits and vegetables, battalions of milk bottles, regiments of chicken eggs, and whole families of happy, smiling white or cocoa-colored people with arms interlocked, mouths open, tongues like cherries, and plaster teeth. Other posters advertise the importance of good health habits or of washing the hands after going to the toilet. A sign in both English and Spanish of local creation further exhorts: "Please do not bring children to this office," although many of the clients are women with children. There are signs prohibiting smoking and notices telling those who wait to take a number and be patient.

Usually, a loud-voiced investigator parades down the aisles between the squares, barking out numbers. When your number is finally called, you go behind a partition to talk with an intake investigator.

Getting on the Rolls

On Stanton Street, as elsewhere in those 16 areas of New York City where most of its 500,000 pauper-clients live, the Department of Welfare does not send out investigators to recruit new clients. Unlike the Social Security Administration and some mental-hygiene consultation clinics, it does not advertise its benefits or otherwise encourage people to come in and apply for them. Welfare caseloads are generally heavy, and the paperwork on each case can be overwhelming. The dedicated worker is in the position of constantly having to rationalize his clients to the system and the system to his clients. Yet, a worker can be dismissed if he is thought to be "overidentifying" with his clients. For a variety of such occupational reasons, there is an annual turnover averaging more than 40 per cent among the employees of the Department of Welfare. The new workers—whatever their intentions—have a difficult time mastering the complex regulations which they must use to govern their clients. Even the veteran workers who stay on year after year at low salaries find themselves so hard-pressed by the continuing demands of the upper-echelon bureaucracy, as well as by their clients, that many of them process applications in only the most cursory fashion.

The intake investigators at a welfare center typically have a certain amount of seniority, since it is presumed that the most experienced hands will be the most skilled in discerning eligibility. They are also, of course, the most skilled in determining ineligibility. Voluminous statements of policy must be checked before action can be taken. One such policy, for example, advises the investigator that legally responsible relatives (spouse, child, parent, grandparent) must by law be considered as potential financial resources for the person applying for assistance. It then counsels the investigator that he should endeavor to make contact not only with these legally responsible persons but also with the applicant's other relations (brothers, uncles, aunts) and even his friends. This same manual later states that the withholding of assistance is as important to the client as the giving of assistance. Presumably, it is the supervisor's function to instruct his worker in wholesome interpretations of such a doctrine (which, of course, is intended to discourage unwholesome dependencies), just as it is also his function to decide when it is advisable to go beyond the rules of legal responsibility into those grey areas where relatives can be shamed and coerced into accepting responsibilities for which they are not legally obligated.[1]

When the applicant is summoned from the bull pen, one of the investigators casually introduces himself and then proceeds to elicit the prospective client's history a second time in more exhaustive detail. *When was the last time you worked? How much did you earn? Are you a veteran? Do you belong to a union? Do you have any bank accounts? How are you living at present? Do you own a car? Is there insurance? Are there relatives? Where did you get that gold watchband?* If the intake investigator decides on the basis of his interrogation that there is "presumptive" suspicion of need, he can give the applicant an

---

[1] For a general discussion of the abysmal statutes and administrative practices of public welfare agencies, see Richard A. Cloward and Richard M. Elman, "Poverty, Injustice and the Welfare State," *The Nation*; Part I, "An Ombudsman for the Poor?," February 28, 1966, pp. 230-35; Part II, "How Rights Can Be Secured," March 7, 1966, pp. 264-68.

immediate grant pending an even more exhaustive social investigation to be carried out by others in the field. Occasionally, where need seems self-evident and severe, he will try to define the person's possible category of assistance and then make him immediately eligible.

There are six categories of public assistance in New York, including Home Relief (the cost of which is borne equally by the city and the state) and five other categories which are partly reimbursed by both the state and federal governments: Aid for Dependent Children, Old Age Assistance, Veteran's Assistance, Aid to the Blind, and Aid to the Disabled. (There is also a federal public-assistance program of medical aid to the indigent which is administered by the Welfare Department for all eligible applicants.) Although benefits in all except the last-named category seem virtually identical, the investigation and rehabilitation requirements tend to be different, as do the rights vested in the recipient, the resources left at his disposal, and the responsibilities of the Department of Welfare to the state and federal establishment. A person receiving Aid to the Disabled, for example, has to be recertified by a competent physician or psychiatrist, whereas a person applying for AFDC may have a relatively easy time remaining eligible for benefits once she has established that she has dependent children. Whereas the recipients of the federally reimbursed programs have the right to a formal administrative appeal (or "fair hearing"), which can be further appealed through an action in court, applicants for Home Relief can only complain.

The variety of possible categories poses crucial problems of discretion. It is regarded as preferable to qualify a candidate for a federally reimbursed category of assistance rather than Home Relief. If an applicant seems alcoholic, he can be declared presumptively eligible for Aid to the Disabled—again, preferable to city-supported Home Relief. Many people who are initially judged qualified for Home Relief are reclassified to one of the federal categories as soon as possible. For the person who fits none of these categories but who is nevertheless needy, the process can involve ludicrous contortions. A kind-hearted investigator may invent some handicap so that such a person can qualify for assistance. When a subsequent investigator examines the case, the client may be accused of malingering. If such a person, moreover, irritates his worker at this initial interview, he and his dependents may receive nothing.

The means-test interview and the constant reinvestigation required in New York are frequently subject to maladministration because so many welfare families must draw upon a composite of benefits—e.g., a father on Aid to the Disabled, mother and children on AFDC. In the case of large families which are receiving supplementary financial assistance because the breadwinners are engaged in low-paid labor, Welfare may be quick to qualify the family but may issue its supplementary payments only once every three months, so that the breadwinner is forced to find other income (which could later disqualify him from benefits) to exist between payments.

By law, all applicants must be advised of their rights under the existing programs of benefits. In practice, they are usually given booklets which describe their rights in vague and abstract language, usually without examples being given. The investigator must follow certain formal guidelines, but the client typically has little specific forewarning of what he can expect to receive. Coming to his investigator in a state of ignorance, the applicant is not able to argue or negotiate; he must beg. To arrive at a decision about such an applicant, the investigator attempts to evaluate information about existing resources sworn to by a client who knows nothing of the advantages and disadvantages of the various types of eligibility. Grants are based upon the difference between the applicant's alleged resources and the maximum amount that can be given out under his presumed category of eligibility. If he is believed to be without any resources, he will receive a full entitlement. If he is thought to have adequate resources (whether actually or merely potentially), he will receive nothing. The choice depends largely upon the moral arithmetic of the investigator, who has the job of subtracting those who are deserving from those who are not. (One such investigator told us, as if speaking about some pampered graduates of the Choate Academy: "We don't believe that these able-bodied Puerto Rican men shouldn't work. It's not good for them.")

Welfare also upholds the right to interview a prospective client in confidence, unimpeded by the presence of his friends, a translator, a social worker, or a lawyer. This policy is followed, it is said, in compliance with state law, to protect the client's privacy, but it also seems to ensure the untrammeled discretion of the Welfare functionary. Throughout the city, DW rejects approximately 40 per cent of all new applicants every month. A typical case is that of Mr. B, a 40-year-old Puerto Rican living with his wife and baby in a tiny three-room walkup on Stanton Street:

> Since coming to New York in 1948, B had been steadily employed with only brief layoffs, but he had never been able to earn more than the minimum wage. He pays ten dollars a week child support to a son by a previous marriage. When laid off by his last employer, B presumed that it might be for only a few weeks so he did not immediately apply for unemployment payments. After two weeks, he was destitute, went to Unemployment, and was told he would have to wait another two weeks for his first check. B then went to Lower Manhattan Center where, after waiting an entire morning, he was told to come back the next morning with a letter from his boss stating that he had been laid off. He was also told to look for work. When he returned the following day with the letter, he was again urged to look for work. When he asked what he should do meanwhile to pay his bills, he was harangued: "DIDN'T YOU SAVE ANYTHING AT ALL?"

Staying on the Rolls

Of the 60 per cent who are given some assistance when they apply, many are abruptly disqualified later, on the ground that their eligibilities have altered. In the more or less typical month of August 1964, for example, the Lower Manhattan Center closed a total of 468 cases, including 123 cases of Home Relief, and 39 cases of TADC. Few of these actions were taken at the behest of clients who had prospered sufficiently to request their removal from the benefit program. Rarely did clients who were denied their benefits take advantage of the "fair hearing" procedures available under law. Although some closings were made because clients had died, found employment, or moved to other cities, the majority came about as a consequence of uncontested contentions about the recipient by investigators at the Center, or because of mistakes due to haphazard administrative procedures. "It is much easier to close a case," one investigator told us, "than to open one." Thus some people were lopped off the lists for allegedly decreased need (i.e., the discovery that they had unreported assets or legally responsible relatives), for allegedly refusing to accept employment (i.e., failure to accept a proffered job which involved distasteful tasks or low pay or which otherwise did not meet the recipient's standards), for allegedly having other sources of income (i.e., taking in boarders), and for the catch-all "refusal to comply with departmental regulations."

In some instances, investigators used the case-closing procedure to discipline difficult clients. In nearly all such cases the investigator was both judge and juror, presenting his allegations as facts and then prescribing suitable punishments. For example:

Mrs. T, a Negro woman with four children, lived in a Stanton Street tenement on her semimonthly AFDC payments of $105.70. One day her oldest child missed school. When the school social worker visited her she smelled whiskey on Mrs. T's breath and concluded that she must be neglecting her children. The Department of Welfare was notified and told Mrs. T that two of her children would have to be placed in a home if she expected to continue to receive benefits. When Mrs. T refused to allow representatives of Welfare to inspect her home without notice and interview her children, her case was closed.

Mrs. X has an 18-year-old son who is a school dropout and a 14-year-old daughter. She has raised them on AFDC payments. When her son reached 18 he was told to report to the employment division of Welfare. When he missed his appointment, the boy was taken off Mrs. X's budget so that she had to feed three mouths with an allotment for two persons.

Mr. G, a single man on Home Relief, received a letter telling him to report to Welfare the following morning to discuss his housing accommodation. When he arrived an hour late, he was severely chastised by his worker. Mr. G answered back and was then disqualified from further benefits for "obnoxious behavior."

Mrs. Y's caseworker arrived very early one morning, ostensibly to inspect her carpet. He found her still in bed and sat down beside her, placing a hand on her bare knee. "You get your hand off me," she insisted. "You don't have to be so nasty about it," he said. "If you ever touch me again," she said, "I'll get you." The worker then went back to his office and wrote Mrs. Y a letter requesting that she appear at his office the next day. He made sure to post this letter so that it would arrive late. When Mrs. Y failed to show up her case was closed. It was three months before she was to receive Welfare benefits again.

Getting Full Benefits

The most galling aspect of the inequities visited upon the people of Stanton Street is their inability to influence crucial decisions about the way they must live. The success of their smallest efforts to improve their living standards—to occupy decent housing, to furnish their homes adequately, to procure ample food allowances, to acquire a sufficient quantity and variety of clothing for themselves and their children—is largely dependent upon their investigator's interpretation of Welfare policies. In many cases these policies are within the law: in other cases they are violations of the intent of the law.

The number of additional benefits that are available by law is impressive, as are the obstacles which have been erected around them. There are some Stanton Street families, for example, which are legitimately eligible for a variety of supplementary grants (for heavy clothing, household furnishings, appliances, etc.). By policy, however, the availability of these grants—which might make the difference between bare subsistence and an adequate standard—is not publicized, and the grants are not issued routinely. Thus relatively few eligible persons know of their entitlement to such funds, and of the requests that are made many are denied.

Similarly, a person who is eligible for a special diet (because he is sickly) or for surplus food (to supplement his cash allowance) is often not told of his eligibility. Indeed, if he does apply, his action may be interpreted as "manipulative" and his request refused. In order to have a telephone or television set, the applicant must obtain medical or psychiatric permission and welfare-panel doctors are customarily instructed not to give such permission. With special permission, welfare families can have washing machines, refrigerators, and perhaps even college educations for their children, but each entitlement requires a special pleading, often accompanied by the recommendations of supporting authorities. If they are able to convince their investigator of the legitimacy of their request, he in turn must petition his unit supervisor, who might have to pass the request on to the central case-consultation unit, which may be acting under a mandate to keep such requests to a minimum.

Because of such mandates, the worker may feel compelled to give his client a pittance; thus if she applies for a washing machine (approximately $100), she may be offered a dresser (approximately $25). The client has to be wary in accepting such a grant, because another worker may subsequently punish her for not having the dresser which she was given money to buy. In any case, the pauperized recipient will find that her request has not been honored, that she has had to settle for less than her wants and needs. If she protests being so defrauded, she may be disciplined for her audacity by being subjected to an inspection visit. When Mrs. J, for example, applied for school clothing for her three children, she was visited by a worker who tried to establish that the presence of a pair of trousers in Mrs. J's closet "proved" that there was a man living in her house capable of providing support.

Stanton Street families are naturally bitter when investigators invade their privacy only to deny them benefits, and they are ashamed when benefits are awarded as a result of such humiliating intrusions. Nearly all think that they are underbudgeted, and even Welfare will admit that as many as 30 per cent are. Many are living in overcrowded apartments because Welfare will not give them "key money" to move to larger quarters. Many are disqualified from public housing because they are on welfare. When they give birth to illegitimate children, Welfare sometimes punishes them by withholding grants for layettes. When Stanton Street women are hospitalized their children are sent to a shelter, even though Welfare is supposed to provide them with trained homemakers. And when a fire guts a Stanton Street tenement, the former occupants are placed for indefinite periods in squalid hotel rooms, although Welfare is obliged to find them new quarters. One woman summed up Welfare's attiture in these words: "When I need a new pair of eyeglasses hell can freeze over."

Sometimes the investigator is ignorant of a client's entitlement and unwilling to reveal his ignorance by passing the request along to his supervisor. Such has been the fate of many requests for the so-called rat allowance—an extra utilities allowance to enable the recipient to burn his lights all night long so as to drive away rats. Stanton Street families often live on less than what is presumed to be the minimal standard (and are given no way of ascertaining what that standard should be) because some investigators never learned how to make up the required minimum subsistence budget.

Some observers of these punitive, exploitative, and impoverishing practices of the welfare state have recognized a need to establish programs to represent the interests of low-income people in their dealings with agencies of government. One such program was established by Mobilization for Youth.

Advocacy on Stanton Street

Mobilization for Youth is a multimillion-dollar investment by government and private philanthropy in the Lower East Side community. It began in 1962 as a broad-scale attempt to deal with juvenile delinquency by providing delinquent youth with "a stake in conformity." Its varied programs and facilities, scattered throughout a 67-square-block area, have generally come to be regarded as the forerunner of the Community Action Programs currently being encouraged by the Office of Economic Opportunity.

Mobilization's short history has been marked by controversies. The agency has been accused of teaching low-income people disrespect for authority, of harboring subversives within its staff, of fomenting race riots, and even of attempting to divert and dissipate genuine revolutionary discontent. For some people on the Lower East Side it has provided employment as nonprofessional workers in various programs. For others it has provided an opportunity to participate in social-action programs (e.g., rent strikes) which hold promise of improving their lives in meaningful and practical ways. It has served many young people in its remedial-education and employment-training programs. To most of the adults on Stanton Street, however, MFY is symbolized by its storefront service centers, where residents are encouraged to bring their daily problems of living under the welfare state.

A Mobilization social worker with one assistant first occupied the storefront at 199 Stanton Street in November 1962. (Additional storefront centers were subsequently opened throughout the area.) Across the street was a *bodega*. Another grocery down the block was the principal numbers drop for the area. MFY partitioned the back of its storefront to provide "private" offices, painted the waiting room in the front of the store, and installed some chairs and couches. Then a sign was painted on the front

windows: CENTRO DE SERVICIO AL VECENDARIO . . .
NEIGHBORHOOD SERVICE CENTER. A sign lettered on the
door said WALK IN! The Stanton Street residents who did so
were invited to describe their problems as they saw them. The
social workers then set out to provide assistance and redress of
grievances. The workers soon found that although people came
in to present a lengthy verbal charge sheet against the hostile
environment in which they were forced to live, the source of
most of their grievances was the welfare state, chiefly public
welfare.

In fact, it soon became clear to the director of the first storefront, Joseph Kreisler, that unresolved problems with public
welfare were a crucial factor in the instability of life along
Stanton Street. If people didn't have enough money from Welfare, they weren't able to pay their bills at the grocer. If they
didn't get their Welfare checks on time, they ran into trouble
with their landlords. If Welfare didn't provide school clothing,
they had to keep their children home from school and had difficulties with school authorities. This day-to-day relationship with
the Welfare bureaucracy was making people bitter and angry
and punitive toward one another. "They would come in and talk
and we would ask questions about them and their children,
about their health, housing, unemployment, education, etc., but
they would keep coming back to Welfare. They didn't have
enough of this, they weren't getting that, could we get them the
other thing. After a while," Kreisler concluded, "the pattern was
clear."

But if the pattern seemed clear to Kreisler and to Sherman
Barr, who was in over-all charge of all storefront centers, those
who complained most bitterly were not often able to pinpoint
the source of their misery. "I feel that the City of New York has
abandoned me," one man told Barr. Others told of harrowing
experiences with Welfare officials as if such dealings were entirely as they should be. Never having been led to expect better
treatment from such an agency, they had no awareness of their
rights under the law, much less any confidence that these rights
could be upheld and defended without recriminations. It became
necessary, therefore, for the workers to assure people that they
did have such rights.

The worker had to have a dogmatic conviction that injustice

had been done in order to apply himself effectively to the sometimes petty pecuniary problems of his clients. One worker put it this way:

> "When I think that Mrs. Cortez hasn't gotten any money for her rat allowance I sometimes want to throw up my hands and say: What difference does it make? Why should people in this day and age have 'rat allowances'? But when I realize that it isn't just the rat allowance . . . that it's a total system of oppressiveness and disrespect for people, why then I've got to get her that rat allowance. I've got to help her get as many things as possible."

Even Kreisler, a veteran of the public-welfare systems of New York and Maine, had his "eyes opened" by the volume of abuses revealed by the testimony of the clients, as well as by the pettiness, vindictiveness, and injustice of the policies and practices they documented. In the center's first few months of operation, hundreds of Stanton Street families came to attest to their antagonistic relationship with the Department of Welfare. Many had learned through the neighborhood grapevine to come directly to Stanton Street after an affront at one of the local welfare centers. Welfare recipients, it is true, accounted for only a third of the total number of clients who found their way to the storefront during those first six months, but of the nonwelfare families, nearly two thirds listed "insufficient income" as their principal problem, which meant, in many cases, that they were not being subsidized even though they were eligible for welfare benefits. One quarter of all the families on welfare were having problems affecting their continued eligibility. Many more had had such problems in the past. Still others listed problems with other city agencies in which their welfare status was a crucial factor. Three years later—when the number of clients seen at Stanton Street had increased tenfold and the original storefront office had spilled over into two adjoining sites—problems with public welfare continued to be the principal complaint. At 199 Stanton Street the social workers discovered that the problems of their clients were so tied to the bureaucratic workings of the city that they could keep their storefront open profitably only from 9 to 5 on weekdays, the normal working hours of public agencies.

This came as a distinct surprise to administrative personnel at MFY, who had originally assumed that the chief function of the centers would be to offer specific and practical advice on problems of health, housing, welfare, education, and employment. Workers had been told to act as liaisons with public agencies, not as adversaries. But many workers soon found that they had to do something more than refer, advise, and counsel if they expected results. They were being called upon to take sides in a pervasive dispute between their clients and the welfare state. When they refused to do so, their clients ceased to ask them for help. The practice that then evolved came to be known as advocacy.

Social Workers as Advocates

An advocate in this context is one who intervenes on behalf of a client with a public agency to secure an entitlement or right which has been obscured or denied. To act effectively, the advocate must accept his client's definition of the injustice, but he must also have sufficient knowledge of the law and of government's administrative procedures to discern remediable issues or disputable questions of fact in the emotional testimony of the client, and then seek a solution in harmony with the client's interests. In practice, the Stanton Street advocates often found that they had to instruct the representatives of agencies such as Welfare in what was the law and how it should be interpreted. Beyond their ability to interpret a client's account without losing his confidence, the advocate's most demanding task was to serve notice on his opposite number in the Welfare Department that he was prepared to move a notch further up the hierarchy if justice was not tendered on the present level.

Thus the advocates listened to endless tales of woe; they totaled up scores of welfare budgets to detect underbudgeting; they placed telephone calls to a bewildering number of functionaries and sometimes accompanied clients when they went to see these people in person. They argued and they cajoled. They framed rebuttals to cases put forward by Welfare, and they also attacked when necessary. When, for example, a Stanton Street woman was charged with child neglect, the alert worker was able to show that she had been consistently underbudgeted for more than a year, which made her child-rearing efforts virtually futile. When another client was evicted for nonpayment of rent, the worker forced Welfare to make such a payment by showing that the Department had failed in its legal obligation to do so. Whether the workers' threats were made politely or in anger, as a technique of careful manipulation or with blustering disregard for the sensibilities of their opposite numbers, they served notice on the low-level Welfare employee that he would be held responsible for his actions to his supervisor—and so on up the line. Thus advocacy on behalf of the clients was the bludgeon by which this city agency was made more responsive to a portion of its Lower East Side constituency. At 199 Stanton Street the workers came to serve as surrogates for their clients with the bureaucratically arranged world outside the Welfare ghetto.

Advocacy, often militant, was always carried on at 199 Stanton Street with a calculated informality. Young people were not discouraged from idling about the place. Any client was free to come and go as he pleased. Neighborhood parties were held on holidays. Local people were employed as janitors, clericals, and translators. Many of the professional workers and "case-aides" were themselves either Negro or Puerto Rican, and there was little attention given to any differentiation of duties according to professional status.

The center managed to keep up an active interviewing and referral practice for clients who requested other kinds of service. When a client came for help with Welfare, it was always possible for him to get a loan or even a small outright gift of cash to tide him over while his case was being adjudicated. An effort was also made to keep a supply of clean used clothing on hand for those whose requests from Welfare might take more than a few hours to resolve. But these small grants and services were not the chief attraction of the center; the major reason that people were drawn to the center was that the workers took sides. They were willing to put themselves out to uphold their clients' rights in the welfare state. One Puerto Rican mother put it this way: "When you go alone to Welfare they treat you like dirt. When you go with a social worker it's different." Another said: "They used to tell me I didn't understand. Now they say, let me talk to them. I like that a lot better because even when you un-

derstand, it sometimes doesn't do you any good . . . no good
at all. . . ."

Legal Advocates

When, after a year, it became clear to the administration of
MFY that the indignation and advocacy of the social worker
was sometimes an insufficient protection against the injustices
of the social welfare state, the agency hired two lawyers to operate a free legal service for clients referred from such neighborhood centers as the storefront on Stanton Street. These attorneys
applied themselves to eviction proceedings in public and private
housing, to consumer frauds, and other specialized areas of
practice among the poor. They also began to challenge decisions
concerning Welfare clients where the facts were at issue, or
where actions had been taken in seeming violation of the intent
of the law. "The legal profession," said Edward Sparer, MFY's
former legal director, "has thus far failed in its obligation to develop a rule of law within the welfare administrative processes
most important to the poorer section of the population."

As a case in point, one might cite the New York State Welfare
Abuses Act, passed in 1962 as a compromise measure to satisfy
demands that New York deny public assistance to applicants
from out of state. It was clearly stipulated by the legislators
that only persons who came to New York for the express purpose
of collecting relief could be lawfully denied such benefits. In
practice, however, the new resident's mere application for relief
was frequently taken as sufficient reason to deny him benefits.
MFY attorneys successfully represented several families on the
verge of starvation as the result of the misapplication of this
statute.

By 1964 four attorneys were employed full time at MFY on
cases brought to their attention by the social workers. It was
because these lawyers threatened to bring suit that the Lower
Manhattan Center no longer invoked the Welfare Abuses Act as
a matter of course. It was fear of litigation which prompted the
department to abandon its policy of after-midnight intrusions on
the residences of AFDC mothers to detect the presence of males
—a policy which seems in clear-cut violation of constitutional
guarantees of privacy. The workers at Stanton Street were en-

couraged to bring to the attention of MFY attorneys cases through which the legality and constitutionality of administrative acts could be contested in open hearings, so that precedents could be established. The lawyers also spent a good deal of time advising workers and clients about strategies by which to exploit those rights which did seem vested. Working closely with the social workers, the lawyers contested capricious eligibility rulings and attempted to reinstate clients whose benefits had been arbitrarily terminated. At times they argued the merits of the case. At other times they argued that the law had been perverted by bad administrative policies. The lawyers were prepared to represent the clients at the formal appeals tribunals of the State Department of Social Welfare, but they found that a majority of client grievances did not need to come before such hearings. Often a telephone call from an MFY attorney expressing interest in a case was enough to persuade a functionary that he was acting without respect to the client's rights.

Because of Welfare's desire to avoid the establishment of precedents and hence to settle out of court, the MFY legal service actually litigated only a small percentage of the cases it was called in on, but its impact upon the legal vacuum within the Welfare ghetto was impressive. The workers at Stanton Street continued to be confronted with cases requiring immediate advocacy, but they could now defend their clients' rights reinforced by the legal expertise of Sparer and his associates. They were able, moreover, to increase their sophistication about Welfare law through their continuing association with the attorneys, and they passed on some of this education to their opposite numbers in the Welfare bureaucracy. Even the clients benefited educationally from the program. Many had never before had any contacts with attorneys, except, perhaps, as their adversaries. Now these attorneys were representing them in adversary proceedings against the Department of Welfare, and they became aware of the power that proper representation bestows upon the private citizen. One AFDC mother put it this way: "I trust the lawyers more than anybody because they would make a living even if there were no poor people. What would a social worker do if there were no poor people?" When a bitter and prolonged strike afflicted the Department of Welfare in the winter of 1964-65,

MFY workers and clients from Stanton Street demonstrated in support of the Welfare workers, to signify that their complaints were directed against laws and policies, not against the personnel of the welfare system.

Reactions to Advocacy

By the summer of 1963, MFY had established three other neighborhood centers along the Lower East Side. The agency's supervisory staff decided to solicit even more clients by publicizing its services through handbills, posters, and mass meetings. Some workers had also begun to seek out clients in distress, among other ways by reading newspaper accounts in the Spanish-language press. The strategy of the centers was now fixed. They were given a definite set of priorities for intervention with city agencies, of which Welfare was to be the preeminent target. This increasing attention to advocacy tactics meant that the workers had to contend with increasing antagonism from the Welfare Department. The Commissioner was angered, for example, by the threats of aggressive court action against Welfare. The lower-echelon functionaries were angered by their harassment by MFY and would often respond with open hostility to calls from Stanton Street employees. "When I go to Welfare," one Stanton Street worker declared, "I don't wait around for the stall. If I don't get treated with respect, I start hollering for the supervisor." Another worker said: "Any way you cut it, they are the enemy." Perhaps this explains what one Welfare worker meant when she described MFY's staff as "rude, angry, and non-professional." Some MFY workers were also accused of lacking information about public-welfare policies in taking on their advocacy positions. But, since many Stanton Street workers were former Welfare employees, it seems more reasonable to suppose that they were merely placing more liberal interpretations upon existing Welfare regulations. Where, for example, the Welfare investigator might cite a client's improvidence as justification for not making an additional grant, the Stanton Street worker would insist upon the client's legal right to such funds, regardless of his supposed characterological defects.

One Welfare employee with more than thirty years in the Department was critical of the MFY policy of giving money to people on some occasions rather than forcing Welfare to make these payments. However, she was generally appreciative of MFY's efforts. "If we were doing our job," she said, "you wouldn't need any neighborhood centers. And if there were more neighborhood centers like this in the city of New York," she added, "we might have to begin to do a better job. . . . I learned what my investigators were doing with some clients from the neighborhood service center. I might never have known otherwise." When this same person subsequently retired from the Department of Welfare, she was hired as a consultant by MFY to help cut through the knotty complex of rules and regulations by which people on Stanton Street were being governed. As one Stanton Street employee put the matter: "What this proves to me is that you have got to work thirty years in the Department to be able to get people what they are entitled to . . . and they expect people to just walk in and apply. . . ."

Such comments reflected an increasing hostility between Welfare and the workers on Stanton Street. But the workers also began to exhibit hostility and impatience toward their clients, who by now had transferred some of their previous dependency on Welfare to the storefront on Stanton Street. "Can't these people do anything for themselves?" was frequently heard among the workers. Many of them developed a resentment against the need to perform the same rudimentary "nonprofessional" services on behalf of their clients over and over again. Some of the clients also were restless, partly as a result of their activities in MFY's various social-action programs. The program heads, Barr and Kreisler, began to wonder whether, if the clients were given support and encouragement, they could begin to take over some of the burden of dealing with Welfare. If fifty clients all needed the same items of clothing, they reasoned, it might be more effective to make one request on behalf of fifty rather than fifty individual requests. They reasoned, too, that this strategy might coerce Welfare into making certain kinds of grants more automatic, or, rather, less discretionary. "It got so," Kreisler points out, "that we just thought there were some things which could be done by a group of clients and some things which could be done better by worker-advocates. We didn't know how far to go. It was like the civil-rights thing, I guess. We were willing to try. . . ."

And so it was, after three years, that the center on Stanton Street decided to hire a "community organizer" to bring together people in the neighborhood around their most commonly shared interest—their problem with public welfare.

Organizing on Stanton Street

Stanton Street people spend the hot summer months worrying about the cold months ahead. They know that if they don't begin then to bother their Welfare workers about winter clothing for themselves and their children, their requests may not be fulfilled in time—if ever. In the late summer of 1965, they came to make their usual requests to the advocates at 199 Stanton Street. Would the workers talk to Welfare? To their surprise they were advised this year to go to a storefront next door and speak to the Committee of Welfare Families.

The Committee of Welfare Families was hardly more than a name at the time, although the concept of social action was certainly not novel to MFY or to the people on Stanton Street. Many of the initial cadre had already participated in rent strikes and civil-rights demonstrations, but whereas these were activities of short duration, the Committee hoped to be a permanent organization. In addition to a few of the local women who had been active previously, there was an MFY attorney and social-work organizer, Ezra Birnbaum.

Clients who went next door to see the Committee were told that the group intended to bring together Negroes and Puerto Ricans who had common problems with Welfare. Each client was advised to make a survey of her family's winter-clothing needs and bring it to the Committee, which would attempt to act as the bargaining agent for all of them. Within a month over 90 families had agreed to the procedure, and the first tentative strategies were proposed.

"We chose the winter-clothing issue," Birnbaum has said, "because it was something that genuinely concerned people, because they had so many small children, and because the injustice was so blatant. Many people hadn't gotten coats in six or seven years. Here was an issue we could organize around that would genuinely benefit people. . . ."

The winter-clothing issue also went to the heart of the perennially nagging question of what constituted a Welfare entitlement. Every Welfare family is budgeted a very small sum semimonthly with which to augment clothing supplies. Invariably these sums are used for ordinary living expenses because grants for food and other necessities are so low. In addition, hearsay had it that the Department's policy was to allow special winter-clothing grants of approximately $150 a year per family,[2] but these grants were usually not given out unless requested and, even then, the investigators would often allot less than the full amount. In October 1965, individual investigators at all the Welfare centers serving residents of the MFY area began to receive neat, concise letters from their clients. It was clear that they had all been prepared by one agency and mailed out simultaneously, but, since they were written as individual requests, it was not yet clear to Welfare what was behind this sudden flurry. The letters read:

> I would like to request winter clothing for my children and myself. I would appreciate it if you would grant this request as quickly as possible, as the weather is cold at this time. My family is in need of the following items of winter clothing:

There followed itemized requests for coats, children's snowsuits, coveralls, boots, scarves, woolen skirts. All these requests had been certified by the Committee as being in accord with stated Welfare policies. When, after a few weeks, the Welfare investigators did not reply, a follow-up letter was sent, with copies to supervisory personnel at Welfare. When this effort also netted scant results, the Committee as a group announced itself to the Acting Commissioner of Welfare:

> Dear Commissioner:
>
> We, as members of the Committee of Welfare Families of the Lower East Side, have written letters to our investigators requesting winter clothing. Our members have already sent 70 individual letters to four Welfare Centers: Lower Manhattan, Gramercy, Non-Residence, and Yorkville. The first 21 letters were mailed between October 12th and October 15th. Of these, only 9 have received any money at all, and none of these 9 have been given enough money to keep their families warm this winter. *More important, the other 12 families have received no money at all!*
>
> We feel that we are being neglected—especially since many of

[2] In 1965, the Department actually expended a mere $40 per person per year for special grants (including both heavy clothing and household furnishings).

our investigators haven't even been in touch with us to find out about the seriousness of the situation.

Winter is here; our children are cold. Many of us are unable to keep clinic appointments because we do not have proper clothing. Many of our children have caught colds which can lead to other serious illnesses. Some of our children haven't been to school since the weather turned cold.

In most years, many of us have had to wait until December, January, or even later to buy our winter clothing. This year, we're not willing to wait that long and see our children have to wear thin summer clothing when it gets below freezing. That is why we asked Mobilization for Youth to help us this year.

Commissioner, we feel we have waited long enough to receive our winter clothing. Now we, the total membership of the Committee of Welfare Families of the Lower East Side, request an appointment with you on behalf of our 21 members whose letters were mailed three weeks ago. We need your help in securing winter clothing for all our members before the weather gets any colder.

We request that our meeting with you be held within the next three days.

> Sincerely,
> THE COMMITTEE OF WELFARE FAMILIES
> OF THE LOWER EAST SIDE

When, after three days, the Commissioner did not respond to this letter, the Committee sent him a telegram:

You received letter from us on Monday November 15 requesting meeting with you to discuss our members needs for winter clothing stop We received no reply stop Our children are cold winter is here stop Our investigators have not answered our letters or have not given us enough money to keep children warm stop We need your help before weather gets colder stop We will be at your office to meet with you Tuesday November 23 1:30 P.M.

That very same day the Commissioner replied by telegram (after attempting to telephone) that he would be able to meet with the Committee on Friday, November 26, and that in the meantime he would try to get information on each of the cases specified in the Committee's original letter.

The November 26 meeting was, in the Commissioner's own words, the first between a Welfare commissioner and a New

York City client group in over thirty years. All of the Welfare recipients had been well briefed by Birnbaum on what they should say to the Commissioner, but protest proved unnecessary. The Commissioner quickly agreed that all Committee members who were entitled to winter clothing would receive it, and he acknowledged the bargaining status of the Committee by outlining a formal grievance procedure. Clients were to continue to make their requests either by mail or in person through their workers at the various Welfare centers. The Commissioner would instruct all workers to acknowledge the receipt of such requests immediately and in writing. If, within ten days, no reply was received to an individual client's request, the Committee was free to contact predesignated liaison personnel at each of the Welfare centers serving the neighborhood, who would be empowered to act to correct their grievances.

The hard-pressed members of the Committee of Welfare Families were quick to interpret their meeting with the Commissioner as a victory. By agreeing to consult with them as a group about their needs, he had implicitly recognized, for perhaps the first time in their careers as Welfare clients, that they had a legitimate interest in helping to determine the rules of their dependency. In the days that followed, many of these families received checks from the Department of Welfare for winter clothing. Further meetings were arranged with the designated liaison personnel at the various Welfare centers to discuss bargaining procedures. The women took a real delight in the fact that they could dictate which and how many of their number could be in attendance at these formal procedures. Thus, when the Department tried to insist that only members of the Committee could meet with Welfare officials, the women held firm in their insistence that the Committee could designate anybody it chose to represent it at these meetings, and the Department of Welfare was forced to give in on this point. The women also decided to take up other pressing issues. For example, they asked that all members request budgets from their investigators and bring them to the Committee for scrutiny. The Committee also elected officers and designated subcommittees to investigate new problem areas having to do with their welfare dependency. The leadership attended briefing sessions with MFY attorneys in an effort to acquire a better understanding of their legal rights. Gradually, as the natural leadership potentials of some of the women emerged more clearly, MFY's paid organizer began to function more as an adviser than as a leader. One of the women gave this explanation for the process: "Some of us know we are going to be on Welfare the rest of our lives. They know it and we know it. So it's about time we started acting like human beings."

But, though the first victory had encouraged hope and ambition, the fact was that the Department had agreed only to allow the Committee to function more efficiently. It had agreed that there was a need for better service, but it was not yet willing to concede that many of its policies interfered with service. After the November 26 meeting, the Commissioner wrote:

> It is accepted Department practice, and it is also my firm conviction, as I expressed it at the meeting, that investigators should visit families when requests for clothing needs are to be considered in order that a family can fully discuss its clothing needs and so that grants can be made on a realistic basis.

It was as a consequence of such visits, however, that many Stanton Street families came to be punished. The Commissioner also affirmed that:

> . . . State law pertaining to confidentiality of records does not permit the social situation of one recipient to be discussed with another recipient even though he may be a group representative.

In fact, it is the confidentiality policy that enables Welfare workers to make dependency so humiliating, for clients have no effective way of putting forth claims and demands. The Commissioner also insisted that the Committee undertake a time-consuming procedure to pursue its grievances. And even after the meetings with Committee members in November and December, the Department remained reluctant to supply the Committee with its grant schedules so that members could more accurately determine their entitlements.

At this writing, it is presumed that the Committee of Welfare Families will grow and form alliances with client groups and other community organizations elsewhere in the city to pressure legislators and administrators to liberalize Welfare regulations. Through the expertise of social workers and attorneys, it is also hoped that the Committee will help to isolate and dramatize welfare issues such as underbudgeting and denial of winter-clothing and utilities allowances—issues which have a relevance for all who are dependent. It is also presumed that the Committee will be a useful mechanism through which welfare recipients can begin to articulate their grievances and acquire the necessary sophistication to defend their rights. But, unless the economic situation for people on Stanton Street changes significantly in the years to come, it seems likely that there will always be dependency and the need for professionals who can deal, if necessary, on a case-by-case basis with the arbitrary power vested in functionaries of the welfare state. Many of the women on Stanton Street are all too aware of this. As one put it, "We are only as strong as you've let us be. If you went away, things could change tomorrow." For the unemployed or underemployed men who have still not been organized, Stanton Street's workers have much to do in beginning to provide them with the entitlements which they have thus far been denied. "It wouldn't be so bad living here," one of these men told us, "if you were rich. We're not rich. All we have is the Welfare. That means freezing in the winter and boiling in the summer. It means living on credit when we can't afford it. It means lying. It means doing without. . . . When I come home in the evening my wife has been at Bellevue which is uptown and maybe at Church Street, all the way across town, and I'm wondering where she got the money for the carfare. . . ."

The storefront on Stanton Street has been in existence a little less than four years. It is still too early to evaluate its permanent contribution to life in the community. Its powers have been limited. It has not been able yet to change substantially the terms of economic dependency, although the consensus among most legislators and their constituents is that such dependency is to be discouraged and abhorred. The center set out to legitimize the dependencies of those who were in fact dependent. This has meant for the people of Stanton Street more generous allowances and a few comforts. Many more people from Stanton Street are on welfare than four years ago. The storefront's clients are better clothed, better housed, and better fed than they were four years ago. Many now have telephones and quite a few washing machines and television sets. Are they better people? Are they worse? Such questions are supremely irrelevant. For if they are not better for their improved economic circumstances, the society is better for their actions against it. Democracy cannot be said to exist where government is allowed to oppress its citizens so blatantly.[3]

[3] The public welfare system—one of the most barbarous government programs—ought to be abolished, and a guaranteed minimum income program substituted. For a discussion of a strategy to generate the political pressure required to secure these changes, see Richard A. Cloward and Frances Fox Piven, "The Weight of the Poor: A Strategy to End Poverty," *The Nation*, May 2, 1966. The article points to a vast discrepancy between the benefits to which people are entitled under public welfare programs and those which they actually receive. But perceptions of the public welfare system are so conditioned by invidious attitudes toward financial dependency that this fact is unrecognized. It is well known, for example, that nearly 8,000,000 persons (half of them white) now subsist on welfare, although it is not known that for every person on the rolls, at least one more probably meets existing criteria of eligibility but is not obtaining benefits. In a society which is self-righteously oriented toward getting people *off* the welfare rolls, therefore, no one has realized how profound a crisis could be precipitated by a massive drive to recruit the poor *onto* the rolls. A widespread campaign by civil rights forces to register the eligible poor for welfare aid and to help existing recipients to press for full benefits would produce bureaucratic crises in welfare agencies and fiscal crises in local and state governments. A series of such disruptions in a number of large cities would, it is argued, impel federal action to abolish public welfare and to end poverty by a new program to redistribute income, for these crises would deepen existing divisions among elements in the big-city Democratic coalition—the remaining white middle class, the white working-class ethnics, and the growing minority poor. To avoid a further weakening of that historic coalition, a national Democratic administration would be under pressure to put forward a federal solution to poverty which overrides local welfare failures, local class and racial conflicts, and local revenue dilemmas. In the internal disruption of local bureaucratic practices, in the furor over public-welfare poverty, and in the collapse of current financing arrangements, powerful forces can be generated for major economic reforms at the national level.

Part Six

THE LAW AND SOCIAL ACTION

CHAPTER SEVENTEEN

Democracy and Public Policy*

by Marvin E. Larson

I would like to talk a bit about democracy. I have an abiding conviction that democratic principle is extremely important to all of us—far more important than most of us appreciate. As a state welfare director, I have an abiding conviction that my program is a valid and binding commitment of a democratic society. Indeed, I have an abiding conviction that a much better welfare program than mine is the valid and binding commitment of a democratic society.

I have often heard it said that grass-roots government is democratic government—that it is most undemocratic for a state or for the federal government to attempt to modify what a county or a city wants to do in public welfare. I am dismayed at this immature concept, which seems to relate solely to who has the authority rather than to the responsibility of local units for good programs. It seems to me that a local unit of government owes a fealty to its state and to its national government, and that what it does to and for the people in its area is done to and for citizens of the United States, and therefore in the national interest. I doubt that a local unit of government should be able to deprive needy people of an adequate opportunity—that local units should be able to deprive children of education and training.

I am dismayed, too, at the comment that the essence of democracy is states' rights. Certainly state government is important. But I believe that each state owes allegiance to the nation as a whole, and that what a state does for the people within it is indeed in the national interest.

* Excerpted from a speech delivered at a conference of the American Public Welfare Association, Dec. 5, 1963, and later, in essence, before the Mobilization for Youth Legal Services Unit. No attempt has been made to alter the informality of the original.

Most of us think of democracy as "government of the people, by the people, and for the people." Since each of us is one of the people, it is pretty easy to think of democracy as government of people like me, by people like me, and for people like me. And this might leave out quite a few people.

Some of us think of democracy as government by popular sovereignty, as opposed to government by a monarch or a dictator, and slip into a false premise that the will of the people should be or is supreme in a democracy—in other words, that democracy is simply the rule of the majority of our people. This, too, is a false premise, because in a democracy mob rule may not have its way, and individuals are protected against danger stemming from the hostility of the general population—even from the hostility of a majority of the general population.

What, then, is democracy? Democracy is government by high moral principle, applicable to all. This means that it may not be violated by the President himself, nor by Congress, nor by any state—indeed, it may not be violated by a majority of the people themselves. This moral principle is set down in the Constitution and its interpretations by the courts. Popular sovereignty is not the essence of democracy—rather, it is the awful commitment of democracy, representing the principle that government should be with the consent of the governed. To retain the consent of the governed we need to provide for the welfare of all the people—not just for the people like me.

Moral principle in government is not an abstraction. Quite the contrary—it is a very personal thing. It relates in a very real way to each and every one of us; to the danger there is for each of us without morality, and to the dignity of our persons.

To me, as a citizen and as a lawyer, the Fourteenth Amendment stands as a perfect and beautiful statement of high moral principle for state government. The Fourteenth Amendment is the most important constitutional provision in relation to civil rights. All persons who administer public welfare should know it:

> All persons born or naturalized in the United States and subject to the jurisdiction thereof are citizens of the United States and of the state wherein they reside. No state shall make or enforce any law which will abridge the privileges or immunities of citizens of the United States; nor shall any state deprive any person of life, liberty or property without due process of law nor deny to any person within its jurisdiction protection of the law.

You will notice that the Fourteenth Amendment is a command to the state governments. It prohibits any state from depriving any citizen of his natural rights. It prohibits any state from taking life, liberty, or property without due process of law. Due process includes notice, the right to be heard, a fair hearing, compensation, and so on.

The equal-protection-of-the-law provision has been interpreted by the Supreme Court of the United States to require states in their laws to provide equal treatment, equal opportunity, and equal privilege as well as equal protection. It stands as a constitutional prohibition against discrimination by any of the states. It requires that if a state provides a welfare program, it must be equal and uniform throughout the state for all persons in need. Throughout the nation there are complaints about state control of local administration of welfare programs, and this is blamed on the federal law. But the federal law does no more than require what is already required by decent moral principle, and by the Fourteenth Amendment, which is to provide a uniform welfare program throughout each state for equal protection of the law.

When we speak of public welfare, of public assistance, we are really talking about the right to life—the right of an American citizen to live and not to die because of starvation or lack of housing, clothing, or medical care. This, in this enormously wealthy country of ours, with its enormous surplus of food, is precisely what public welfare means to a great many of our citizens—it means the right to life, the right not to die, the right not to be a beggar.

How, then, are we applying the principles of the Fourteenth Amendment to the very right to live? How are we applying the equal-protection clause, which means equal privilege and equal treatment under the law?

Let me repeat the first sentence of the Amendment. It reads: "All persons born or naturalized in the United States and subject to the jurisdiction thereof are citizens of the United States and of the state wherein they reside." It does not say "citizens of the United States and of the state wherein they have resided five out of the last nine years and the last year continuously."

I am sure there is no difference in the need, in the hunger, in the coldness and suffering of a citizen of the United States who has been a resident of the state for the last year continuously and for four years and eleven months out of the last nine years, and one who was strong enough to stick it out for the whole five years. Surely residence laws are unconstitutional, and surely residence laws violate high moral principle.

I think another violation of the Fourteenth Amendment, another denial of the civil rights of clients, another violation of high moral principle is the maximum grant. I doubt if any court in America could figure out the difference between the food and clothing needs of a child with one brother or sister and the food and clothing needs of a child with a dozen brothers and sisters. Let me salute the Polk County (Iowa) District Court and the Supreme Court of Iowa, which found that a legislatively imposed maximum was unconstitutional, on the ground that a child in a big family needs as much food as a child in a small family.

The case is *Collins* v. *State Board of Social Welfare*, a 1957 decision. I like the language of the district court in the statement of its findings of fact and in its decision:

> The case presents a sad picture indeed. Plaintiff and her husband have six children ranging in age from fifteen to five years. Plaintiff is unable to work due to a lung disease. She has lost 26 pounds during the past year. A protein diet has been prescribed for her but no funds are available for purchase of the necessary items of food. The husband has bursitis, prostate trouble, bone disease in his left arm and rectal bleeding. He cannot work.
>
> The eldest child is bright but unable to attend school for lack of funds. The other children are put to considerable embarrassment and disadvantage in school activity because of their cast-off clothing and other effects of poverty. The entire family is without needed medical and dental care and proper clothing and diet. They have no money, car, or other property of any kind save a few sticks of old furniture and the clothing on their backs.
>
> Under the program of Aid to Dependent Children the board has computed the minimum sum necessary to provide a reasonable subsistence compatible with decency and health. On this basis the budget for the Collins family came to $291.50 per month until June 1, 1955. The family was able to subsist on this amount. On that date the budget was recomputed at $277.89 per month. Then, as a result of a proviso in the appropriation act that no family should receive more than $175.00, their budget

was cut to that figure, which is the amount they presently receive.

It is the latter reduction which placed the family in its present plight. The family exists on the verge of starvation, seeking a little here and a little there from some charitable soul or the Salvation Army, and sinking gradually lower.

On this finding of facts, it should not require a constitutional provision to establish the utter immorality and stupidity of a maximum grant, even if the maximum is set at an amount that some employers consider an adequate wage.

The court in its decision said:

> The distinction which the legislature has taken between families under $175 and those which are over is not real, it is arbitrary. It is a distinction without a difference. The size of the two families is not the same, but the need of each member is not different.
>
> They suffer the same hardships, entertain the same hopes, are stirred by similar ambitions, and are faced with similar economic problems. It is as though the legislature had written, "Children in small families shall receive their full needs. Others shall receive two thirds."

The court decreed:

> That part of Section 4, Chapter 6, Iowa Laws 1955, as follows: "provided, however, that no family shall receive a grant hereunder in excess of $175 per month" is unconstitutional and of no effect.

In this case, Mr. Collins could not be employed because he was seriously ill. As valid a reason for unemployment would have been the unavailability of a job within his skill and capacity. His family would have been in precisely the same situation—"and sinking gradually lower," as the trial court put it—regardless of the reason for his unemployment. I have difficulty understanding that children must starve if their father can't get a job, but if he runs off or is crippled, then they can be fed. It seems to me that all children have precisely the same needs for food, clothing, housing, and education and that we as a nation have the same needs for the proper physical and intellectual nourishing of these children of unemployed parents—future citizens too, may I remind you. Yet look at the timid and slow approach Congress has taken, especially in the face of national and increasing unemployment. Look at the states, leaving these children to the contemptuous program of locally administered general assistance —in some cases leaving them to virtually no program and, except for the states that have adopted AFDC of unemployed parents, leaving them to inadequate state general-assistance programs. It seems to me that a logical extension of the Iowa case would be to say that high moral principle and the Constitution dictate that all children in need are entitled to assistance in an equal and uniform degree.

Rent maximums also represent a violation of the equal-protection clause. When a county or state department of social welfare sets a maximum above which it will not provide money for rent, and when the family on assistance (indeed, even the welfare department itself) cannot find housing for the family at this amount, then the family must pay rent above the maximum by taking funds from its food and clothing allowance. The rent maximum especially hurts families with many children, who require large and hard-to-find houses or apartments. These children have less food and clothing than the children of families who find housing within the maximum. In any case, rent maximums ensure inadequate housing for all families on assistance.

Percentage payments of need I suppose do represent equal protection of the law. Percentage payments violate high moral principle only in the sense that everyone in need is equally and uniformly deprived of the right to life. They are uniformly hungry. And this in the wealthiest nation in the world, a nation that pays millions of dollars daily for the storage of surplus food.

In the public-assistance program we see serious evidences of a basic retreat from fundamental democratic principles, from fundamental constitutional guarantees, and from basic high moral principle. I am talking now about the methods used by some investigative units to invade the privacy of the homes of some of our citizens.

Here, suddenly, we have precisely the same violation of basic human rights which we have deplored in authoritarian states. Can it be that constitutional principles apply to those of us who violate the law, but not to those of us who, because of matters entirely beyond our control, are hungry and cold? We need to stop to examine, not only our commitments as members of a democratic society, but also our commitments as members of a religious society.[1]

God provides us with rewards and punishments—with pleasure and pain. The Lord's greatest reward, his greatest pleasure for us, is the parent–child relationship. Nothing else equals the bringing up of an adult child with our values, who still communicates with us, and who carries on with his or her own family the destiny of our tribe, race, and nation. The Lord provides no greater pain or punishment than for a person to have a child and then to lose this child, to have it be hurt or go wrong. The parent–child relationship is a sacred thing, a basic right in society.

The law has done a little to recognize this fact, by providing safeguards in juvenile proceedings. The law has also ignored it by permitting "suitable home" provisions in public-assistance laws, which make it possible for babies to be starved because parental conduct unrelated to child care makes the family ineligible for funds. Under the Louisiana law, for example, which was passed in 1960, a child, in order to be eligible for Aid to Dependent Children, must be living in a "suitable home." According to the provisions, a home was not considered suitable in which parents and other relatives of the child were living together without being legally married. Assistance was terminated to a home in which the mother gave birth to an illegitimate child, and it could not be reinstated unless the mother produced proof—satisfactory to the parish board of public welfare—that she had ceased illicit relationships and was maintaining a suitable home. Many innocent children were removed from the rolls. Secretary Arthur S. Flemming ruled that Louisiana was out of conformity with the federal requirement of equal and uniform treatment of people in order to qualify for federal funds. We should surely salute the federal agency for its "Flemming rule" in relation to the Louisiana suitable-home law. The fact remains, however, that the Flemming ruling merely withholds federal participation from a state that violates fundamental moral princi-

[1] Let me refer you to two articles prepared by Charles A. Reich, associate professor at the Yale Law School, on the constitutionality of these kinds of activities, "Searching Homes of Public Assistance Recipients, The Issues Under the Social Security Act," *Social Service Review*, Vol. 37 (September 1963), pp. 328 ff.; and "Midnight Welfare Searches and the Social Security Act," *Yale Law Journal*, Vol. 72 (June 1963), pp. 1347, 1359-60.

ple. I am wondering if democracy does not need a stronger moral enforcement than the withholding of money, which, after all, can only result in further deprivation and hardship for some of the citizens of the United States.

Perhaps the dirtiest violation of the civil rights of clients occurs in some agencies in connection with intake. The stall, the delay, the referral to other agencies, the referral to nonexistent employment—all are deprivations of the statutory and constitutional rights of United States citizens. The casting upon the applicant of the burden of proof—"We can't do anything unless you show us you are eligible"—amounts to the same thing. This type of intake policy—and I am afraid it is not infrequent, and I am more afraid it has popular approval—is a systematic robbing of the poor. Any other larceny would be grounds for prosecution—certainly it would constitute grounds for dismissal which would be sustained by the state civil service board. But how many civil-service dismissals on this ground have you heard about?[2]

I have confined myself thus far to the client's rights in relation to financial assistance. These rights have been so poorly dealt with that I hardly dare talk of his other rights. But I think we must look at the whole picture. Surely the right to life means more than the right not to starve to death. There must be a right to some emotional security and to some normal satisfaction —some outlet for a creative urge, and hence something interesting and rewarding to do. Why, indeed, when our economic and social institutions fail some of our citizens, should they not have the right to social, medical, educational, and rehabilitative services? I think they should, and that such services may not for long be optional with the states.

On the matter of public-welfare policy, I have pointed out that we have not done a very good job of protecting the rights of clients. We also have done a poor job of protecting the rights of the general public. I think America is entitled to a welfare program that is constitutional, that abides by high moral princi-

---

[2] I could give numerous other examples of basic violations of civil rights in our public-assistance programs. I hope you will read the mimeographed memorandum of the National Social Welfare Assembly, by Elizabeth Wickenden, called *Poverty and the Law—The Constitutional Rights of Assistance Recipients* (Feb. 25, 1963), and *The Right to Life*, by the late A. Delafield Smith (Chapel Hill, N.C.: University of North Carolina Press, 1955).

ple, and that meets the needs of people for the right to life. This we do not have. We have residence laws, maximum grants, suitable-home laws, and restrictive administration in our welfare programs, all designed to deny some of our citizens the right to life. We have welfare programs which include practically no services at all.

The American public's right to a decent welfare program is founded upon more than abstract principle. Its right to a decent welfare program is founded upon that sacred institution, the taxpayer's dollar. Poor welfare programs reflect the added cost in hidden places, but places that are very real and very costly— in perpetuated dependency, in general hospitals and medical services, in nursing homes, in mental institutions, in penal institutions, to mention just a few. Think of the appalling and horrible waste involved in the Collins family, which got caught in the Iowa maximum-grant law.

I have mentioned the money value. The shocking waste in human values is even more apparent. And here we get to the fundamental reason for the American public's right to a decent welfare program. It was for the preservation of human values that our democratic nation was founded, and only by the preservation of human values can it survive. I mentioned earlier that popular sovereignty was the awful commitment of democracy. If too many people must go without their reasonable expectations being met in the most affluent society in the world, at least some of these people are bound to be attracted by nondemocratic forces.

It has recently been estimated that in these wealthy United States, there are 32 million people living in poverty. This is something a democracy simply cannot afford.

You and I have a very real responsibility to our nation. Our responsibility is to defend the poor, and to do it with courage and conviction. Public-welfare administration has too frequently and too long been a matter of mealy-mouthed appeasement and apology. But the extreme rightist, the ignorant, and those who are thoughtlessly selfish cannot be appeased. Everyone who administers public welfare, in the federal, state, and county agencies, stands on an important outpost for the preservation of democracy and for the preservation of our nation as we know it. I hope we all develop a little more knowledge—and, above all, a little more courage.

CHAPTER EIGHTEEN

Social Welfare and Social Justice*

by CHARLES F. GROSSER and EDWARD V. SPARER

The residents of the inner-city slum live at the vortex of the complex industrial metropolis, where they daily confront the social issues debated in the public press and professional journals. Technological unemployment, deteriorating housing, discrimination, juvenile delinquency, proliferating drug use, and a spiraling crime rate are part of the life of the slum family.[1] It hardly needs to be noted that few such families are prepared to deal with these manifestations of social pathology.

Coping with city slum life has many legal ramifications. It brings the slum dweller into frequent contact with public agencies created by legislative action, such as housing authorities and welfare departments, as well as with public agencies charged with responsibility for upholding the law, such as the police and the courts. As tenants, complainants, defendants, suspects, welfare recipients, public-housing residents, receivers of unemployment-insurance benefits, taxpayers, litigants in Workmen's Compensation cases, and holders of installment-buying contracts, the youth and adults of the inner-city slum constantly interact with the legal establishment.

Life has conditioned the poor to regard the law as an instrument of the privileged which is usually used against them. The poor have, in fact, often been the recipients of punitive rather than equal justice. Furthermore, they are seriously disadvantaged in both the quantity and the quality of legal representation available to them.[2] A study recently completed by Columbia

---

* Adapted from *Social Work*, January 1966. Reproduced with permission of the National Association of Social Workers.

[1] Cf. Gertrude Samuels, "A Peace Corps for Our Own Bleak Areas," *New York Times Magazine*, Nov. 23, 1962; A. Schoen, "Problems in A.D.C. Programs," *Social Work*, Vol. 2 (April 1960); Conference on Economic Progress, *Poverty and Deprivation in the United States*: Washington, D.C., 1962.

[2] Robert F. Kennedy, "The Indigent Defendant," excerpts from an address to the American Bar Association House of Delegates, San Francisco, Calif., Aug. 6, 1962, *Legal Aid Briefcase*, Col. 21, No. 1, Oct. 1962, p. 20.

University's Bureau of Applied Social Research, for example, found that fewer than 5 per cent of the lawyers practicing in New York City had clients whose median income was less than $5,000, whereas more than 60 per cent had clients whose median income exceeded $10,000.[3] Small wonder that impoverished persons, in their continuous contact with the legal establishment, tend to react with defensiveness, caution, and recalcitrance. Either they must attempt to "con" the establishment so as to avoid being punished or forced to comply, or they must resign themselves to their fate, taking no recourse in the various legal alternatives available to them.

What little attention has been given to the legal disadvantages of impoverished persons has focused in the main upon law enforcement. The adverse position resultant from lack of funds for counsel, bail, pretrial investigations, and appeal has been extensively noted. Remedies to ameliorate the situation have also been limited largely to enforcement issues. Thus, publicly funded public-defender offices, increasingly advanced as a solution, generally represent only the accused and accept only criminal cases. Privately funded legal-aid organizations, many of which handle both criminal and certain civil cases, tend to emphasize the former and sharply circumscribe their representation of the poor man as plaintiff. Even the most highly developed legal-aid organizations rarely involve themselves in what may well be the most significant legal need of the poor—clarification of their relationship to welfare, housing, unemployment, and other agencies created in connection with a host of new legal rights.

It is to this need that this paper is addressed. The legal ramifications of the engagement of low-income people with government bureaucracy have been largely ignored; yet the principal arena of the poor man's interaction with the legal establishment is no longer the courtroom (criminal or otherwise) but the anteroom of a city, state, or federal agency, as he awaits a determination of vital significance to him and his family. One professor of jurisprudence put the matter as follows:

> The new expectations progressively brought into existence by the welfare state must be thought of not as privileges to be dispensed unequally or by arbitrary fiat of government officials but

[3] *New York Times*, April 17, 1964.

as substantial rights in the assertion of which the claimant is entitled to an effective remedy, a fair procedure, and a reasoned decision. Anything short of this leaves one man subject in his essential interests to the arbitrary will of another man who happens to partake of public power; and that kind of unequal and demeaning encounter is repugnant to every sense of the rule of law.[4]

Social work has long held that the provision of services to citizens, when it is stipulated by specific legislation, is a matter of right, not a "charity" or a gratuitous privilege. When these services are not provided as stipulated, the service agency or its administrative staff has abrogated the rights of the client and is guilty of subverting the intent of the law, if not of violating the letter. Redressing grievances of this kind cannot be a matter of noblesse on the part of the public agency.

Neither law nor social work, the professions most directly concerned, has devoted itself to this issue. The rights of clients to public services as a matter of inherent social justice, although articulated by some social-policy planners,[5] have been observed more in the breach than in the reality.

To illustrate both the need for a definition of the rights of those involved and a means of protecting these rights, we might choose the unemployment-insurance programs, old-age assistance, public-housing programs and private-housing protection, or various education efforts. We are focusing here on the welfare-relief program, as perhaps the most extreme example.

Some of the most flagrant violations of the civil rights of clients, according to the director of the Kansas State Department of Social Welfare, occur in connection with intake practices which have the effect of turning away the poor.[6] Social

[4] Harry W. Jones, "The Rule of Law and the Welfare State," *Columbia Law Review*, Vol. 58, p. 143.

[5] Cf. Neva L. Itzin, "The Right to Life, Subsistence and the Social Services," *Social Work*, Vol. 3, No. 4 (Oct. 1958), p. 4; and A. J. Altmeyer, "Some Assumptions and Objectives in Social Security," in William Haber and Wilber Cohen (eds.), *Social Security: Programs, Problems, and Policies* (Homewood, Ill.: Richard D. Irwin, 1960), pp. 6-7. See also J. Douglas Brown, "The American Philosophy of Social Insurance," *idem.*, p. 66; and Charles I. Schottland, "Basic Characteristics of OASDI," *idem.*, p. 143.

[6] Marvin E. Larson, "Public Welfare and Public Policy," *APWA Round Table*, December 5, 1963; reprinted above, pp. 283-91, as "Democracy and Public Policy."

workers who are outside the public-welfare system but in contact with public-welfare clients report a widespread tendency to ignore schedules relating to the amount of assistance due welfare recipients. There seem to be no observable criteria for granting significantly different amounts in identical situations. A wide range of discretion exists within welfare departments, since normative guidelines and standards are often absent, and the basis of decisions made by the public-welfare agencies is rarely questioned.[7]

One means of reducing arbitrary decision-making is through an appeals procedure. However, "fair hearings," although guaranteed by federal law to applicants who are denied assistance, are infrequently utilized. Prospective recipients are often unaware of the procedure, and regulations require a degree of sophistication which discourage its use. Furthermore, unless the client has access in his appeal to legal assistance which is independent of control by the government agency with which he is in contention, no remedy to arbitrary decision-making can be wholly effective.

The price of welfare assistance frequently is the imposition of higher moral standards on welfare clients than on the population at large. Professor Charles Reich, of the Yale Law School, contends that the practice of paying unannounced visits to the homes of welfare recipients at odd hours of the night and morning, to gather evidence of immoral conduct or unreported sources of income, violates the Fourth Amendment, even where the relief client has apparently given the welfare agent permission to enter the house.[8]

Mr. Larson has also expressed the judgment that welfare laws requiring state residence for eligibility violate the United States Constitution.[9] Whatever the merits of his opinion, it is significant that, in the many states with residence laws, only one old and rather dubious case[10] has been developed to test the proposition.

[7] Alan Keith-Lucas, *Decisions About People in Need* (Chapel Hill, N.C.: University of North Carolina Press, 1957).

[8] Charles Reich, "Midnight Welfare Searches and the Social Security Act," *Yale Law Journal*, Vol. 72 (June 1963), pp. 1347, 1359-60.

[9] Larson, *op. cit.* See also Elizabeth Wickenden: *Poverty and the Law: The Constitutional Rights of Assistance Recipients*, National Social Welfare Assembly, Feb. 25, 1963.

[10] People ex rel. *Heydenreich* v. *Lyons* 374 Ill. 557, 30 N.E. 2d 46 (1940).

The New York State "Welfare Abuses" Law offers a further illustration of the need to define the rights of clients who receive welfare assistance. The law, an attempted compromise between political demands for residence requirements and contrary demands from humanitarian organizations, provides that assistance shall be denied to persons coming to New York State for the purpose of receiving relief although nonresidents coming for other purposes are entitled to aid. When an application for assistance is rejected, temporary emergency relief is a stipulated requirement of the law. Although certain criteria are specified by which to assess the applicant's motivation in coming to the state, there is much that is vague. The law does not define "temporary" in regard to emergency relief, nor does it define "emergency" itself. There is reason to believe that the law may be impossible to administer. As a consequence, we may assume that decisions will depend upon the whims of officials or the political pressures upon them. Harsh and arbitrary interpretations are likely to be common.

The violations of the rights of welfare (and other) clients do not stem from character defects or malicious intent on the part of welfare officials. Obviously, any large bureaucracy will include workers of varying convictions and competencies. Inadequate salaries, overburdened workloads, and thankless tasks result in unusual personnel turnover within welfare departments, but they do not create the basic problem.

In part, the problem stems from broader societal attitudes. As one observer notes:

> . . . persons who find themselves impelled to receive governmental assistance are not in general, or at least always, considered to have the same political and social rights as those who can provide for themselves and their families from their own economic efforts or resources. There is behind the present welfare picture a long tradition of English and American "Poor Law," of the equation of poverty with moral inferiority, and of fear of according rights to paupers who might thereby find some satisfaction in dependence on government aid.[11]

Welfare officials are, of course, not immune to these attitudes. More importantly, however, they are subject to pressure from powerful persons and organizations who strongly hold these

---

[11] Keith-Lucas, *op. cit.*, p. vii.

beliefs. They are often held responsible for the very conditions they are trying to alleviate. Thus, a New York City councilman challenges a welfare official to justify rising relief rolls,[12] as if this were the responsibility of the administrator. Counterpressures from humanitarian sources tend, on the other hand, to be weaker and more diluted, and those from the poor themselves are virtually nonexistent.

Operating within a "means system" framework is dehumanizing. Attempts to check eligibility and to prevent cheating, combined with pressure from unfriendly "watchdogs," inevitably lead to an abrogation of client rights. A system which requires such finely computed budget allowances as 48 bobby pins per year for a woman, 12 haircuts for a man if he is employed and nine if he is not, must result in the abuse of human values and rights.

Welfare officials are not individual entrepreneurs. They are members of an organization, subject to the requirements of their roles within the organization. Administrators in particular must keep one eye on their service to consumers and the other on the well-being of their organization. Their maneuverability on behalf of the client group is circumscribed. In short, even the most well-meaning administrator is no substitute for a clearly defined set of rights and effective means of vindicating those rights.

Other nations, beginning with Sweden, have sought systematic redress of personal grievances arising from interaction of the individual and society in the services of the ombudsman, "a special parliamentary commissioner whose job is to receive complaints from citizens who are aggrieved by official action, to investigate these complaints and, if he finds they are justified, to seek a remedy. . . . [The ombudsman is] appointed by and responsible to Parliament . . . as its own defender of the law."[13] In this country, such public guardianship does not seem possible at the present time. But social workers and lawyers can combine in an attempt to defend the rights of indigent clients vis-à-vis administrative agencies.

Frustration and futility have dogged the steps of the social-service practitioner in his efforts to deal with the social milieu of his impoverished clients and to establish the concept of service

[12] *New York Times*, May 1964.
[13] D. Rowat, "An Ombudsman Scheme for Canada," *Canadian Journal of Economics and Political Science*, Vol. 28, No. 4 (Nov. 1962).

as a right rather than a charity; yet he has not enlisted lawyers and the legal profession in these attempts. Where social workers have sought the services of a lawyer, it has been mainly in connection with specific problems, such as family discord and debt adjustment. Through cooperation with a lawyer, the social worker occasionally seeks to wrest concessions from the social system on behalf of a client. Cooperation to this end performs valuable services for individual clients, but it represents a purely instrumental use of the lawyer, not an effort on behalf of whole classes of people.

On the social worker's part, this undoubtedly reflects his normal method of working. His concern is with the solution of social problems and the attempt to influence prominent others. The focus of his practice, however, is upon the persons with whom he or his agency interacts, rather than upon broad social issues or categories of people. When a client of a social agency is denied welfare rights, for example, the agency worker ordinarily communicates with a "contact" in the department to reverse the decision. Accommodation often results. Concessions made as a matter of accommodation, however, do not alter systems so as to preclude future problems of a similar nature. In fact, the gratuitous granting of case-by-case accommodation actually provides the public agency with a viable strategy for maintaining the status quo, for it disarms the petitioner without establishing precedent, and thus vitiates issues.

The social worker's lack of involvement in this area may also stem from his tendency to define problems in individual professional or personality terms. Keith-Lucas notes that what little writing there is about welfare decision-making "seems to take for granted that with a professional social work staff little or no questions as to values need be raised."[14] Social-work practice has not yet sufficiently incorporated a political and organizational perspective.

Legal perspective and practice do provide the necessary tools, since lawyers seek to establish and use precedent. In this advocate's role, they can cut through city, state, and national laws and regulations which often constitute a smokescreen, effectively blocking the fixing of responsibility for welfare decisions. The presence of pro-claimant lawyers for welfare clients will not

[14] Keith-Lucas, *op. cit.*, p. vi.

necessarily make administrative or court decisions fair or right, but it can help to limit the power of government agents to give or deny, help or hurt, without sufficient statutory and constitutional basis. The significant role of claimants' lawyers in the struggle for civil rights suggests that much might be accomplished if their efforts were devoted to righting welfare-program abuses.

The lawyer's current lack of involvement stems in large measure from the fact that the practice of law affecting the slum dweller does not ordinarily provide great financial reward. Ensuring the participation of lawyers is ultimately, of course, the responsibility of the legal profession. Voices within the profession have spoken of its moral obligation to the poor, noting that "the poverty which makes them unable to enforce their legal rights makes those rights doubly important for them."[15] Until more basic solutions are feasible, such as the English system of governmental subsidies, which enables the attorney to receive his full fee regardless of the client's financial resources, idealism engendered by the civil-rights and anti-poverty crusade needs to be exploited. Law schools and bar associations might be persuaded to recruit volunteers, and some enlightened firms might even be willing to subsidize associates and members who wish to donate their services to this cause, as many doctors donate their services to clinics. Social-welfare organizations can perform a catalytic function in this regard.

As the profession most closely concerned with the problems of the poor and trained to deal with social problems, social work can play an even more central role in encouraging the development of poor man's law and the establishment of poor man's rights. The social worker has contact with the poor, can locate clients, can encourage their use of legal remedies, and can support them during the process. He has first-hand knowledge of bureaucratic inequities and their debilitating consequences. He is in a position to indicate priorities of attention.

Private social-welfare organizations are in a unique position to employ lawyers for this end. Using legal talent and expertise to develop strategies of influencing public programs affecting categories of people requires only a shift in perspective. An

---

[15] E. E. Cheatham, *A Lawyer When Needed*, New York: Columbia University Press, 1963, p. 40.

agency seeking to have an impact upon social issues needs to maintain a clarity of objective so that it can accept the gain to the individual client through settlement of his particular case while still pressing for a change in policy on the underlying issue.[16]

This approach, which insists upon the granting of rights rather than favors, challenges the penchant of social-work organizations for integrative strategies, for promoting change through "good relationships." Successful negotiation for policy change between any two parties depends, in part at least, upon the sanctions which can be marshalled by the change agent. Legal action, as well as the threat of legal action implicit in the very existence of a legal staff, strengthens the negotiating hand of the organization.

Counteraction can be expected from public officials. They may exert pressure through interlocking board directorates and the intercession of influential persons. Mutual obligations and the sharing of professional concerns with public-agency staff also tend to be limiting factors. These need not be insurmountable, however. Public argument will support the contender who maintains the legal rights of impoverished clients. Pressure can be withstood by a commitment to the objective and a willingness to risk tension. Indeed, farsighted public officials may even welcome the intercession of the social-welfare organization, since it offers a counterforce to other, less humanitarian, influences.

The poor themselves are a further source of support for intervention on behalf of the indigent. "There is only one proved method of avoiding the growth of the sense of dependency. . . . That method is to make him who is dependent the legal master of that on which he depends."[17] In civil rights an unusual combination of legal, judicial, and legislative activities has taken place in conjunction with a mass movement of heroic proportions. The organized activity of the Negro community, the group with the greatest stake in the outcome of the struggle, guaranteed that legal and quasi-legal alternatives on behalf of civil rights

[16] In order to prevent cases from being "adjusted" out of existence, it may be necessary to confront the department with a large number of clients who are affected similarly by welfare handling. With a sizable list of cases, the "adjustment" strategy becomes difficult for a welfare department to maintain without losing the issue.

[17] A. Delafield Smith, *The Right to Life* (Chapel Hill, N.C.: University of North Carolina Press, 1955), p. 3.

would be mounted by conventional institutions, public administrators, and workaday attorneys, as well as by idealistically
motivated professionals. Like the Negro, the poor man has been
excluded by the establishment and thus has little to lose by
abrasive activity. He is therefore not constrained, as public,
social, and legal institutions often are, to bargain for privileges
within the status quo. Social workers committed to and acting
out of the traditional democratic concept of self-help can provide the impetus for organizing the myriad poor. Although this
is an exceedingly problematic task,[18] it offers an additional and
important means of bringing about increased social justice for
the disadvantaged.

[18] See George Brager, "Organizing the Unaffiliated in a Low Income
Neighborhood," *Social Work*, Vol. 8, No. 2 (April 1963).

CHAPTER NINETEEN

The New Public Law: The Relationship of State Administration to the Legal Problems of the Poor*

by Edward V. Sparer

A phenomenon of extraordinary importance to any serious effort to cope with the legal problems of the poor has taken place within the last thirty years. Government has abandoned its passive role in the lives of our citizens and has undertaken the role of mediator and regulator, dispenser of services, and source of what Reich has labeled the "new property."[1] Government has undertaken these roles for all citizens, including the poor; in addition, for the poor, government has made special efforts in public housing, unemployment and other social insurance, juvenile-court reform and youth rehabilitation, a variety of public-welfare programs, private housing codes and mandatory repair laws, various educational programs, minimum labor, health, and safety standards, and other laws designed to relieve the harsh conditions of poverty and promote the common good.

With the change in the role of government, both national and local, has come a profound though insufficiently noticed change in the legal relationships of the poor. The primary contact of the poor man with the law no longer is with law-enforcement agencies and personnel but with various administrative agencies, city, state, or federal.

Most of the public—including the relevant professionals in social work, law, and agency administration—did not and still do not infer from this situation that the poor need legal assistance and advocacy in dealing with government agencies. It is widely believed, first, that there is generally no right to governmental intervention and assistance; secondly, that governmental agen-

---

* Presented at the Conference on the Extension of Legal Services to the Poor, sponsored by the United States Department of Health, Education and Welfare, Washington, D.C., November 12, 1964.

[1] Charles Reich, "The New Property," *Yale Law Journal*, Vol. 73 (1964), p. 731.

cies dealing with the poor are created to help, not to exploit, the
poor, and that, therefore, legal help is hardly needed to contend
with such agencies; and thirdly, that such agencies often base
their judgments on expert social evaluations of what is best for
any given poor person or family, and that for lawyers to advocate
against the position of the agency is, in effect, to militate against
the best interests of the poor themselves.[2]

The hard test of any position, however, is concrete analysis of
the experiences which flow from it. The closer we move toward
the concrete experiences of the impoverished, the more disturbing are the questions raised for analysis. Is a need for a lawyer's
counsel—and possibly his militant advocacy—demonstrated in the
suspension of a deserted mother and her children from a welfare
program because of anonymous complaints that she occasionally
sleeps with a man, or in a family's eviction from a public housing
project because one of their six offspring has been imprisoned,
or in the school-suspension hearing of a child, a hearing which
left the child on the streets and out of school for several months,
or in an unemployment-insurance referee's determination that
a client had "provoked" his own firing from the job and is therefore ineligible for such insurance?

In this article we shall attempt to examine three related aspects of the relationship of state administration to the legal
problems of the poor:

1. The scope of the new legal problems involved, as indicated
   by an analysis of some of the issues raised by one major
   area: welfare administration.
2. Decision-making in local governmental agencies and the
   role of the lawyers, as illustrated by the history of the
   welfare-abuses law.

[2] The philosophy underlying the agencies' concern for the client's best
interests rather than his procedural or substantive "rights" is nowhere
more highly articulated than in the literature dealing with juvenile-court
reform. For an early but unusually clear exposition, see Miriam Van
Waters, "The Socialization of Juvenile Court Theory," *Journal of Criminal
Law and Criminology*, Vol. 13, p. 61. A recent example of this "best interests" argument is a speech delivered on April 18, 1964, to a Columbia
School of Social Work Alumni Conference by Philip Sokol, Deputy Commissioner and Chief Legal Officer of the Welfare Department of New
York City. However, at the September 11, 1964, Northeast Regional Conference of the American Public Welfare Association, the same speaker
modified his position and emphasized the legal entitlements of welfare
clients in a context of obligations.

3. Legal needs of the poor in relation to other governmental agencies, and a problem of ethics for lawyers interested in representation for the poor.

We contend that the new public law, dealing with the legal relationship of administrative agencies to the poor, requires the vigorous participation of lawyers representing the poor, both for the development of the law and for the protection of the poor man's interests. Such representation, in turn, raises an old problem: can lawyers paid from government monies effectively contend against government decisions?

The Scope of the Problems at Issue: Welfare Administration

We chose welfare administration for an exposition of some of the many unattended legal problems for two reasons. First, the welfare program is enormously important, a matter of life or death to many Americans. In New York City alone, nearly 450,000 persons receive public aid under the several welfare programs; 320,000 are assisted under the Aid to Dependent Children Program alone.[3] By estimate of Welfare Commissioner Dumpson, a million persons are "poverty stricken," including members of families whose total income is less than $2,000 per year and unattached individuals who earn less than $1,500 per year.[4] The second reason is that no other long-range governmental program for the poor has been torn by so much dispute concerning what is a matter of legal "right" and what a matter of charitable "privilege."

The list of legal issues of significance to welfare administration which have come to light in various parts of the country is endless. Here we shall focus on some of the issues which have arisen in one corner of one city, the Lower East Side of New York, where I work and have some experience. Each of the problems noted below is based upon an actual case in the Mobilization files.

Does a family suspended from welfare assistance on the charge of wrongdoing or fraud have a right to know the precise ground for the suspension? May the client know who his accusers are? If the client, even aided by a private social worker, cannot obtain

[3] New York State Department of Social Welfare, *Social Statistics: A Monthly Summary*, June 1964.
[4] *New York Times*, January 11, 1964.

such information, is there any way in which he can effectively disprove the charge? Are not these legal issues requiring legal assistance in the face of negative agency determinations?

May a local welfare department refuse assistance to a New York State resident and her baby (born in New York and living in New York for over a year) on the ground that it is more "socially valid" for the resident to live in another part of the country, where her stepmother has allegedly offered shelter (though nothing else), even though the woman is not eligible for welfare aid in the other state because of her New York residence? Are there constitutional issues in this case which only a lawyer could raise? If the client challenges the factual allegations made by the welfare department (e.g., that her stepmother really did offer to give her shelter), who can better help her establish her challenge at a hearing than a lawyer?

If a client needs beds for her children to sleep in, or a motorized wheelchair for her paralyzed body, or a bigger rent allotment than that given as the result of a caseworker's mistake—is there a limit to how long the bureaucratic process may take in resolving the family's request for help? Or can the rent checks go unadjusted for over half a year and the wheelchair ungranted for more than a whole year (despite clear need and a private social worker's help in presenting the requests)? Is there a remedy in law to force a reasonably prompt determination and grant? Under New York law there is, but how is it to be obtained without a lawyer's help?

If the head of a family on relief defrauds the welfare department by earning $100 and not reporting that income, may the welfare department suspend aid to the client's three children (all under the age of four years) and thus create a danger of starvation? Is this an issue of the intent of the social-welfare law? If the welfare department may suspend aid, for how long may it do so? Can the babies be punished indefinitely for the mother's "sin"? Can they be so punished for one year? For six months? Is this an issue that needs a lawyer's assistance?

In a state which bars welfare aid to those who came for the purpose of obtaining such aid, what facts are relevant in the determination of purpose? Does the very need for aid give rise to a presumption of purpose? If a young mother of six children, abandoned by her husband, comes to New York with her children to be near her relatives, including her own mother and father, but needs welfare assistance, can she be said to have come here for the purpose of obtaining welfare aid? Are not these matters on which legal assistance is warranted for the client?

If a needy family is under investigation for alleged "failure to cooperate," shall the children get emergency assistance pending the investigation's final result? New York law is clear that they "shall" receive emergency aid. When they do not, as will happen, and a social worker's effort to help fails, do they have an effective remedy in law? The writer believes so—but surely it would require a lawyer to effect the remedy.

If an abandoned mother is the subject of anonymous complaints that a certain man slept with her, is the welfare department justified in having the woman's home "raided" by a special investigator and a uniformed policeman at 6:30 A.M., without a warrant? (The theory of the welfare department apparently is that if a male sleeps with the client, he is presumably a source of income. If he is a source of income, then suspension will result if the client failed to report the income.) Suppose that a man was found in the apartment; is the presumption of support reasonable? Is the client's alleged though disputed consent obtained to the search sufficient in law? Is this method of obtaining evidence legal?[5] Failure to report income is also a criminal offense. Should the welfare mother be entitled to the same legal protections as the ordinary criminal suspect?

How pervasive are these problems? The most frequent problem encountered by persons already on the welfare rolls appears to be unreasonable delay in the granting of needed items of aid. The "welfare abuse" problem (dealing with alleged purpose in coming to New York) has been extensive and is discussed in detail below. The case of the lady who originally came from another state appears to be quite similar to the problems of some 1,347 people described in the 1962 Annual Report of the New York State Department of Social Welfare covering the 20-month period preceding the report.[6] The practice of suspending aid without explanation to the client is very common.

---

[5] William Stringfellow, a young lawyer who spent seven years in East Harlem practicing law for poor people, reports in his recent book, *My People Is the Enemy*: "I had one case in which an investigator climbed a tree at two o'clock in the morning in order to perch there and spy into the window of a project apartment of a welfare family waiting to see or hear something that could be used against the family to disqualify them from further assistance" (p. 75).

[6] *Public Welfare in New York State in 1961*, Annual Report of the New York State Department of Social Welfare, issued Feb. 15, 1962, p. 25. The 20-month period immediately preceded August 31, 1961. The persons in the category described were referred to as residents of other states. When

Similarly, when cases are closed, are reasons given? Again—not always. In one county, for example, 35.7% of those interviewed claimed they were not told why assistance was cut off, and the case records failed to indicate that the former recipient had been given a reason.[7]

Several of the cases referred to above involve the question of initial eligibility rather than administration. Does this reflect too much concern for eligibility issues on the author's part? In 1961, there were more than a quarter of a million applications for public assistance in New York; 39 per cent were rejected.[8] Consider this rejection rate in view of Commissioner Dumpson's estimate, cited earlier, that a million persons in New York City are poverty-stricken, living below the margin of adequate subsistence. At the same time, less than half that number actually receive public aid. In Westchester County, just north of New York City, a recent study found that "more than five times as many people are living in abject poverty [defined as an income of less than $3,000 a year for an urban family of four or more] as are receiving aid from the Westchester County Department of Public Welfare."[9]

The Moreland Commission reports that rooting out the supposedly ineligible is a primary preoccupation of welfare workers. Is this a matter deserving of careful scrutiny by an advocate for the supposedly ineligible? We know that one major consequence of the effort to "root out ineligibles" is that less time and effort are devoted to actual help and rehabilitation efforts with the families.[10] Commenting on this emphasis on eligibility, Greenleigh Associates, the research organization for the Moreland Commission, declared:

An applicant becomes eligible for assistance when he exhausts his money, gives a lien of his property to the welfare department, turns in the license plates of his car, and takes legal action

it was established that one of these claimants was in fact a New York resident, the Welfare Department contended that that fact was irrelevant since the claimant "belonged" in another state despite the acquisition of residency here.

[7] Moreland Commission, *Report on Public Welfare in the State of New York*, 1963, p. 68.

[8] *Public Welfare in New York State, op. cit.*, p. 32.

[9] *New York Times*, October 29, 1964, p. 37.

[10] Moreland Commission, *op. cit.*, p. 27.

against his legally responsive relatives. When he is stripped of all material resources, when he "proves" his dependency, then and then only is he eligible. Welfare policies tend to cast the recipient in the role of the propertyless, shiftless pauper. This implies he is incompetent and inadequate to meet the demands of competitive life. He is then regarded as if he had little or no feelings, aspirations or normal sensibilities. This process of proving and maintaining eligibility in combination with the literal adherence to regulations and procedures tends to produce a self-perpetuating system of dependency and dehumanization.[11]

If needy people are to be rejected because of a caseworker's "literal" interpretation of a regulation, is it possible that a lawyer's advocacy of the proper interpretation might be desirable? If the result of present policies tends to dehumanize welfare clients by treating them as devoid of feelings and sensibilities, is it possible that a lawyer's dedicated representation could contribute, not only to the client's financing, but to his self-recognized status as a man, an equal American citizen? Indeed, is it possible that representation of clients by lawyers can improve the humane administrator's ability to effect better policies?

Decision-Making in Local Governmental Agencies; the Role of the Lawyer

Most of us are inclined to place a great deal of faith in the "good guy" theory of government. If there are problems regarding the legality of various agency practices, put in a "good guy" to head the agency. If the agency ineffectively carries out its enforcement duties, it must be because it is led by a "bad guy"— throw him out and replace him with a "good guy." Good guys will see to it that good policies are effectively carried out and fairly applied.

Unfortunately, the functioning of government is somewhat more complex, particularly on the municipal or local agency level. No matter how dedicated and competent he may be from a professional point of view, the agency head must continually make a high politicalized effort to maintain his own survival and that of the agency, while he accepts a compromise here to

[11] Report to the Moreland Commission, Greenleigh Associates, Inc., November 1962, p. 78.

win a professional gain there. Sayre and Kaufman analyze the administration of New York City line agencies in this way:

> . . . the strategies of the line administrator—winning internal control of his agencies, and manipulating his environment—require accommodations with all the participants in the contest for the stakes of politics who are concerned with the agency decisions. To render himself less vulnerable to all the conflicting and contradictory demands and instructions, and to all the forms of resistance and opposition to his will, the agency head has to muster the support of all the friends he can find and strike bargains with everyone around him. To preserve his discretion in some areas of his jurisdiction, he must surrender in others. He has to placate his allies to keep them on his side and pacify those who are rarely active in his aid lest they use their influence to injure him and his agency. He has to balance a welter of factors to survive, let alone to progress, for virtually everyone he deals with has an independent source of power.[12]

The line administrator, then, no matter what his personal excellence, almost invariably has to bargain and compromise. He does not and cannot call his own shots, developing his own policies in the manner dictated by his best professional instincts. This is as true at least in welfare administration as in any other local government administration.

Among the many extraordinary pressures with which large-city welfare administrators must contend are the ordinary pressures for economy; the extraordinary pressures for economy that continually arise; the organized and strident antiwelfare demagogues who constantly seek material to exploit for their claims that all welfare clients are lazy and fraudulent; the constant internal pressure from an overworked, underpaid, and ever-changing staff; internal maneuvering from would-be successors; and external relations with a state agency which may be led by an administration of the other political party.

In addition, as Dean Rostow notes, the administrator, in the face of such pressures, must work with statutes which are often made purposely ambiguous so as to allow room for shifting compromises resulting from a lack of any effective political consensus

---

[12] Wallace Sayre and Herbert Kaufman, *Governing New York City* (New York: Russell Sage Foundation, 1960), p. 305.

on what should be done.[13] Moreover, though the pressures are many, one of the weakest pressures of all—indeed, it is virtually nonexistent—is that which comes from the welfare clients themselves.

In the context of the problems and politics of agency administration, the lawyer who represents the impoverished client introduces a new element. By fighting for his client, by engaging the issue involved in his client's cause with the judicial or quasi-judicial process, the lawyer not only creates the possibility of reversing an improper interpretation of law which affects many others in addition to his client but also increases the administrator's potential for effecting humane policy and the clientele's rightful entitlements.

It is helpful at this point to examine in some detail the history of one major issue in New York welfare administration and the lawyer's contribution to its solution.

The History of an Issue: The "Welfare Abuses" Law of New York

New York has never had a residence law which required a person to live in the state for a certain period of time before he became eligible for welfare. In 1960 and 1961, however, certain groups in the state, disturbed by recent migrations, undertook a strong campaign in behalf of such a law. A hue and cry was stimulated by the antics of City Manager Mitchell of Newburgh,[14] who alleged that undesirable newcomers were flooding the state relief rolls. Although less than 2 per cent of public assistance furnished by the state went to persons who had lived in the state for less than a year, in 1960 the legislature passed a bill restricting aid to residents. It was vetoed by the Governor.[15]

---

[13] Eugene Rostow, "Law, City Planning, and Social Action," in Leonard Duhl, ed., The Urban Condition (New York: Basic Books, 1963), p. 357.

[14] Mitchell's infamous 13-point plan, promulgated in 1961, was designed to drive people from the welfare rolls in a variety of ways. It was based in part on the charge that great numbers of "undesirables" go to Newburgh to get public assistance. In point of fact, only $205 was spent by that city for home relief in 1960, and that sum was fully reimbursed by the state. Nothing was spent on ADC for nonresidents in 1960. Annual Report, op. cit., p. 6. Upon motion of the State Department of Social Welfare, the New York Supreme Court enjoined the City of Newburgh from effecting the plan. State Bd. v. Newburgh, 28M 2d 539 (1961).

[15] See Governor Rockefeller's veto message of March 22, 1960. The "less than two per cent" figure is taken from that message.

In 1961, the effort for a residence restriction was again under way. Commissioner Dumpson of New York City, vigorously opposing a residence law, answered the argument that newcomers come to the state for the purpose of obtaining relief:

> . . . In recent years, due to the restricted immigration laws, in-migration to New York has come largely from Puerto Rico and from the southern states. Our experience in the Department of Welfare clearly indicates that people migrate to New York City in search of a "better life." They are seeking employment opportunities, a better employment experience, better housing, better educational opportunities for their children, for health reasons, and to join friends and relatives. These are the reasons for which five million Americans move within the nation every year. They are the reasons which prompted migration to the United States from the beginning of our history. People do not move to New York in order to receive public assistance. People come to New York City in response to the lure of many of our industries. Indeed, our state and local economy, in large part, is dependent on this in-migration of workers. In simple justice, we cannot enjoin the benefits of our health and welfare services when need arises. . . .[16]

In the spring session of the state legislature, the pro- and anti-residence-law forces seemed deadlocked. Finally, a bill was proposed to <u>deny welfare aid to those who</u> came to New York for the <u>*purpose* of obtaining welfare aid</u> but to grant it to other newcomers. The bill, in an effort to please the humanitarian groupings, also provided that temporary emergency assistance shall be given to those who are in immediate need, regardless of their purpose in coming to New York. The bill, then, was a compromise between varying political factions. Each faction anticipated a different result. The pro-residence-law forces could say that the law now barred aid to the "freeloaders." The anti-residence-law forces knew that hardly anyone really came to New York for such a purpose; no one would suffer. Thus the bill was passed into law, labeled the "welfare abuses" law. The legislative contentions were over. It was time for the varying pressures concerning the administration of the law to begin.

In the first ten months of the law's existence, 2,730 people were denied aid on the ground that their purpose in coming to New York was to receive aid. Of these 2,730 persons, only 387

[16] *Here It Comes Again* (New York: State Charities Aid Association).

were given emergency aid.[17] The total number rejected was, to
say the least, surprising in light of the firm conviction of social
workers and others, including the New York City Commissioner
of Welfare, that people simply do not migrate for the purpose of
receiving welfare aid. The minuscule number who received
emergency aid—about one out of every seven rejected applicants
—seems even more surprising. If the 2,730 were rejected because
of their purpose in coming to New York and not because of their
lack of pressing need, would not more than one out of seven
need temporary assistance?

Two years went by. The numbers of rejectees continued to
mount. The numbers denied emergency aid grew. In 1964, a
lawyer interviewed the heads of several families who had been
denied aid, emergency or otherwise. We shall spare the reader
the details of their stories. We note only that to both the rejected
applicants and the lawyer it seemed clear that they had come to
New York, *not* to obtain welfare aid, but for a variety of other,
perfectly legitimate reasons. It also seemed clear that in each
case a terrible need for emergency aid existed.

As the lawyer interviewed clients, a pattern seemed to emerge.
The same two erroneous presumptions by welfare workers appeared regularly. These were:

1. A person who comes to New York without an adequate
   plan of support, and possibly knowing that he or she will
   need welfare help, therefore comes for the purpose of obtaining welfare help.
2. Emergency aid under the welfare-abuses law should be
   given only to those who agree to leave the state.

How did two such presumptions become established—presumptions inconsistent with the law that was actually passed?
In part, it was the pressure of overworked and undertrained
caseworkers whose "social evaluation" plays an enormous role
in any such case. Partly also, it was a variety of "political" forces
that pressured for and gradually enforced the interpretations we
write of. In any event, a liberal Commissioner of Welfare had
been rendered largely powerless to reverse the process. Indeed,
by the time of the hearing of a test case on the welfare-abuses
law, the welfare department's lawyer argued in his brief that if
the claimant's arguments were accepted:

[17] Moreland Commission, *op. cit.*

. . . then we can no longer deny public assistance to anyone seeking better education, better hospitals, better health facilities, better municipal concern for the downtrodden and the underprivileged. This city and state could then become the Mecca for all disadvantaged persons, regardless of their origins; and the taxpayers of this state would be required to assume the burden for all who come or are induced to come here.[18]

Nevertheless, the hearing process, the briefing of the case and reply briefs, the readiness for further court appeal if necessary, the light of rationality and quasi-judicial and judicial decision-making power, also had effect. The presumptions were declared in error and the determination of ineligibility was reversed. Every other case in this area which was brought to the lawyer's attention was reversed and aid granted; each was based on similar error. It is the writer's belief that of the 2,730 cases denied in the first ten months of the welfare-abuses law's existence, 2,700 could have been reversed on appeal to the State Board of Social Welfare or the courts—if the claimants had had the vigorous advocacy of a lawyer. How many others since the first ten months—or even today, due to lack of uniform application of the law—needed and need such advocacy?

In any event, the contribution of legal representation on this issue was to establish the *right* to entitlement, to expose erroneous social evaluations, and to make more possible the humane policy urged from the first by the administrator of the agency.[19]

Other Areas of Legal Need, and a Problem of Ethics

This article began by suggesting that the poor have a need for legal counsel—and at times militant advocacy—in their dealings with virtually all agencies charged with administration of the new public law. We have concentrated on the legal needs arising in connection with one agency, welfare administration,

[18] Welfare Department brief *in the matter of R*, Fair Hearing held before N. Y. State Department of Welfare, June 1964.

[19] The history of this issue is not yet complete. In welfare administration generally, hearing decisions do not have the precedent effect they should. Indeed, the decisions are often unknown from department to department or area to area. Social agencies generally have not carried out an effective informational campaign since they are largely unattuned to the legal process in welfare administration.

only to illustrate the more general point. Perhaps discussion of some issues from other significant agencies is here appropriate. We shall consider the public housing authority and the local board of education.

Public Housing

The New York City Housing Authority, established in 1934 to provide homes for families of low income and to clear slums, is today the city's biggest landlord, housing several hundred thousand persons. A low-income family seeking decent apartment quarters in New York City today will either be fortunate enough to obtain public housing or will probably have to suffer the consequences of living in a substandard slum home. The Authority receives approximately 85,000 applications per year but there is room for only a fraction of that number. In 1962, for example, 10,000 families moved into public housing apartments. Obviously, the grounds used to reject an application or to evict a family already admitted are of fundamental importance to the poor.

The public landlord quite properly objects to tenants who do not pay rent, who destroy the landlord's property, who spoil the possibilities for good relationships among the other tenants. So, too, does the responsible private landlord. Nevertheless, even the most pro-landlord lease designed by a local real-estate board usually prohibits a landlord from arbitrarily terminating that lease. If the landlord does so act, the tenant will have remedy either in court or in an arbitration proceeding.

But the typical public landlord offers his tenants no such protection. Upon the recommendation of the federal Housing and Home Finance Agency, the typical public-housing lease is drawn on "a month-to-month basis whenever possible." Is this a recommendation designed to protect the tenant? Hardly. The agency states: "This should permit any necessary evictions to be accomplished with a minimum of delay and expense on the giving of a statutory Notice to Quit *without stating the reasons for such Notice.*"[20]

However, where housing authorities choose to assert an arbi-

[20] *Local Housing Authority Management Handbook*, The Public Housing Administration—Housing and Home Finance Agency, Part IV, Sec. 1, No. 5(d). Emphasis added.

trary ground for denying admission or terminating a tenancy, such authorities have exceeded their legal power. Said one court:

> The government is under no duty to provide bounties in the form of low-rent housing accommodations for its citizens. If it elects to do so, however, it cannot arbitrarily prevent any of its citizens from enjoying these statutorily created privileges. . . .[21]

Is it not time for lawyers representing public-housing tenants to review the statutes and other decisional material to determine whether the quiet refusal of a housing manager to state reasons for termination is consistent with law?

In New York City in the late 1950's, hundreds of tenants were evicted from city housing projects on loosely stated charges of "undesirability," without opportunity for fair review. Citizen groups publicly stated their "outrage" at such "unjust evictions." Wide-scale demand for a change was made, and a change was indeed instituted. A Tenant Review Board (composed of authority representatives) was created to consider and make a final determination of all proposed evictions regarding undesirability. An opportunity is given to the tenant to appear and hear the charges against him, make a statement, and present his own witness.

But the tenant is not allowed to cross-examine those who made the charges against him; he cannot even learn who they are; he cannot have a record of the hearing; no official notes are even kept of the hearing which he may see. If one of his sons has been imprisoned, that is a ground for his eviction; if another son has played on the grass, that fact is recited—to show "the whole family pattern"; the loosest sorts of hearsay statement are quoted against the family—and if a tenant questions the source, he is told it is from a trusted employee of the project; if a tenant's lawyer then questions whether the statement was made by the trusted employee acting as a witness or merely repeating what

[21] *Peters v. N.Y.C.H.A.*, 128 NY 2d 224, 236, *aff'd* and *modified*, 283 App. Div. 801, *rev'd on other grounds*, 307 N.Y. 519 (1954). See also *Chicago Housing Authority v. Blackman*, 4, Ill. 2d 319 (1954); *Housing Authority of Los Angeles v. Cordova*, 279 P. 2d 251 (1955); *Lawson v. Housing Authority of Milwaukee*. 270 Wisc. 269 (1955). These cases deal with efforts to impose loyalty oaths as a standard of eligibility for public housing. Few cases treat the adequacy of eviction standards and procedures on "non-desirability" issues. See e.g., the dissent of J. Hofstader, in *Watson v. N.Y.C.H.A.*, 27 M. 2d 618 (1960).

another person told him, the lawyer is frequently met with a blank stare on the part of Review Board members or is asked, "What do you want, a regular trial of all these incidents?"

There is enormous need for lawyers to test eviction standards and procedures in public housing. Such tests will have the further desirable effect of clarifying some of the admission standards which affect even greater numbers of persons.

Education

Some of the most subtle and yet important issues for lawyers to be devoting their attention to are in connection with public education. There is at least general familiarity with the difficult legal issues relating to de facto segregation and integration in the public schools. How about the ordinary school-suspension hearing, however? Is adequate attention given to the factual issues which must form the basis for the disposition reached by such hearings? The consequences to the life of the child in question may be far more severe than a minor criminal charge in later years.

The hearings that I have been informed about do not deal with trivial matters—as they should not if a suspension is involved. They deal with alleged assaults, thefts, indecent exposure, extortion, and various conduct patterns which often appear in a juvenile court proceeding. Lawyers—if they have any virtues—are presumed to be experts in the methods of determining facts. Nevertheless, I know of no effort anywhere—even on a study basis—to analyze fact finding in suspension hearings with a lawyer's eyes and skills.

Equal in importance to the fact finding at such hearings is the disposition of suspension cases. Yet it is not unusual, at least in New York, for suspended children to be left without any plan whatsoever for months at a time, while their case records churn through the bureaucratic procedures or are left to rest in untouched files. Such results can be unfortunate to the well-protected middle-class child. To the slum child they can mean personal disaster.

Statute, at least in New York, requires the Board of Education to take "immediate steps" to institute an alternative plan of education for a suspended child. When a suspended child is ignored for months, has there been a failure in legal obligation? Does the legal obligation itself imply that the parent can take legal steps to require the Board to perform its legal duty? Would not such an action force a revision and improved procedure generally? Questions, not answers, are here being offered. But they are questions which require the involvement, the time, and the dedication of lawyers. To those who would argue that these are matters for educators and social workers, the writer contends that a lawyer's role may at times be that of impelling educators and social workers to do their duty.

A Problem of Ethics

There is a peculiar aspect of striving for legal representation of the poor in their dealings with government agencies. The rich pay for their own counsel; the antagonism of their opposite parties customarily has little effect on the dedicated nature of their legal representation. The impoverished cannot pay for their own counsel. With regard to the legal needs we have been speaking of, it is the same government with which the poor are contending that must pay the bill or develop and fund the institutional entity that employs the lawyer.[22] That is why the reaction of the government agencies to representation of the poor is a subject to be considered.

The subject becomes a particularly pressing one when the board of directors of the institutional entity that employs the lawyer is the "microcosm of the total community"[23] that is typical of antipoverty or antidelinquency projects. Such a board typically includes leading representatives of each of the local agencies with which the lawyer must contend.

There is, of course, no uniform reaction on the part of agency representatives to the results of legal service for poor persons in contention with the agency. Particularly with agencies which, for

[22] Of course, some legal-aid societies are voluntarily financed. To so expand the work of such societies as to allow comprehensive coverage of legal needs relating to governmental agencies would probably be beyond the capacities of voluntary financing.

[23] For a description of the varying forces that constitute the Board of Mobilization for Youth, Inc., in New York City, see Grosser, *Neighborhood Legal Service: A Strategy to Meet Human Need*, presented at the Conference on the Extension of Legal Services to the Poor, Washington, D. C., Nov. 12, 1964.

varying reasons, are not unused to the lawyer's role, problems caused by reaction to advocacy are often minimal.[24] With others, the reaction can be sharply different. Still elsewhere, the worst of the matter might result from anticipation of reaction on the part of the project's friends in local government who are interested—quite legitimately—in the maintenance of good relations between the project and the local government.

Neither is there a uniform reaction based on the nature of the issue which has become the source of legal contention. Earlier we spoke of legal advocacy for claimants which makes it more possible for humane administrators to effect policies they endorse. Yet legal action may produce strains, irritations, and a sense of being threatened which cloud all else. Who, after all, readily accepts the notion that additional pressure of a compelling sort is something to be directed at oneself? When the nature of the issue involved produces direct conflict with policies the administrator favors—or flouts the professional pride of a specialized group—the reaction may be even sharper.

The lawyer who represents the poor in contention with government while being paid with government money in an institution partly directed by government personnel may find that his position is not fundamentally different from that of the line administrator as described by Sayre and Kaufman. He is soon involved in a highly politicized effort to maintain his own survival and the survival of his agency—while he accepts a compromise here to win a professional gain there. To preserve his discretion in some areas, he may surrender in others. Accommodation with those who are concerned with his agency's decisions is often needed to render himself less vulnerable to the conflicting demands of others who may affect his agency's future.

How does pressure make itself felt? If the lawyer writes to a local board of education for a copy of its suspension rules, he may find that his letter has been brought to the attention of others in the project. If he takes his client through a state welfare-department hearing, he may learn to his surprise that a complaint has been lodged with the referee of the hearing

[24] For example, the MFY Legal Services Unit has experienced no hostile reaction whatsoever on the part of housing authority representatives, although the unit is currently engaged in court challenge of existing practices.

charging him and his organization (erroneously) with "the un-
authorized practice of law."[25]

If the lawyer is too persistent and too militant in his advocacy
with certain agencies, he may find that a high official writes to
his organization's director to state that the lawyer's activity on
behalf of his client "raises a serious situation in our interagency
relationship."[26] A well-connected and highly placed person may
tell the lawyer that he must not "threaten" litigation on behalf of
certain clients already retained; perhaps a "study project" will
provide the best solution.

The lawyer may go to his organization's director and find that
he is fortunately situated with a decent and dedicated man who
supports the lawyer's work. The lawyer may go to his university
faculty advisors and find extra sources of strength. In the end,
like all of us, he must look toward himself.

There is a lawyer's ethic requiring him not to betray his client;
observing this ethic is both his duty and his greatest source of
strength. Meanwhile, he will slowly learn that open and frank
discussion of the pressures and problems he meets is, in the long
run—though perhaps not immediately—the very best contribution
he can make toward the provision of adequate legal services for
the poor in their dealings with governmental agencies.

The lawyer's ethic in serving his client, poor or rich, is a well-
established one. That ethic applies, however, only to a lawyer–
client relationship already established. It does not and cannot
prevent a policy decision which bars him from establishing a
lawyer–client relationship on certain matters or in relation to
certain agencies. It is in this connection that government, if it
is truly interested in making counsel available for the poor with
whom it deals, must establish its own ethic: it will make lawyers

[25] Fortunately, however, the lawyer will be able to explain that his organization has been authorized to practice law by the appropriate court and
that he is a member of the bar; he will also note that state welfare-department rules make it clear that a representative of a social agency (which
lacks authorization to practice law) is entitled to represent claimants in
state board hearings. The referee will be satisfied and the lawyer will wonder—who could have made the complaint?

[26] The letter will also note that "we agreed to work co-operatively in the
use of your Legal Services Unit." The lawyer will wonder who agreed to
what. He will speculate on how such formulations affect the duties he
owes exclusively to his client—and not to his employing organization or to
local agencies before which he represents his clients.

available without any conditions or limitations other than those imposed by the lawyers' own legal judgment and sense of duty.

The government's obligation to establish legal recourse for the poor in their dealings with governmental agencies is today merely in the argument stage. It is an obligation, however, which should be assumed, particularly in the war against poverty: partly because the poor themselves need representation; partly because the law is best developed with representation; partly because the war against poverty needs that "civilian perspective . . . of dissent, of critical scrutiny, of advocacy and of impatience"[27] which lawyers for the poor can bring to it.

The assumption of such an obligation on the part of government will mark the beginning of a new blossoming of civilized and dignified human relationships within our country. Assumed without conditions attached, it will establish a new and higher ethic for government. Surely this should be done.

[27] Edgar S. Cahn and Jean C. Cahn, "The War on Poverty: A Civilian Perspective," *Yale Law Journal*, Vol. 73 (July 1964), pp. 1317, 1318.

CHAPTER TWENTY

Experiments in Serving the Indigent*

by Marvin E. Frankel

It is no new discovery that the promise of equal justice is a hollow one for people too poor to retain counsel. What is new—though the novelty does no credit to the Bar or to the public—is a widespread, spirited, and growing determination to work at the problem.

The Bar has at last made this a matter of prime concern. But lawyers are by no means alone on the fronts of study and activity. To cite a single but notable illustration, a Washington conference sponsored by the Department of Health, Education and Welfare on November 12-14, 1964, featured among its panelists many social workers, social scientists, and authors as well as lawyers.[1] Most important, the Economic Opportunity Act of 1964 has made it a national purpose to include new and expanded forms of legal service among the weapons for fighting poverty.

"Suggested Policy Guides" of the N.L.A.D.A.

Responding to and vitally interested in the call for action, the Executive Committee of the National Legal Aid and Defender Association on December 16, 1964, adopted a statement of "suggested policy guides" with the stated "objective of giving maximum cooperation" to the projected extension of "legal assistance for the poor . . . [as] part of the so-called antipoverty programs under the Economic Opportunity Act."[2] The source of this state-

*Reprinted from *The American Bar Association Journal*, Vol. 51 (May 1965), pp. 460-64. *Author's Note*: I acknowledge gratefully the assistance of Richard S. Granat, a 1965 graduate of the Columbia Law School, in the preparation of this article.

[1] The proceedings of the conference have been published under the title "The Extension of Legal Services to the Poor," which is available from the Government Printing Office. This volume is hereafter cited as "*H.E.W. Conference Proceedings*."

[2] The statement is printed in full in the *New York Law Journal*, December 23, 1964, p. 1. For the text of the recommendations, see *American Bar Association Journal*, Vol. 51 (1965), p. 275.

ment—embodying so much experience and so impressive a record of service to indigent clients—commands respectful attention. The content of the statement—largely instructive and constructive—raises some questions of strategy and attitude that may well become subjects of controversy in the days ahead.

In a "statement of facts" the outline of policy guides briefly sketches the long history (over seventy-five years), the variety of facilities, and the extent of existing services of organized legal aid in the United States. Acknowledging that there are "many gaps in this legal service for the poor," the statement notes that continual efforts are being made "to extend and broaden the legal aid and defender programs." Then, in its last two "statements of fact"—propositions that a technical lawyer might label mixed statements of fact and judgment—the document says:

> L. With ample funds, traditional legal aid and defender organizations can be broadened to meet the full legal needs of indigent people in metropolitan centers.

> M. The creation of separate, duplicating agencies to offer legal services under Economic Opportunity [Act] programs will be more costly and less effective than will proper use of existing facilities, and serious ethical questions will be raised where non-lawyers attempt to practice law.

Here, in what is presented quite simply as a matter of fact, the National Legal Aid and Defender Association appears to stake out a claim to monopoly. The "traditional . . . organizations," it says, are enough; give them the money and they'll do the job; other agencies not only would be "duplicating" service but also would be likely to pose "serious ethical questions. . . ." If this should harden as the N.L.A.D.A. position, it amounts to a declaration of war, not on poverty, but on competition.

Following the "statement of facts" the N.L.A.D.A. lists its "recommendations as to policy guides." These make the cogent point that existing legal-aid agencies and the organized Bar should be consulted about and involved with developing plans for legal assistance. Then, in what sounds like a reaffirmation of the insistence on exclusivity, the statement urges that "where expansion or modification of existing programs appears warranted, resources available through the Economic Opportunity Act be used through established systems to supplement, broaden and make more meaningful for the community the existing services." The final recommendation, however, appears to suggest that there may be room for alternatives: "where the development of *new* or traditional legal assistance is contemplated, the legal profession *and the other professional disciplines*, all of whom are concerned with helping people, [should] work closely together in each community to implement the Economic Opportunity Act" (emphasis added).

Here the wisdom of common-law lawyers seems to prevail over the earlier threat of rigid hostility to change. This ultimate recommendation would picture the Bar as engaged, deeply interested, watchful, but sympathetic and receptive to the prospect of experimental change.

It is to be hoped that this will indeed be the stance of the National Legal Aid and Defender Association and of the Bar generally. For, as a thoughtful scholar has recently observed, the multifarious problems entailed in attempting to make legal services available to those in need call for a sense of "creative dissatisfaction" and "for variety as well as continuity of method."[3] Expressing the same view, Attorney General Nicholas Katzenbach has urged the development of "new techniques, new services, and new forms of interprofessional cooperation to match our new interest."[4] Similarly, Lewis F. Powell, Jr., President of the American Bar Association, has insisted that "the organized Bar must explore broadly, and with an open mind, the possibility of other solutions" than those already in the field.[5]

Existing Limitations of Legal Aid

It does not diminish the splendid contributions of established legal-aid organizations to recognize (as they do) that enormous needs of the poor for legal services remain unfilled. As declared

[3] Elliott E. Cheatham, *A Lawyer When Needed* (New York: Columbia University Press, 1963), pp. 57-58.

[4] *H.E.W. Conference Proceedings*, p. 11.

[5] *American Bar Association Journal*, Vol. 51 (1965), pp. 3, 20. The same outlook is now embodied in official American Bar Association policy. In a notable resolution adopted on February 9, 1965, the House of Delegates announced the Association's determination "to improve existing methods and to develop more effective methods for meeting the public need for adequate legal services." For the text of this resolution, see *loc. cit.*, p. 339.

in the N.L.A.D.A. statement, the gap could undoubtedly be narrowed by increased financial support for legal aid. It is arguable, nevertheless, that the traditional forms and policies of established legal-aid organizations are intrinsically unsuited to the task of satisfying completely the legal needs of the indigent.

The established agencies are old, frequently well organized, directed by prominent community leaders, and—established. It takes no revolutionist to be aware of the defects of these virtues. The negative impact of habit, of routine, and, it should be said, of settled bureaucratization is well known and has been noted as a possible flaw in legal-aid operations.[6]

A related problem inheres in the essentially charitable character of most legal-aid organizations—in the fact that their services are seen to be bestowed by affluent donors on supposedly grateful but passive recipients. Among the relatively new—or at least newly implemented—hypotheses expressed in the antipoverty legislation is the conception that there must be "maximum feasible participation" by the poor themselves in programs for their betterment. Similarly, experimental programs like New York's Mobilization for Youth are premised on the belief that "[when] the poor wage their own war against poverty, they win a new image of themselves."[7]

It is conceivable that such thinking could be implemented in legal-aid agencies by suitable changes in policy, in the composition of directing boards, and perhaps in other respects. Even so, the problem invites experiment and diversity. The critics are surely entitled to an opportunity to demonstrate whether new devices and new organizations can avoid the aura of philanthropy.

Another aspect of the same criticism is the charge, accompanied by some documentation, that the paternalist attitudes of existing legal-aid agencies have entailed discriminations against the poor in access to theoretically universal remedial rights. Consider, for example, the recent statement of a legal-aid attorney on the marital problems of the poor:

> People may say that poverty prevents the poor from having the same rights to get a divorce as a person with money, yet we must remember obtaining a divorce is not a right but a privilege.

[6] Cf. Charles F. Grosser, "The Need for a Neighborhood Legal Service and the New York Experience," *H.E.W. Conference Proceedings*, pp. 73, 76.

[7] *Action on the Lower East Side: Progress Report and Proposal* (New York: Mobilization for Youth, 1964), p. 69.

For most legal aid clients, a separation is just as useful and practical as a divorce.[8]

It may turn out in fact that judgments like this are somehow in the best interests of the impoverished client. Today, however, the predication is an unacceptable one, premised as it is on the assumption that poor people are afflicted with special forms of stupidity or fecklessness to which the affluent are immune. Discriminations that the law has not made (and probably could not make) against the poor should not be imposed upon them by their lawyers.

There is also the argument, and some evidence, that centralized legal-aid offices are frequently inaccessible and unknown to the people who need them. Writers with some claim to know tell us that the urban poor tend to be bound by the most straitened physical horizons (the block or the slightly larger neighborhood); a journey "downtown" or to a distant neighborhood is likely to be a rare and perilous enterprise. Coupled with this is the fear of and hostility to official types generally but most particularly "the law"—shared widely, but most acute for the poor and excluded.

In the face of such realities, strange and distant legal-aid offices may be in effect nonexistent for numbers of potential clients. Moreover, these offices have not made it a practice to publicize their wares, commonly contenting themselves with discreet telephone listings that are not immediately discoverable by moderately literate researchers.

Finally, it is said that existing legal-aid agencies, although they issue publications for this purpose, have failed effectively to educate the poor about the law—about their rights as tenants, as consumers, as applicants for governmental benefits. The result, again, is a large reservoir of unknown and inevitably unsatisfied needs.

These criticisms may be overdrawn. Some of the suggested problems may not lend themselves to ready solution by any proposed means. But responsible experimental efforts to solve prob-

[8] Wayne Theophilus, "Determining Social Need," *Legal Aid Brief Case*, Vol. 22 (1964), pp. 211, 213. The quotation in the text and other references to the same effect are given in Jerome Carlin and Jan Howard, "Legal Representation and Class Justice," *UCLA Law Review*, Vol. 12 (1965), pp. 381, 413-15.

lems—these or others—must not be stifled or met with a priori opposition by the Bar.

One form of suggested cure for at least some of the asserted defects in existing services is the neighborhood law office.[9] To describe this current concept in most general terms, it contemplates a law office as part of or in close relation with an agency or agencies offering a spectrum of social services. The thought is that lawyers in such units will team with social workers and other professionals in detecting needs for service, in preventive legal education, and in providing necessary representation before agencies, courts, and legislative bodies. Varying forms of this device are already operating in Boston, New York, and the District of Columbia.

In itself, the idea of a law office in a neighborhood, although it has been implemented rarely and only recently, represents no radical departure from traditional legal aid. Indeed, the National Legal Aid and Defender Association is one of the sponsors of such an enterprise in New Haven, Connecticut. However, recent thinking outside legal-aid auspices points toward new directions, attitudes, and functions. As described by its director, the experimental legal unit in New York conducted under Mobilization for Youth

> . . . differs from the traditional legal aid office in at least five characteristics: (1) its main efforts are directed towards representation before government bureaucracies dealing with the poor, ranging from welfare to housing agencies, to [the] . . . police; (2) it is a neighborhood-based law office; (3) its operation is closely integrated with the work of scores of private social workers and community developers within the neighborhood; (4) it makes particular efforts to select cases for representation whose outcome will have a broad impact on the quality of living for the poor of the neighborhood; (5) its educational methods on legal rights of the poor are oriented towards practical work with neighborhood groups rather than . . . the writing and distribution of brochures on various areas of the law.[10]

[9] As is true of most ideas, the essence of this one is not new. A well-established system of neighborhood offices exists in Philadelphia, for example, differing from the types now under consideration in that fees are charged for service. See Robert D. Abrahams, "The Neighborhood Law Office Plan," *Wisconsin Law Review*, 1949, p. 634; "Twenty-five Years of Service: Philadelphia's Neighborhood Law Office Plan," *American Bar Association Journal*, Vol. 50 (1964), p. 728.

[10] Edward Sparer, "The Role of the Welfare Client's Lawyer," *UCLA Law Review*, Vol. 12 (1965), pp. 361, 366 *n.* 14.

There is unquestionable occasion as such experiments proceed for concern and scrutiny by the Bar in the interests of legitimately cherished professional standards. It is to be hoped, on the other hand, that we can adapt creatively to this neighborhood-office concept as well as to other new devices. For example, it may be suggested that traditional notions about solicitation do not fit comfortably the plight of the poor and the alienated. Programs of consumer and slum-tenant education may generate "legal business," to be sure, but this is a world away from the evils against which the relevant canons were drawn. And it is no mere coincidence but a pertinent and hopeful sign that the American Bar Association is embarked on a re-examination of these canons along with its current studies of legal services for the indigent.

Other Experimental Possibilities

The Private Lawyer, Privately Retained

As existing and projected organizations compete for the poverty business, one may hope that the Bar will seek ways in which the unorganized, unbeholden, merely private lawyer may serve and earn at least minimal fees in this burgeoning field. The indigence of the clients is no insuperable obstacle; the whole discussion of this problem proceeds in recognition that public funds will finance the legal and other tools for the attack on poverty. And it is a familiar fact that those who serve the poor—with food or medical care or buildings or clothing—are paid large amounts of such funds. The problem is to seek techniques through which the unique values of the private practitioner may be preserved and extended to the poor while the community (properly) shares the burden.

One prototype that has become increasingly well known is England's broad program under its Legal Aid and Advice Act of 1949, as amended in 1960. The genius of that scheme, particularly on its civil side, is its arrangement for public financing without governmental intrusion upon the lawyer–client relationship. Under means tests providing for partial or total payment by the government, local bar committees determine eligibility, subject to appeals by rejected applicants to area committees. Persons found eligible are free to choose from panels of solicitors and barristers who have agreed to serve under the plan. Evidence of the vigor and wide acceptance of the scheme is the fact that virtually all of England's barristers and solicitors have placed their names on the panels.

This cursory account is offered here merely as an invitation for inquiry. It is at least conceivable that American communities, or even entire states, might find the English model adaptable to their needs. There appears to be no reason that pilot plans of this type could not qualify for support under the Economic Opportunity Act.

More limited variants of the same idea may also merit exploration. To suggest a single possibility in a field wide open for creative thought, private lawyers might be made available for poor persons with complaints (or supposed complaints) against one of the many administrative agencies to which they look for assistance. These agencies—welfare, housing, unemployment compensation, and others—exist by definition and purpose to aid the disadvantaged; the welfare applicant or recipient is the agency's "client." Nevertheless, quite apart from the "insolence of office" and other human failings, it is inevitable that officials, particularly at the low levels where dispositive action often occurs, will misconceive or misapply the law. There are indications of huge needs for lawyers in this area, not only to serve in the standard forms of administrative and judicial review, but also to perform their vital function as lawmakers, testing and pressing for doctrinal change in the trouble spots of welfare administration.[11]

How can private lawyers be retained by the poor and paid for their services? Thorough answers could come only from the interest and hard study proposed here. Perhaps it would be possible to provide that the rejected welfare applicant or the public-housing tenant threatened with eviction should be en-

[11] The legal literature reflects a growing dissatisfaction with the notion of welfare grants as mere "privileges" subject to unreviewable denial in official discretion. See Harry W. Jones, "The Rule of Law and the Welfare State," *Columbia Law Review*, Vol. 58 (1958), p. 143; Charles Reich, "The New Property," *Yale Law Journal*, Vol. 73 (1964), p. 733. The lawyer is needed to press for the changing theories in litigation and otherwise. It appears, too, that there is broad scope for the adversary lawyer's energies at the administrative level, where views too long untested and unquestioned may yield to persuasive opposition. See Edgar S. Cahn and Jean C. Cahn, "The War on Poverty: A Civilian Perspective," *Yale Law Journal*, Vol. 73 (1964), pp. 1336-38; Sparer, *op. cit.*

titled automatically (and carefully informed of his entitlement) to consult one of a panel of lawyers registered for this purpose. Relatively small fees could be paid administratively for the lawyer's review of and advice on the problem. If further steps were taken within the agency, with broad latitude for the lawyer's judgment short of the frivolous, additional compensation could be payable by the agency. Finally, where the path of judicial review is taken, suitable fees might be awarded by the court.

Perhaps this is visionary. It may seem at first blush that an automatic right to see a lawyer is an unjustifiable luxury. But people with money enjoy that right, and it is open to question whether this modest benefit would really add unbearably to the cost of administration. What, after all, are we willing to pay for the ideal that justice may be seen to be done? My plea is for open-minded inquiry with a view to experiment.

Public Counsel

To turn 180 degrees from the preceding suggestion, it may be that some communities will want to consider the retention of publicly salaried lawyers as advocates for the poor. Agencies of this kind would not be wholly unprecedented. It is reported that there are at least five small "public bureaus" now in existence that are supported entirely by local government.[12] Other legal-aid establishments are partially financed in this way. The widely debated but apparently growing institution of the public defender for criminal cases is a close counterpart. The familiar arguments for and against the public defender are likely to be revived if this suggestion is pursued. There is a prima facie appeal in the idea that government itself should provide legal representation for people who cannot afford it even when the adversary is in a sense that very government. There is, on the other hand, the respectably held view that vigorous independence, at least against governmental opposition, is automatically precluded when the lawyer is a public employee.

The latter view appears to have prevailed in the enactment of the federal Criminal Justice Act of 1964; the Senate provision

[12] National Legal Aid and Defender Association, *Summary of Conference Proceedings*, Vol. 26 (1963); and see Emery A. Brownell, *Legal Aid in the United States* (Rochester, N.Y., Lawyers Cooperative Publishing Co., 1951).

for public defenders as one of the locally available alternatives for representation of indigent criminal defendants was deleted in the House and failed of enactment. But the sentiment favoring tests of this device remains strong and widespread. There is no mathematically certain decision of the controversy. It is an ideal subject for local experimentation and study.

The Ombudsman

Much has been written in recent years concerning this significant Swedish contribution to the perennial struggle against governmental arbitrariness. The idea has spread from its country of origin through Scandinavia to West Germany and far-off New Zealand. It has been urged as worthy of adoption here.

The ombudsman is kin, but by no means identical, to the public counsel mentioned as a possibility just above. Unlike the functions of such a counsel, those of the ombudsman relate solely to the operations of government agencies and officials. Varying somewhat from country to country, he is generally equipped with investigatory authority and powers (commonly respected) to criticize, recommend administrative changes or corrections, and publicize his views and findings. In addition, he may bring proceedings in the courts against allegedly derelict officials. He may act either on the complaint of a person claiming to be aggrieved, in which case he seeks correction of the specific grievance, or on his own motion.

The idea is an obviously attractive and provocative one. Whether it is suited to parts or all of the United States is a question that awaits thorough testing.[13] Here is another opportunity to explore, at least locally, new ways of making justice a reality —perhaps for the poor in the first instance, perhaps for everyone later on. The material resources are available; what are needed now are the imagination and the willingness to invest in promising new departures.

[13] Some portions of the ombudsman's functions on the national level— investigation, criticism, recommendations—have been assigned to the now permanent Administrative Conference of the United States established by Pub. L. No. 88-499, 78 Stat. 615 (August 30, 1964). For earlier proposed or temporary variants, see Kenneth C. Davis, "Ombudsman in America: Officers to Criticize Administrative Action," *University of Pennsylvania Law Review*, Vol. 109 (1961), p. 1057.

"Let Our Minds Be Bold"

When it committed the federal government, in the Economic Opportunity Act of 1964, to the support of community-action programs, the Congress called for diverse, individualized plans suited to the special needs and preferences of local people. It was indicated that the "range of programs and projects that may be undertaken by a community . . . is limited only by the needs of the area and the ingenuity of its leaders in developing practical and promising ideas." This is a heady challenge and a potentially rich opportunity for rich and poor alike. For we are all impaired when there are "millions of Americans—one fifth of our people—who have not shared in the abundance which has been granted to most of us, and on whom the gates of opportunity have been closed."[14]

It is more than a lawyer's occupational prejudice to say that access to equal justice, including the indispensable assistance of counsel, is high on the priority list of gates to be unlocked. As we set to work on that task, we should be skeptical of deep preconceptions. This is not to say that the basic canons of loyal professional service and discipline ought to be scrapped. It is only to urge receptivity to new and varied ways that may better serve the joint goals of the profession and of all the people.

We would do well to borrow from a not-too-distant context the wisdom of Mr. Justice Brandeis:

> To stay experimentation in things social and economic is a responsibility. Denial of the right to experiment may be fraught with serious consequences to the nation. It is one of the happy incidents of the federal system that a single courageous state may, if its citizens choose, serve as a laboratory; and try novel social and economic experiments without risk to the rest of the country. . . . If we would guide by the light of reason, we must let our minds be bold.[15]

---

[14] Message of President Johnson submitting the poverty bill, H.R. Doc. No. 243, 88th Cong., 2d Sess. 1.

[15] Dissenting in *New State Ice Company* v. *Liebmann*, 285 U.S. 262, 311 (1932).

Conclusion

Mobilization for Youth has been both a part of and a contributor to an era—an era in which, for the first time since the innovative New Deal days of the 1930's, government has undertaken to redefine its responsibilities toward the citizenry. Indeed, the role of the state in protecting citizens from inequities of government itself has been a major concern of the project. That the age of the specialist and the bureaucrat should spawn the specialist-bureaucrat to defend people against the power of other specialist-bureaucrats is not so untoward a notion as it may seem.

Conservative critics of publicly financed welfare programs have maintained that excessive power accrues to government officials who have the authority to award or deny significant benefits. As a consequence, they say, large sectors of the population become dependent upon the bureaucracy and therefore inhibited in voicing legitimate complaints and pursuing independent judgment. This argument is frequently used to support a proposed diminution in government services and welfare programs (but not so frequently to oppose special tax benefits, such as oil-depletion allowances). Human-relations professionals and liberals generally have contended that in a complex, urbanized, industrial society, human want and suffering can be relieved only through government action. They have, as a consequence, tended to ignore the cogency of the conservative argument. Although they believe that citizens are entitled to services specified by legislation as a matter of inherent social justice, they are less sensitive to the consequences for the recipients of the community's perception of these services as a "charity" or privilege. To the extent that citizens are subject to the arbitrary whims of officials and powerless to affect decisions basic to their dignity and well-being, to that extent is the conservative case valid.

Public services are pervasive and will inevitably become more so. Bureaucratic systems are difficult to negotiate, and low-income persons, who need them most, are least able to understand and manage them. Their own sense of powerlessness and its objective reality compound the problem. The consequence is

332

that a large segment of the populace is effectively denied its democratic and legal rights.

Sir George Haines, National Chairman of Great Britain's Citizen's Advice Bureaux, has succinctly defined the issue.

> Protection of the individual is the heart of the matter in present day society. . . . People are faced with a scale of events and new powers that dwarf them . . . a world in which impersonal forces operate over which they have no control—a vast complex of communal regulations that impinge on their lives. . . . We must give strength to the private individual even as we give the state a larger share of responsibility.[1]

Several of the articles in this volume emphasize protection of the interests of consumers of public services. The success of this effort requires government support, financial and otherwise, of such activities as challenging the constitutionality of administrative rulings and statutes adversely affecting the users of public services; advocating the interests of the poor directly in dealings with public institutions; exploiting the helping capacities of the clients themselves and developing a new partisanship among members of the helping professions in behalf of the indigent; exerting pressure to bring about greater institutional responsiveness to client needs; and helping clients to organize on their own behalf, both as a spur to institutional accommodation and as a means of exercising control over their own destiny. These are recurrent themes in this collection.

One method of protecting consumer interests—the encouragement of collective action by the clients themselves—requires further comment. While the method is the subject of many of the preceding papers, the role of government support of such efforts is dealt with only by implication. It is clear that the authors of at least some of these articles, and the architects of Mobilization's first three program years, support the granting of public funds to a private organization for the purpose of organizing the poor to challenge public programs and policies affecting their lives. There is, however, a strong case to be made for the reverse position—i.e., that social change which requires the mobilization of the poor should not be government-supported.

[1] Quoted in Mildred Zucker, "Citizen's Advice Bureaux," a paper prepared for the Conference on the Extension of Legal Services to the Poor, Washington, D.C., November 1964, mimeo., p. 1.

It can be argued, first, that it simply is not possible to mobilize the poor to act in their own behalf with government encouragement. This was the early position of one of MFY's top policymakers. To suggest, he said, that a largely government-financed institution, such as MFY, would be allowed to organize the poor was at best romantic and at worst a fraud. Such an objective might gain support from some funding-source officials and thus constitute an element in the art of grantsmanship, but the constraints of government financing pose an insuperable barrier. If Jesus had been on the Roman payroll, he noted, the history of Christian civilization might have been different. Other policymakers agreed that local officials were unlikely to support pressure against themselves, and that neither local nor national officials would view with equanimity activities as controversial as Mobilization's were likely to be. They insisted, however, that the attempt to organize the poor nevertheless be made. The subsequent attack upon the project confirmed the earlier analysis. Only one substantive charge was developed: agitation. In support of the indictment were MFY's representation of indigent clients against public agencies such as the Department of Welfare, its facilitation of the withholding of rents in tenements in violation of code regulations, its encouragement of participation in antidiscriminatory protest events such as the school boycott, and its refusal to try to dissuade local residents from individual or collective direct action.

The Mobilization experience offers a Scotch verdict on the matter. On the one hand, the agency very nearly went out of existence as a result of an attack which would not have been launched if MFY had refrained from community action.[2] Although it survived, its course may well have been irrevocably deflected from the encouragement of effective social action by the poor. On the other hand, a number of local but substantive accomplishments may be cited: drastic revision of the city's interpretation of the Welfare Abuses Law, changes in the administration of the local schools, and legislation easing and legalizing rent withholding in New York State. Nationally, a consequence of the attack was that public attention was directed to the issue, which was resolved in favor of the use of public funds to sup-

---

[2] This was not the only reason for the attack, however. Control of poverty funds—whether by the central city machinery or by nonpolitical groups in the neighborhoods of the city—was an important underlying issue.

port community self-help efforts. (One of MFY's chief City Hall detractors was moved by political considerations to agree that MFY-sponsored groups should be permitted to "fight City Hall.") "Resolved" may, of course, be an overoptimistic interpretation, as attested by the recurrent controversies surrounding the role of the poor in poverty projects. It can accurately be said, however, that discourse regarding the engagement of the poor has moved to a different level.

More troublesome, however, than the pragmatic argument against government-financed social-change efforts is the philosophic one. The case has been put as follows:

> The emotional thrust behind nearly all such programs is bound to carry them over into the field of political action. Voter registration, civil rights, tenant councils, and the like are programs possessing a strong political color. What the government through its subsidization of such programs is in fact doing is providing them with an organizational framework and a degree of legitimacy. This is not only contrary to American political practice and tradition, but serves as a potentially dangerous precedent. "The poor today and some other group tomorrow" is a slogan that flows easily from the premise for government-sponsored social-action programs. Such programs, finally, could be exploited by unscrupulous or overzealous persons for their own partisan or personal ends.[3]

Such risk is undoubtedly inherent in government support of social-change programs. The line between social action and partisan political action is a thin one indeed. (MFY was accused, for example, of supporting reformist elements in the local Democratic party, although it scrupulously attempted to avoid political involvements.)

New York's senior senator, meeting with MFY officials, raised a further objection. Taxes, he said, should not be used to the advantage of one group of citizens at the expense of another; specifically, it is inappropriate to use public funds to organize citizens against taxpaying landlords. This position had a court test during the MFY imbroglio when a real-estate company unsuccessfully sought an injunction against MFY's use of funds for this purpose. Tax funds are frequently used for the advantage of

[3] Murray Silberman, *Securing Change Through Government-Supported Social Action Programs,* Columbia University School of Social Work, March 6, 1965, mimeo., p. 9.

one group to the detriment of another, of course; farm subsidies, for example, hardly benefit the taxpaying urban consumer. Nor is there a dearth of examples of government succor to special groups—i.e., on the basis of age, occupation, industry, economic category, etc. The essential difference in the Mobilization form of assistance to the poor is that it generates controversy. These programs, Silberman notes, "have little if any prescriptive sanction, and do not (or are not likely to) enjoy widespread public support of a substantial body of public opinion and antagonize important economic, professional and political groups in the community. . . ."[4] The controversial nature of a program is, however, essentially a strategic issue rather than a moral or an ethical question. The very controversial nature of the program may argue for its necessity. Because the poor have been unable to influence political processes, they are disadvantaged in the distribution of societal resources. Because they do not have the resources, their political influence is meager. Their lack of power in turn accounts for the controversy concerning government assistance. The argument is circular; the need of the poor is for help to break the cycle.

One accepts the risk of political abuse inherent in engaging the poor in social action if one assumes that poverty can be reduced if the poor develop a stake in their community, contribute their special perspective and experience to devising solutions to the problem, and acquire the political influence necessary to bring about a more equitable distribution of resources. At some point in the sociopolitical history of the nation, the risk may be too costly for the desired end. At present, however, there is sufficient check within our political processes, and the poor are so severely underrepresented in decision-making councils, to warrant courting the danger of abuse.

It is true that troublesome philosophic objections are obviated when private groups organize social-action programs; this is, after all, in keeping with the American political tradition. The greater freedom and lesser accountability of the private sector theoretically serve to shelter action attempts from the shifting winds of controversy as well. Nevertheless, to relegate the job to the private sector is to relegate it out of existence. Private groups are in fact no less ready supporters of controversy. More im-

[4] *Ibid.*, p. 5.

portant, they do not have the necessary resources to undertake the task. Private programs cannot hope to provide the aid and protection required by the poor in dealing with so massive a purveyor of services as the government.

Just as Mobilization has played a role in the redefinition of government responsibilities, so its theoretical espousal of social structure as a primary behavioral determinant has placed it within a trend in the helping professions to devote greater attention to issues of social policy.

To locate the source of social dissonance in institutions rather than exclusively in individuals is not to denigrate the importance of remedying the pathology in the individual. Strategies aimed solely at basic causation ignore the vast reservoir of human misery and injustice already created. Furthermore, the accumulation of human benefits achieved at given points in time contributes to the continued development of our social system. Reforms designed for individual remediation, such as, for example, the current spate of youth-work training programs, can lead to more basic and institutionally oriented change—for example, the development of a vast public-works program for youth. (Social security is a classic example of a reform which, though initially decried by some as a palliative which ignored causation, has presaged a revolution in the role of government and the economic life of the country.)

A new mood of change and challenge is being felt, as the helping professions increasingly turn their attention to issues of social policy. (The vastly expanded responsibility of government, as noted above, encourages this development by seeking solutions at the national level.) In the public-welfare field, for example, social workers no longer offer the increased professionalization of welfare staff or the addition of a complex of rehabilitative services as the only—or indeed the major—solution to the dependency, apathy, and anger of public-welfare clients. Their concern is with such matters as family allowances, financial support for poor students, finding alternatives to work as a source of income, and bridging the gap between the role of welfare in a modern society and the Horatio Alger myth, which still stigmatizes clients.

Concern about changes in social policy inexorably leads to programs of social reform. Social reform has had a long tradition within social work. The profession's missionary zeal has in fact come to be identified as "do-goodish" and "fuzzy-mindedness"—epithets which carry the clear connotation that while the heart is in the right place, the head is somewhat askew. Perhaps the most novel aspect of the reformist orientation of Mobilization for Youth and the other government efforts which followed it was that it represented an alliance of social reform with social science. (It is indicative of this development that the epithet changed to "sociological subversives," an accusation directed against MFY by a New York City official.) As a result, reformist social workers need no longer apologize for the lack of a knowledge base intrinsic to their efforts. A scientific body of knowledge is now available to draw from and reshape for practice purposes. More important, social-science knowledge put to the service of social reform offers strength and sanction for change attempts.

The articles in this volume reflect the fledgling nature of the alliance between social reform and social science. We are convinced, however, that the MFY experience from which they were drawn constitutes a step toward the ultimate maturity of the collaboration.

Index of Authors

Index of Authors

341

Index of Subjects

Index of Subjects

Ad hoc groups, 149
Advocacy, 20, 174, 264, 267, 302
Aid to the Blind, 258
Aid to Dependent Children, 258, 261, 269, 270, 286, 288, 289, 304
Aid to the Needy Disabled, 258, 261, 269, 270
Alcoholics Anonymous, 217
Alienation, 137
American Public Welfare Association, 283, 303
Anti-poverty projects, 21, 151
Area Redevelopment Administration, 127
Authoritarianism, 69

Bedford-Stuyvesant, 21

Case work, iii, 64, 239, 241
Client perception, 73
Change agent, 111
Chicago Area Project, 171
City administrator (N.Y.C.), 93
Citizens' Advice Bureau, 333
Citizens Housing and Planning Council, 229
Civil-rights movement, 135, 301
Civil-rights violations, 290, 294
Columbia University Bureau of Applied Social Research, 292
Committee of Welfare Families, 273, 275
Community development, 89, 133, 243

Community life, 67, 142, 157, 263
Community organization, 143, 243, 273
Concrete services, 157
Conference on the Extension of Legal Services to the Poor, 317, 333
Conflict, 118, 138, 336
Consolidated Edison Co., 230
"Cooling-out" tactics, 103, 152
C.O.R.E., 237, 250, 251
Council of Economic Advisors, 35
Council of Federated Organization, 250
Criminal Justice Act of 1964, 329

Delinquency, 18, 87
Democracy, 283
Demonstration projects, i, 24, 83

Economic Opportunities Act of 1964, 17, 20, 321, 328
Emergency Committee for More Low-Income Housing, 231
Enabler role, 190, 245
Ethics, 313

Family Service Association, 42, 50
F.B.I., 22
Federal government, 83, 100
Ford Foundation, 21, 92
Fourteenth Amendment, 26, 284, 285, 286